The Saving Line

The Saving Line

Benjamin, Adorno, and the Caesuras of Hope

Márton Dornbach

NORTHWESTERN UNIVERSITY PRESS
EVANSTON, ILLINOIS

Northwestern University Press
www.nupress.northwestern.edu

Printed in the United States of America

10 9 8 7 6 5 4 3 2 1

Library of Congress Cataloging-in-Publication Data

Names: Dornbach, Marton, 1973– author.
Title: The saving line : Benjamin, Adorno, and the caesuras of hope / Márton Dornbach.
Description: Evanston, Illinois : Northwestern University Press, 2021. | Includes bibliographical references and index.
Identifiers: LCCN 2020027631 | ISBN 9780810142992 (paperback) | ISBN 9780810143005 (cloth) | ISBN 9780810143012 (ebook)
Subjects: LCSH: Hope. | Benjamin, Walter, 1892–1940. | Adorno, Theodor W., 1903–1969. | Philosophy, German—20th century. | Literature—Philosophy.
Classification: LCC BD216 .D67 2020 | DDC 121.66—dc23
LC record available at https://lccn.loc.gov/2020027631

CONTENTS

ABBREVIATIONS OF WORKS CITED

AA Kants gesammelte Schriften herausgegeben von der Deutschen [Königlichen Preussischen] Akademie der Wissenschaften*, 22 vols. (Berlin: Walter de Gruyter, 1902–). Known as the Akademieausgabe.

AT Theodor W. Adorno, *Aesthetic Theory*, ed. Gretel Adorno and Rolf Tiedemann, trans. Robert Hullot-Kentor (London: Continuum, 2002).

DE Max Horkheimer and Theodor W. Adorno, *Dialectic of Enlightenment: Philosophical Fragments*, ed. Gunzelin Schmid Noerr, trans. Edmund Jephcott (Stanford, Calif.: Stanford University Press, 2001).

EA Johann Wolfgang von Goethe, *Elective Affinities*, trans. David Constantine (Oxford: Oxford University Press, 1999).

"GE" Theodor W. Adorno, "Geschichtsphilosophischer Exkurs zur *Odyssee* [Frühe Fassung von Odysseus oder Mythos und Aufklärung]," in *Frankfurter Adorno Blätter V*, ed. Rolf Tiedemann (Frankfurt: edition text + kritik, 1998), 37–88.

"GEA" Walter Benjamin, "Goethe's Elective Affinities," trans. Stanley Corngold, in *Selected Writings*, vol. 1, ed. Marcus Bullock and Michael W. Jennings (Cambridge, Mass.: Harvard University Press, 2004), 297–360.

GHA Johann Wolfgang von Goethe, *Goethes Werke*, 14 vols., ed. Erich Trunz (Hamburg: C. H. Beck, 2005). Known as the *Hamburger Ausgabe.*

GS Walter Benjamin, *Gesammelte Schriften*, 7 vols., ed. Rolf Tiedemann and Hermann Schweppenhäuser (Frankfurt: Suhrkamp, 1991).

HBA Friedrich Hölderlin, *Sämtliche Werke, Briefe und Dokumente in zeitlicher Folge*, 12 vols., ed. D. E. Sattler (Munich: Luchterhand, 2004). Known as the *Bremer Ausgabe.*

MM Theodor W. Adorno, *Minima Moralia: Reflections on a Damaged Life*, trans. E. F. N. Jephcott (London: Verso, 2005).

ND Theodor W. Adorno, *Negative Dialectics*, trans. E. B. Ashton (New York: Continuum, 2007)

SW Walter Benjamin, *Selected Writings*, 4 vols., ed. Howard Eiland, Michael W. Jennings, Marcus Bullock, and Gary Smith (Cambridge, Mass.: Belknap, 2004–06).

"VRJ" Gottfried Keller, "A Village Romeo and Juliet," trans. Paul Bernard Thomas, in *Stories*, ed. Frank G. Ryder (London: Bloomsbury, 1982).

INTRODUCTION

The Pausing of Speech

The line of inquiry pursued in this book originated in a moment of puzzlement. Preparing to teach a seminar session on Max Horkheimer and Theodor W. Adorno's *Dialectic of Enlightenment*, I was rereading the chapter principally authored by Adorno that had found its place in the book under the title "Excursus I: Odysseus or Myth and Enlightenment." What gave me pause was a remark on, precisely, pausing. The remark in question occurs near the very end of the excursus, where Adorno reflects upon a harrowing episode that darkens the Homeric account of the hero's triumphant homecoming. Given its importance for my argument, the passage calls for extensive quotation:

> The pausing of speech is the caesura that allows the events narrated to be transformed into something long past, and causes to flash up a semblance of freedom that civilization has been unable wholly to extinguish ever since. Book 22 of the Odyssey describes the punishment meted out by the son of the island's king to the faithless maidservants who have sunk back into harlotry. With an unmoved composure comparable in its inhumanity only to the *impassibilité* of the greatest narrative writers of the nineteenth century, the fate of the hanged victims is described and expressionlessly compared to the death of birds in a trap, with that silence whose arrest is the true remainder in all speech. This is followed by a statement reporting that "For a little while their feet kicked out, but not for very long." The exactitude of the description, which already exhibits the coldness of anatomy and vivisection, keeps a record, as in a novel, of the twitching of the subjugated women, who, under the aegis of justice and law, are thrust down into the realm from which Odysseus the judge has escaped. As a citizen reflecting on the execution, Homer comforts himself and his listeners, who are really readers, with the certified observation that the kicking did not last long—a moment, and all was over. But after the words "not for long" the inner flow of the narrative stands still. "Not for long?" the gesture of the narrator asks, giving the lie to his composure. In being checked by this gesture, the report is prevented from forgetting the victims of the

> execution and lays bare the unspeakable endless torment of the single second in which the maids fought against death. (*DE* 61–62, translation modified)

The provocatively offhand reference to Homer as a "citizen" and to his audience as "readers" cannot but startle Adorno's readers, confronting them as it does with the sheer oddity of Adorno's reimagining of the *Odyssey* as a novel. It would seem that Adorno here envisions the epic as the work of a distinctively modern type of novelist, one who is not above donning the guise of a journalist reviewing the forensic physician's protocol to write his report on an execution. While this attribution is curious enough, my rereading of the excursus in preparation for the seminar turned up an even more puzzling detail. In previous approaches to this chapter of *Dialectic of Enlightenment*, my main concern had been to make sense of the philosophical claims advanced by Adorno. This time, however, it occurred to me that perhaps the full implications of the argument might only come into full view if I paid closer attention to the Homeric passage under discussion, and in particular to the matter of narrative stance foregrounded by Adorno's elliptical remarks. This hunch prompted me to reach for the text of the *Odyssey* to look up the relevant passage in book 22.

It was then that I became aware of a problem so basic that its apparent triviality may actually explain the apparent lack of scholarly notice paid to it. Regardless of whether one consults the original Greek text available to a reader today or the classic translation by Johann Heinrich Voss that Adorno repeatedly quotes, no trace whatsoever of a "pausing of speech" can be found after the words "but not for long" in line 473. Having executed the maids, Telemachus and his fellows promptly turn their attention to the goatherd Melanthios, whom they mutilate, castrate, and then leave to die—whereupon, with this strenuous work accomplished, they wash their hands and feet to prepare for a joyous celebration of the homecoming. No discernible pause separates the two episodes. At first glance, then, Adorno's comments regarding a pause in narration would appear to be a wishful fabrication. So blatant is his departure from the protocols of philology that one must wonder if perhaps Adorno felt that the gruesome violence of the narrative had to be countered with a mitigating act of invention.

As I struggled to make sense of Adorno's remarks in light of the Homeric passage at issue and in the broader context of Adorno's concluding meditation, I noticed something else. The pivotal term of the passage—"caesura"—has its native terrain in classical prosody, where it refers to a pause that cuts in half and thereby structures a poetic verse. In Adorno's remarks, however, the term was clearly used to mark a feature that interrupts and divides a continuum on a scale far exceeding the individual verse. Adorno's idiosyncratic use of the concept of caesura, his employment of the unusual adverb "expressionlessly," the reference to "hope," and the close attention paid to the narrator's stance all pointed in one direction. They hearkened back to an earlier philosophical reflection on literature that occupies a central place in the Frankfurt School canon, and which explicitly asserts the need for criticism to deploy a certain kind of violence: namely, Walter Benjamin's probing and intensely difficult essay "Goethe's Elective Affinities," which was intended by him as "an exemplary piece of criticism."[1]

This association precipitated a cluster of interests into a coherent line of inquiry. Could it be, I wondered, that reading Adorno's remarks on the putative caesura of book 22 in conjunction with Benjamin's essay might dispel the impression of arbitrariness that attaches to those remarks? And what if such an indirect approach to Adorno's excursus could throw fresh light on Benjamin's essay? In short, I began to suspect that the conclusion of Adorno's excursus was written in tacit dialogue with the older friend who only two years earlier had fallen victim to the lethal regression that Adorno and Horkheimer were trying to explain.

The chapters that follow aim to flesh out this intuition by examining the interpretive strategies and philosophical considerations at play in Benjamin's and Adorno's caesura markings. This undertaking will require me to focus large portions of my argument on a handful of critical passages, submitting Benjamin's and Adorno's writings to the type of micrological interpretation that they themselves practiced. To appreciate the advantages of this approach, it should suffice to recall a basic point made by Albrecht Wellmer apropos of Adorno's writing, which applies with equal or even greater force to Benjamin's works: since these texts possess the qualities of a literary work of art, by taking on the role of a magnifying glass, critical interpretation can enable us to discern "layers of meaning which appear fused to the naked eye."[2] Wellmer compares the type of interpretation he has in mind to the work of a stereoscope that produces "a three-dimensional image in which the latent depth of the texts became visible." My argument in this book will develop a stereoscopic image in a further sense as well. By interpreting Benjamin's and Adorno's critical writings in light of one another, I will bring into focus a deep structure common to both arguments, one that would not be discernible in either of the texts considered on its own. The "saving line" of my title is a shorthand for this structure.

In an investigation of this type, the ratio of close reading to broader explorations of the two authors' oeuvres must be weighted in favor of the former. It is, in fact, one of the broader aims of this book to demonstrate by example that the much-maligned practice of close reading need not be an exercise in sophistry or scholastic pedantry, that it can be philologically rigorous and philosophically disclosive at the same time. This is not to say that close reading focused on the two critical texts will be the sole methodological tool used in my argument. Written at an early stage in each author's career, Benjamin's essay and Adorno's excursus introduce theoretical concerns that continued to animate the authors' subsequent works. At least some of the relevant concerns are, in fact, more fully articulated in these later texts. Making sense of Benjamin's and Adorno's caesura markings will therefore require me to draw on a number of other works by them as well. Moreover, at key junctures it will be helpful to place their works in dialogue with other authors to whom they are responding or who contend with similar problems, including Kant, Hölderlin, Hegel, Nietzsche, Flaubert, Luxemburg, Kraus, and Bakhtin.

This strategy will enable me to shed new light on matters of long-standing scholarly interest having to do with the bodies of writing produced by Benjamin and Adorno. Before outlining these issues, I want to address the most basic question provoked by the two texts that stand at the center of this study: what does it mean, to begin with, to write about literature philosophically? It is best to approach this question first in broad terms and only then to examine the inflection it receives in Benjamin's essay on *Elective Affinities* and Adorno's meditation on the *Odyssey*.

Philosophical Reading and Critical Succession

A suitable starting point can be found in a simple consideration about the form of thought that Socrates bequeathed to Western philosophy. For centuries, philosophical thought has tended to conceive of its own activity in terms of the language game of question and answer. Although most works of philosophy do not have the overt form of dialogues, nevertheless the concepts, distinctions, and arguments deployed in philosophical texts are more often than not geared toward answering questions regarding the good life, the nature of reality, the significance of beauty, and so on. Exceptions to this rule do exist, of course. In particular, the intellectual landscape of modernity has been shaped to a great extent by thinkers who practiced philosophy with a view toward its overcoming, and hence most decidedly not with the aim of answering philosophical questions. Thus Nietzsche allowed his very subjectivity to be pulled into a perilous vortex of interrogation; Heidegger persisted for decades in cultivating an attitude of questioning openness; instead of trying to answer questions, Wittgenstein struggled to dissolve them; and, as we will see, Benjamin's early conception of philosophy centered on a question that cannot be posed but whose idea may be displayed in the medium of art.[3] Yet even in these boundary cases, which are characteristic of philosophy in its crisis, the act of questioning retains its role as an orienting paradigm.

Questioning, however, has also tended to figure as a key element in various answers to the question of what happens when we encounter a text. Thus, theorists of hermeneutics following Gadamer have maintained that significant texts owe much of their power to the questions they pose to us—a claim that has been countered with the reminder that our sense of being interrogated by a text already presupposes the horizon of the questions that we as readers bring to the table.[4] In this respect, a special situation arises when we read a verbal artifact *as* literature. For in such cases our stance is not defined by a single question to which we might expect to learn the answer. Rather, insofar as we take literature to be a domain inviting the type of aesthetic play that Kant so influentially described, we approach the literary work with a constant readiness to ask, "might one not understand this text otherwise?"[5] This sort of openness may have an affinity with the questioning attitude favored by some of the post-philosophical thinkers mentioned previously, but it is difficult to reconcile with the pursuit of definite answers that constitutes the default practice of philosophy. It is certainly at odds with that aspiration to distinguish true from false answers, and desirable from undesirable forms of life, which defines the varieties of philosophy called critical.

For the reasons just outlined, the undertaking to write philosophically about a literary work is fraught with risk. Someone who approaches a novel or a poem with this sort of interest is subject to the conflicting demands of argumentative cogency and sensitivity to the characteristically literary forms of imaginative play, aesthetic semblance, and semantic polyvalence. In addition to the challenges arising from the dissimilarity between literature and philosophy, however, a further source of complication lies in the proximity between the two practices. If, to quote a well-known quip, writing about music is like dancing about architecture, the situation is not necessarily more simple when the medium of the art form under consideration is identical with that of our response: namely, language. For this coincidence makes it particularly easy to mistake the rules of our language game for those of the work, and conversely, it also raises the specter of contamination by the object of our discourse. Such contamination may of course be seen as desirable. Thus, Friedrich Schlegel envisioned a form of poetic criticism that might constitute a literary creation of a higher order, an artistic presentation of the presentational form peculiar to the literary work under consideration.[6]

Even if one sets oneself a more modest goal in writing philosophically about literature, the tightrope act involved in any undertaking of this sort must be hazarded without the aid of a straightforwardly applicable method. Guidance can be found, however, in preexisting works of criticism that succeed to an exemplary degree in combining illumination of a literary work with philosophical insight. To be sure, the emulation of a critical model raises a host of new difficulties. Because outstanding works of philosophical criticism themselves instantiate philosophical thinking as well as literary writing, any consideration of their procedures with a view to their adaptability requires the successor in her turn to combine conceptual rigor with literary responsiveness. It should also be obvious, furthermore, that a given critical model can only be properly appreciated in light of the particular work that stands in its focus, and its relevance to another literary work cannot simply be taken for granted.

In parsing a work of philosophical criticism whose author followed a preexisting critical model, we are therefore dealing with at least three distinct readings: first, the successor critic's reading of his chosen literary object; second, a reading of the critical model that is being emulated; and third, the successor critic's implicit rereading of the literary work that stands in the focus of the critical model. Even if the last two of these readings remain hidden as palimpsests beneath the first, overt one, they are not necessarily any less illuminating than the latter. In most cases, in fact, none of these three readings are going to be self-evident, and the difficulty of reconstructing them will be compounded by the impossibility of treating them in isolation from one another. In an interesting case, however, the illumination to be gained from a joint reading of the type outlined can be commensurate with its difficulty.

An interesting case of this sort is the subject of this book, which may be read as a case study in how a critical encounter with a literary work can draw guidance from perceptions and concepts articulated in a prior critical text about another literary work. The main theses of this book are easy enough to outline, though substantiating them will require a good deal of work. For reasons that will emerge from my argument, both Benjamin and Adorno turn to canonical literary narratives in order to determine why the Enlightenment project has been derailed and how this failure might be remedied. The critical model of the caesura enables Adorno, as it enabled Benjamin two decades earlier, to construe literary narration as the site of a philosophical truth that can dispel a thoroughgoing mystification generated by the failure of the Enlightenment. This truth has to do with an elusive species of hope that philosophical thought can best articulate through reflection on literary narration. Far from being a straightforward application of the Benjaminian model, however, Adorno's excursus on the *Odyssey* is, among many other things, an esoteric dialogue of sorts with the older friend who had taken his life in 1940 on his flight from the Nazis. As such, not only does the excursus develop a philosophical account of the origins of modern subjectivity by way of reflection on the *Odyssey*, it also indirectly illuminates some puzzling features of Benjamin's essay as well as Goethe's novel. My argument will thus bring fresh light to an important juncture in the relationship between Benjamin and Adorno, affording an improved understanding of the aporias they faced, as well as of key points of disagreement between them.

The teasing-out of implicit readings could in principle be extended further in two directions. The first route would take us to Friedrich Schlegel's celebrated review "On Goethe's *Meister*" (1798), which epitomizes the early Romantic idea of literary criticism reconstructed in Benjamin's doctoral dissertation and also served as the critical model he sought to emulate and amend in his essay on *Elective Affinities*. More important for the present argument, however, is the second line of succession, which leads us back to Friedrich Hölderlin's audacious transposition of Sophoclean tragedy into a modern register, for it was in this context that the concept of caesura that Benjamin invokes was first elaborated. This line of succession is all the more important because it implicates my argument in the highly consequential relation between antiquity and modernity, a matter of obvious relevance to the dialogue between two critical texts dealing, respectively, with Goethe and Homer.

For this reason, it will be necessary to outline relevant aspects of Hölderlin's conception of the tragic caesura. However, my discussions of Hölderlin will have to be kept relatively brief, so that the argument can remain squarely focused on the two most recent works in this chain of critical succession reaching back to the 1790s. Considerations of economy dictate this restriction of my scope. Given the radically solitary character of Hölderlin's voice, the sheer complexity of the philological, poetological, and theoretical issues raised by the relevant texts by him, and the width of the historical divide separating his writings from those of his twentieth-century readers, an attempt to keep his theory of caesura in the forefront of the discussion would have forced my argument on to sharply divergent tracks. By contrast, there is just enough historical and theoretical proximity between Benjamin's and Adorno's critical texts to permit a coherent investigation into the relation of critical succession that connects them.

To uncover the distinct layers of reading identified above, my argument will first move from Benjamin to Adorno and then return to Benjamin. The initial puzzlement that gave rise to this study suggests a road map at least for its first, longer half. I begin by laying out in chapter 1 the critical model of the caesura as it was originally developed by Benjamin in reference to a remark made by the narrator toward the end of *Elective Affinities*. With this reconstruction of the Benjaminian model in place, it will then be possible to clarify in chapter 2 the philosophical motivations and the literary basis of Adorno's postulation of a caesura in book 22 of the *Odyssey*.

In chapter 3, my argument will take a somewhat unexpected turn. As will become abundantly clear by that point in my argument, Adorno's excursus does not simply adopt the Benjaminian model but significantly reworks it. Not the least of the modifications involved in this reworking is that—as I show in chapter 3—Adorno posits a second, less sharply marked caesura in book 23 of the *Odyssey*. This move answers to a theoretical exigency at the heart of Adorno's thinking, which I will elucidate by drawing on a number of other texts by him. In chapter 4, I demonstrate that the doubling of the caesura in Adorno's excursus throws into sharp relief an analogous structure that remained implicit in Benjamin's essay on *Elective Affinitites*. For Benjamin's argument aligns the key remark by Goethe's narrator with another moment of transcendence that in certain respects exhibits the formal features of a caesura, namely, the novella "Strange Neighbors" embedded in the novel. I will argue that Benjamin's reluctance to identify this embedded story as a caesura can be explained, on the one hand, by the role of theological commitments in his thinking, and on the other, by a significant blind spot in his interpretation of *Elective Affinities*. My argument will yield a corrective in both respects.

In my conclusion, I demonstrate the adaptability and the heuristic power of the double caesura model by commenting on selected passages by Gottfried Keller, Thomas Mann, and Franz Kafka. This extension of the line of critical succession linking Benjamin's and Adorno's texts will open up a historical perspective and thus allow me to summarize the broader lessons that have emerged from my argument. The limits of the applicability of the double caesura model will be specified first with respect to its object domain, and then—against the foil of Hans Jonas's reflection on mythos and logos—with respect to the historical emergency that warrants its deployment.

Reason's Hope against Reason

Maintaining a focus on the tacit dialogue between Benjamin's and Adorno's texts will allow me to devote sustained attention to some of the central animating concerns shared by the two authors. Let me offer a preliminary survey of these concerns. To begin with the most general point, if Benjamin and Adorno pursue their philosophical agendas via reflection on literary narratives, they do so because they are preoccupied with a topic that does not lend itself to established forms of philosophical inquiry. I am referring to hope, a concept that is most obviously at home not in philosophy so much as in theology, and especially in Jewish messianism and Christian soteriology. Of course, the concept of hope is not entirely absent from the philosophical canon. Yet it would be difficult to deny that this concept has played a relatively marginal role in the mainstream of modern philosophy. In this respect, Kant's way of conceding philosophical relevance to hope is instructive, indeed symptomatic. Since, moreover, Kant's philosophy constitutes a crucial point of orientation for both Benjamin and Adorno, a review of Kant's arguments regarding hope can help us establish the basic parameters of their thinking about this matter.

In the *Critique of Pure Reason*, Kant famously declares that reason's aspirations are "united" in three questions:

1. What can I know?
2. What should I do?
3. What may I hope?[7]

In a drastically abbreviated form, Kant's answer to the last question is that in order to endow our awareness of moral duty with motivating force, we must believe that it is possible for us to partake of happiness in a degree proportionate to our morality, which in turn requires reason to postulate the unprovable but unrefutable ideas of immortality and God.[8] Under the heading of hope, then, Kant subordinates religion to philosophical reason. It could be argued, however, that Kant's answer to the third question of reason does not shed much light on hope as such. This answer and Kant's arguments in its support revolve around the proper object of a hope guided by reason; what they neglect to address is the specificity of hoping as a subjective stance. Instead, Kant effectively assimilates hope to knowledge and willing. For, after rephrasing the third question in a more elaborate form ("If I do what I should, what may I then hope?"), Kant declares that it is "simultaneously practical and theoretical."[9] By this he means that the question seeks a piece of predictive knowledge that is conditional upon the fulfillment of a moral duty. *If* we act morally—so we might paraphrase Kant's argument—*then* we may reasonably expect that we will partake of a proportionate degree of happiness. This way of framing the problem loses sight of hope's essential tentativeness and thus forecloses every possibility of understanding hope as a distinctive subjective orientation that differs in kind from both knowing and willing.

That possibility is restored, however, in the third and final work of Kant's critical edifice, the *Critique of the Power of Judgment*. For something akin to hope turns out to play a central role in Kant's account of how reason projects a hierarchical system of natural-scientific knowledge. When we form new classificatory concepts we must proceed, or so Kant argues, "as if" we knew in advance that nature in its concrete particulars were amenable to such classification, even though we know that no prior guarantee for this agreement exists.[10] Kant's account of the "regulative" idea of "purposiveness," as he calls it, is arguably the closest he comes to identifying something akin to hope. To be sure, his subordination of this principle to the aims of natural-scientific knowledge prevents this theoretical construct from shedding light on the role that hope might play outside the cognitive context, and notably in the sphere of practical agency. Nevertheless, the idea of a desirable state of affairs that we anticipate "as if" we had predictive knowledge of it at the very least suggests a conceptual framework for thinking about the distinctiveness of hope as a subjective orientation.

Even more promising in this regard is Kant's understanding of the peculiar pleasure we feel when an object of experience actually confirms our heuristic assumption of nature's conformity with reason. This notion of a pleasure attendant on a cognitive orientation is the linchpin of Kant's account of aesthetic experience. For our purposes, the key feature of the Kantian account is that it ascribes pleasure and displeasure to the faculty of feeling (*Gefühl*), one of the three basic mental powers alongside knowing and willing.[11] If the basic powers of knowledge and willing correspond, respectively, to the first two of the questions expressing reason's interest ("What can I know?" and "What should I do?"), then it seems natural enough to suppose that the question "What may I hope?" concerns the rational determination of feeling. To be sure, Kant himself does not bring the concept of feeling employed in the third *Critique* to bear upon the concept of hope elaborated in the first. In a sensitive reconstruction, however, Rachel Zuckert has done just this, with results that can help prepare the ground for some of the key themes that will emerge in my argument and are therefore worth reviewing briefly.[12]

According to Zuckert, Kant's conception of feeling comes closest to capturing the distinctive character of the hope envisioned in the question "What may I hope?" What Kant calls feeling, it must be stressed, is sharply distinguished by him from the cognitive faculty of sensation.[13] Whereas in sensation we relate passively to an object, feeling is the subject's passive relation to its own state—in the case of a representational state, the way in which the subject is affected by its own representational activity. This relation of self-affection can be further specified as a relation to the subject's aims that bears a temporal index to the future. That is to say, a state that conforms to our aims is accompanied by a feeling of pleasure that motivates us to maintain that state, for instance by realizing the object represented in it; whereas states inimical to the attainment of our aims are displeasurable and as such prompt us to flee them.

Hope, as Zuckert cautiously puts it, is "at least *like* feeling" in the sense just outlined.[14] With respect to a desirable state of affairs, hope is an affective orientation that is "positively inclined" toward the potential realization of that state of affairs. While not itself a rational motive, hope is a necessary aid to the motives set by reason. As finite beings whose pursuits cannot succeed without the cooperation of a world beyond our control, we need the tentative expectation of hope to muster the vigor and confidence required for action. Precisely because we are finite, however, hope is not to be understood as the product of a pure self-affection, as something engendered by reason's activity alone. Rather, hope is the always already given, default disposition of "a healthy animal that trusts in its place in the world, in the world's fit to its desires or requirements, as it needs to do."[15] In other words, hope is a futural orientation peculiar to the human being as a sentient organism.

As Zuckert observes, Kant's formulation of the question "What may [*darf*] I hope?"—with the verb *dürfen* connoting permission—suggests that reason's task lies in clarifying the proper object of hope and protecting hope from corruption and despair. Assuming that hope is rationally enlightened in this sense, its significance according to Zuckert lies in its power to insert the ideas of reason—which designate unknowable, timeless entities such as God and the immortal soul—"into the temporal arc of lived experience, as had by actual, individual, empirical subjects."[16] We will have occasion to return to Zuckert's point about the temporal arc of experience. For the purposes of a first approach to Benjamin's and Adorno's critical texts, however, it is above all the construal of Kantian hope as a feeling that needs to be underlined. Deeply responsive to Kant's philosophy, Benjamin's essay on *Elective Affinities* too concludes, as we will see, by identifying the "feeling [*Gefühl*] of hope" as "the innermost basis for 'the narrator's stance' " ("GEA" 355).

It must be stressed, however, that Zuckert's account of hope as a type of feeling is an ingenious piece of reconstructive interpretation rather than a doctrine propounded by Kant himself. Zuckert arrives at this account by projecting the Kantian concept of feeling, developed in the third *Critique*, back into the doctrine of rational hope elaborated in the first. Kant himself did not make this connection. In fact, in the second and the third *Critiques* Kant no longer relies on hope safeguarded by rational theology to explain the motivating force of moral duty. Instead, that motivating force is henceforth explained solely in terms of a feeling produced through pure self-affection, namely, the feeling of "respect" for the moral law.[17] In Kant's very last work, the unfinished *Opus postumum*, the postulated God of rational theology is superseded by what Kant calls "Deus in nobis," the self-positing "spirit" inherent to the human mind, and the laconic stipulation that "religion is conscientiousness" altogether obviates the question of what we may hope.[18] What this necessarily foreshortened survey of Kant's thinking about hope shows is that the intricately constructed edifice of the critical system does contain conceptual resources for thinking about hope as a distinctive orientation. The fact, however, that Kant does not make full use of these resources and instead ends up marginalizing this topic suggests that hope, with its characteristic tentativeness, can play at best an ancillary role in a system that—like much of post-Cartesian philosophy—prioritizes certitude.

The problem of hope moved to the forefront of philosophical interest in the wake of the First World War, as humankind's attitude toward the future underwent seismic changes. The nineteenth-century alternative between optimism and pessimism was rendered moot by upheavals that outpaced every prediction, as well as by the realization that humans' technological powers burdened them with a radical alternative between apocalyptic and utopian outcomes. Under the pressure of this predicament, which has only grown more acute since the Weimar era, a number of philosophers began to reckon with hope as a fundamental orientation toward the future. This interest in hope is especially pronounced in the works of German-Jewish thinkers whose broadly Marxist, secular orientation combined with a willingness to adopt figures of thought borrowed from theology. Ernst Bloch, Siegfried Kracauer, Walter Benjamin, and Theodor W. Adorno shared an attunement to intimations of a counterfactual state of things that would be free of all those forms of unnecessary suffering, blind compulsion, and ideological delusion that characterize the shared form of life dominant in Western modernity. This counterfactual state would have to be, in their view, so radically different from the historically given framework of reality that no positive conception of it can be elaborated from the standpoint of the present. Again and again, the transition to it is imagined in messianic terms. The conjunction, characteristic of these thinkers, between a broad commitment to Enlightenment reason and a utopian projection indebted to theological models has remained in the forefront of the controversies surrounding their legacies.

The radical notion of hope just outlined underwrites a critique of the attenuated forms of hope authorized by the philosophical tradition. Not surprisingly, it is the Kantian conception that serves as the target of what is arguably the paradigmatic instance of this critique. In the "Meditations on

Metaphysics" that conclude Adorno's late magnum opus *Negative Dialectics*, he zeroes in on an impasse reached in Kant's postulation of God and immortality (*ND* 384–98). The cognitive limits stipulated by Kant's critical philosophy bar him from asserting immortality and the existence of God as items of ascertainable knowledge. The dynamics of his thinking nevertheless impels Kant to claim that these metaphysical postulates are more than just figments of subjective imagining. What sort of objectivity the metaphysical postulates of practical reason might possess was, however, a question that Kant was unable resolve on the basis of his overly restrictive conception of knowledge (*ND* 391). In broad agreement with the critique of idealism developed by Georg Lukács, Adorno views Kant's restrictive epistemology as a philosophical expression of "the eminently bourgeois affirmation of one's own confinement"—in other words, as an absolutization of the socioeconomically conditioned self-understanding inculcated in bourgeois subjects (*ND* 375). In particular, the doctrine of noumenal ignorance owes whatever plausibility it has to the experience of bourgeois subjects bent on self-preservation in an economy defined by equivalent exchange and a separation between physical and intellectual labor, sensibility and thought (*ND* 382). With the metaphysical postulates of God and immortality, Kant transgresses, albeit hesitantly, the limits imposed by this conception. In so doing, his thinking gestures toward a properly historical, dialecticized conception of experience that would allow practical agency to modify the limits of experience as well as its qualitative character (*ND* 384).

The post-Kantian idealists, and Hegel in particular, espoused precisely this dialectic to claim that human knowledge can, in fact, escape the limitations of finitude and eventually become absolute. Absolute idealism thus replaces hope with a certainty of the full actualization of reason's aspiration. Premised on a belief in the sovereign authority of philosophy, such assertions of the absoluteness of spirit overlook the fact that, as Adorno puts it, "even if Kant's doctrine of the block [i.e., of humans' insurmountable cognitive limitation] was part and parcel of societal semblance, it is still as solidly well-founded as humans are factually ruled by semblance."[19] Although the critique of ideology can unmask the hypostatization of the bourgeois subject to a fixed standpoint of finitude, such unmasking does not suffice for eliminating the real socioeconomic forces that constrain subjects in ways that make this hypostasis appear deeply plausible. This being so, Adorno concludes that the inconsistency in Kant's clinging to hope is more truthful than are idealist assertions of absolute spirit. That inconsistency testifes, as Adorno puts it, to "the Kantian desire for rescue [*Rettung*]." And so Adorno concludes: "That no ameliorations within the world sufficed to do justice to the dead, that none of them touched upon the wrong of death—this is what moves Kantian reason to hope against reason. The secret of his philosophy is the unthinkability of despair" (*ND* 385). This line of thought suggests that the tremendous exertion of secular reason in Kant's work still answered to a need that was formerly met by religion. Benjamin and Adorno are of course much more willing than was Kant to draw on theological figures of thought. Indeed, Enlightenment rationality is so closely intertwined in their writings with theological figures of thought that clarifying the relationship between the two aspects remains a daunting task. The chapters that follow will bring some fresh light to this murky area.

In this connection, at least brief mention must be made of a question that will surface repeatedly in the course of my argument. In the passage quoted above, Adorno suggests that Kant's clinging to a hope against reason stems from a "desire for rescue [*Rettung*]." Yet what does it mean to rescue something that we value? A first approach to this question can be made by rehearsing a series of philological observations developed by Roland Reuss in his recent manifesto on behalf of "philology as rescue."[20] These observations concern the verb *retten* (to save), whose present participle form modifies "critique" in the Benjaminian term for rescuing critique (*rettende Kritik*). In his grammatical-historical dictionary, Johann Christoph Adelung gives the meaning of this verb as the act of swiftly tearing something or someone out of great danger. Adelung further notes that the verb stem of *retten* is descended from the Greek verb *rhuomai*, which has the same meaning; it is used by Homer, for instance, in relating how Odysseus forcibly drags his shipmates, who would rather stay in the land of the lotus-eaters, back into the ship.

In New Testament Greek, as Reuss points out, this verb expressing a forceful removal from danger, which leaves the destination of the movement open, stands in a rivalry of sorts with the verb *sózó* ("to redeem," as in the word *sotír* for "redeemer"), which implies a telos of integration, restitution, and closure in the sense of the healing of a wound. Interestingly, however, it is the non-integrative, negative verb *rhuomai* that figures in the final line of the Lord's Prayer ("*alla risai imas apo tou ponirou*," i.e., "and deliver us from evil"). What the idea of deliverance from evil suggests is thus less a closure through admission into the kingdom of God than a forcible opening made so that something valuable can be torn out of "the essentially fatal dynamics of history," as Reuss puts it—even if the outcome is uncertain. This idea is actually "decidedly more Jewish," as Reuss notes, than the word *erlösen* (equivalent to the integrative-restitutive *sózó*) that Luther uses in his translation of the final line of the Lord's Prayer. Reuss suggests that the clearest modern formulation of this idea of rescue is Benjamin's rejoinder to Marx's claim that revolutions are the locomotives of history, a claim that still implied a telos of redemptive integration. "But perhaps it is quite otherwise," Benjamin replies to Marx: "Perhaps revolutions are an attempt by the passengers on this train—namely, the human race—to activate the emergency brake" (*SW* 4:402).

It is not hard to see why Benjamin and Adorno, who both repeatedly invoked the Jewish prohibition of images in connection with utopian projection, should privilege the negative conception of saving over the integrative idea of redemption. Yet Reuss's finding that the most important Christian prayer concludes on a note that is more Jewish than Christian suggests that keeping the two conceptions apart may not be as simple as it initially appears. As readers of Benjamin's essay on *Elective Affinities* know, both the terms "redeem"/"redemption" (*erlösen/Erlösung*) and the term "rescue" (*retten/Rettung*) figure prominently in Benjamin's argument, without any sharp distinction between the two. To be sure, the fact that Benjamin is writing about a work of literature—and in particular about a work by a nominally Christian writer who was routinely reproached by his contemporaries for his pagan sensibility—means that distinctions such as the one between "rescue" and "redemption" need not necessarily be observed with definitional rigor. Still, it will not be possible to evade the question: what sort of salvaging is undertaken by Benjamin and Adorno?

This question is bound up with Benjamin's and Adorno's interest in literary narration. Adorno's argument about Kant's concession to a hope against reason already hints at an explanation for the fact that the effort to make sense of hope pushed Adorno, as it had pushed Benjamin, beyond the confines of a "pure" philosophy governed solely by the immanent movement of concepts. A further, more specific suggestion as to the direction in which philosophical thinking must extend its reach can be found in Zuckert's claim that Kantian rational hope has to do with the "temporal arc of lived experience." In the critical works examined in this study, philosophical thought turns to literary narratives to account for the paradoxical character of hope and to avoid its assimilation to more readily intelligible attitudes. What Benjamin and Adorno share, however, is not just an interest in literary narrative, but a more specific focus on narrative caesuras as moments that register a fugitive but fundamental hope through interruptions of the continuous flow of narration. Benjamin's and Adorno's interest in moments of interruption would seem to suggest that the negative idea of rescue takes precedence in their thinking over the positive one of redemption. Whether this means that they can dispense with a positive idea of redemption is one of the questions that I will attempt to address in the following chapters.

While these prefatory remarks on hope are necessarily general, it is worth pointing out that the turn to literary narration enables Benjamin and Adorno to address the problem of hope in concrete terms. Their reflections gravitate toward a specific area of life where the need for rescue or redemption is particularly acute in their view. That area is erotic love committed to an ideal of fidelity enshrined in the institution of marriage. When Benjamin's and Adorno's saving intent surfaces in their markings of narrative caesuras, that impulse arises in direct or indirect connection with marriage as a nodal point in the existing order of things, a point at which ethical and political questions become charged with the infinitizing energy of eros. A close examination of Benjamin's and Adorno's markings of caesuras in literary narratives by Goethe and Homer can bring into focus a series of searching reflections on the temporal trajectory of love between humans, on mortality, and gender relations. Benjamin's and Adorno's caesura markings thus make an important contribution to that modest discipline which Adorno terms "minima moralia" in his book of that title.

The fact that some of Benjamin's and Adorno's most suggestive meditations on these matters respond to works by Goethe and Homer, respectively, is far from accidental. Greek antiquity and the age of Goethe were the two correlative centers around which was constructed the classical canon of Germany's educated bourgeoisie. Benjamin's and Adorno's critical projects are animated by a shared resolve to submit this canon to a comprehensive critique in light of recent and impending historical catastrophes. How much violence, and what kind of violence, their critiques must deploy in response to a perceived emergency will be a recurrent question in my examination of their caesura markings. At issue in these critical junctures is the tension between Benjamin's and Adorno's aspirations for a radical transcendence of the existing order of things and their wish to make critique immanent, which is to say reliant on self-reflective moments in the historically given material. On this topic as well, my reconstruction of the dialogue between the two authors promises to be revealing.

Before embarking on the investigation just outlined, one more remark is in order, which concerns my guiding methodological premise. To gain access to the philosophical substance of Benjamin's and Adorno's reflections on literature, they must themselves be read as what they are, namely, densely woven literary texts of great allusive resonance. Equally, however, it is necessary to pay close attention to the ways in which these critical texts are responsive to their literary objects. The nature of this responsiveness emerges with exemplary clarity in Benjamin's remarks concerning the relation between philosophical truth and philological immersion in the literary work. Famously, Benjamin begins his essay on *Elective Affinities* by distinguishing philological commentary on the work's "material content" from criticism proper concerned with the philosophical truth content of the work. Crucially, however, the latter cannot be severed from the former. As James McFarland summarizes the complementarity of the two levels of inquiry, "truth content is not itself constrained by philological deference toward the posited work, but is the truth of a material content that is."[21] Without its anchoring in philological commentary, philosophical criticism would become arbitrary.[22]

The relevance of this requirement to the critical works examined in this study may not be immediately apparent. To state the obvious, neither Benjamin's essay nor Adorno's excursus is a work of academic scholarship. This much may be inferred already from the terms in which the titles chosen by Benjamin and Adorno delineate what their texts are about. During much of the twentieth century, literary scholars took for granted that their proper object of study was the literary work conceived as a self-contained artifact. By contrast, the ambiguous genitival construction "Goethe's Elective Affinities" suggests a dual focus on the work and the author, while "Excursus I: Odysseus or Myth and Enlightenment" implies that attention will be focused squarely on the hero rather than on the canonical text celebrating him.

Of course, both Benjamin and Adorno make sensitive observations about the literary works that they are writing about. However, if they delineate the scope of their reflections in ways that threaten to disrespect the integrity of the literary works at issue, much of what they have to say about these works invites the related charge of overinterpretation. An instructive reflection by Adorno addresses this very issue head-on. In the opening paragraph of his essay from 1959, "On the Final Scene of *Faust*," Adorno ponders the situation of someone writing in the wake of a civilizational collapse who refuses both the false consolations of traditional metaphysics and the equally complacent certainties of "official nihilism."[23] What remains for such a writer is "alexandrinism, interpretive immersion in traditional texts." Denied the possibility of directly expressing "metaphysical intentions," thought "seeks refuge in texts," in which it can discover what it is prohibited from straightforwardly affirming. With great sobriety, Adorno stresses that the discovery of metaphysical contents in a text does not prove their truth, and that such interpretations therefore remain bracketed by a tacit "if only it were so." On this point he makes the following comments:

> Interpretation does not seize upon what it finds as valid truth, and yet it knows that without the light it tracks in the texts there would be no truth. This tinges interpretation with a sorrow wholly unsuspected by the assertion of meaning and frantically denied by an insistence on what is the case. The gesture of interpretive thought resembles Lichtenberg's "neither deny nor believe"; to reduce this to mere skepticism would be to miss the point. For the authority of great texts is a secularized form of the unattainable authority that philosophy envisions as doctrine [*Lehre*]. To regard profane texts as sacred texts—that is the answer to the fact that all transcendence has migrated into the profane sphere and survives only where it conceals itself.[24]

It is no accident that this line of thought echoes Adorno's earlier characterization of Benjamin's "alexandrinism" as a strategy of "treating profane texts as though they were sacred."[25] Indeed, this formula offers a fitting characterization of both authors' approach to the literary passages that they identify as caesuras. Their critical operations at these junctures take place in a triangular force field charged with tensions between the poles of philology, philosophy, and theology. Thus, in marking caesuras, Benjamin and Adorno knowingly take the risk of what must count as overinterpretation from the point of view of professional scholarship. "The philosophical literary critic," writes Ulrich

Plass apropos of Adorno, "treats a literary text as if every word mattered; he overestimates the significance of literature because he lacks the professional distance of the literary theorist."[26] As this formulation makes clear, the diagnosis of overestimation presupposes the standpoint of a scholar whose self-understanding as a contributor to specialized knowledge mandates a methodologically controlled approach to literature. There is, of course, much to be said for such modesty—especially in comparison with the high-minded celebrations of literature that are sometimes meant to compensate for the embattled position of literary studies. A different way of estimating literature may be available, however, to a philosophical reader.

To characterize the discipline involved in philosophical reading of a specific kind is one of the central aims of this study. Because the interpretive strategies that Benjamin and Adorno bring to bear upon particular literary passages are no less central for understanding their conceptions than are their explicitly philosophical pronouncements, it is necessary to pay fine-grained attention to these strategies. Thus, in the chapters that follow, I will take seriously the claim implicit in Benjamin's and Adorno's texts to be *about* their respective literary objects, and I will inquire into the conditions of their "aboutness." This undertaking calls for a modified version of the stereoscopic approach that Wellmer adopts in interpreting Adorno. That is, in examining Benjamin's and Adorno's texts, not only do we need to keep both texts and their relation of critical succession in view; we must also be ready to shift our focus whenever necessary to the literary works that Benjamin and Adorno are considering.

Chapter 1

✦

Benjamin's Hard Caesura

The Hopeful Narrator of *Elective Affinities*

Kantian Reason Decisively Transformed

Written between 1919 and 1922 and published in two parts in 1924–25, Walter Benjamin's major essay "Goethe's Elective Affinities" confronts the reader with an unusual set of challenges. Apodictic and incisive, Benjamin's formulations throughout the essay never stop short of the utmost of semantic compression. His train of thought—readers must remind themselves that this impersonal discourse was produced by a person—alternates between philological arcana and rarefied speculation, and is made all the more opaque by an idiosyncratic use of concepts that are often left undefined. The rhythmic progression of the argument—what is called *Duktus* in German—follows a rigorously constructive, quasi-musical sequencing that places each sentence in a determinate relation to the one that came before as well as to the ensuing one, a stringency that seems all the more noteworthy because straightforward argumentative continuity is often lacking. The fabric of the resultant text is uniformly taut. Reading and rereading the essay, one sometimes has the impression of dealing with a vast hermetic prose poem masked as a work of philosophical criticism.

Nowhere in the essay are these qualities more conspicuously on view than in the highly elliptical and suggestive passages that mark a caesura in *Elective Affinities*, and in the related reflections on the concept of "the expressionless." These junctures have to be approached from a long way off if we are to make any sense of them. In my own approach to them in the first half of this chapter, I will initially bracket the particular textual observations that support Benjamin's claims about the ultimate significance of *Elective Affinities*. Benjamin interprets Goethe's novel with a distinctive philosophical interest, and we must first gain a preliminary understanding of the type of philosophical truth that he pursues before we can examine the specifically literary logic at work in his remarks on the caesura in *Elective Affinities*.

In trying to characterize Benjamin's philosophical orientation, however, we run up against a second difficulty. Hermetic writings are typically self-enclosed and shun direct engagement with interlocutors. Notable exceptions to this rule include the works of Johann Georg Hamann and Karl Kraus—and those of Benjamin, who was an appreciative reader of both these authors. A polemic directed against a multiplicity of targets compounds the challenges posed by Benjamin's hermetic discourse. The philosophical conception that he elaborates through a patiently immersive consideration of *Elective Affinities* is inextricably bound up with a critique of cultural tendencies that have distorted the reception of the novel. Benjamin subsumes his polemical targets under the heading of "myth." What these disparate intellectual formations have in common is, however, far from obvious—and with good reason, since myth, according to Benjamin, is a realm of indistinction in which any two things may appear as mysteriously connected.

Still, the most immediate target of Benjamin's polemic is readily identifiable. It is a book on Goethe published in 1916 by the literary scholar Friedrich Gundolf, a revered member of the esoteric circle of aesthetes gathered around the poet Stefan George. Gundolf's book elevates Goethe to a superhuman hero with a divine mandate, not just to devise works of art, but to create in an emphatic sense. Goethe's life and works are said by Gundolf to constitute a single organic unity that unfolds by a purposive, organic necessity dictated by Goethe's essential "daemon" and his divinely mandated "task." According to Benjamin, this view amounts to mythic obscurantism because it negates the all-important distinctions on which reason depends. In particular, the celebration of the poet as a creator erases the distinction between humans and God; and the postulation of an organic unity connecting life and works erases the distinction between the realm of ethical responsibility and that of artistic activity. The resultant damage done to ethics should be obvious. Less obvious but equally pervasive is the distortion wrought in the aesthetic domain. By construing Goethe's works as spontaneous expressions of lived experiences demanded by the poet's daemon, Gundolf undercuts every possibility of identifying a "layer of meaning in which the meaning of that novel autonomously reigns," as Benjamin puts it, and reduces the literary work to its archaic precursor, namely, "magical writing" ("GEA" 323).

The mythic conflation of life and work proves especially pernicious in relation to *Elective Affinities*. For in the case of that novel, the problem of myth surfaces in the work itself, and it does so in a way that implicates its author. The novel portrays mythic forces of the sort that haunted Goethe throughout his life, and these forces also leave their imprint on the novel's modes of representation and aesthetic form. Gundolf's interpretation of the novel thus documents an unholy encounter between an artwork compromised by myth and a mythic approach to art. As such, Gundolf's book is an ideal target for a wide-ranging critique of myth. This critique will find its ultimate vindication in its positive corollary, that is, in Benjamin's demonstration of a "luminous kernel of redemptive content" that *Elective Affinities* succeeds in preserving precisely because it is a work of autonomous art that resists reduction to the promptings of lived experience.

In order to arrive at this positive demonstration, however, we must traverse the negatively critical argument. Benjamin singles out Gundolf's book for polemical treatment because it crystallizes in a relatively sophisticated form certain intellectual tendencies that permeated German letters at the time Benjamin wrote his essay. For one thing, the book is an exemplary manifestation of the deeply conservative cult of art for art's sake whose high priest was Stefan George. For another, Gundolf's glorification of Goethe accords with various currents of post-Nietzschean vitalist irrationalism, as well as with a psychologizing preoccupation with lived experience that became widespread in the wake of Dilthey's work. An attempt to appropriate Goethe in the name of such a deeply conservative agenda, in a country whose unstable identity had all but become bound up with that author's legacy, was bound to be perceived by a left-leaning intellectual as an ominous development.

Benjamin's countermeasure, however, is not a simple one of repudiation. Rather, he sets out to uncover the deeper reasons for the seductive appeal that this blend of retrograde ideas evidently held in the eyes of so many contemporaries. This strand of ideological criticism in Benjamin's essay clearly anticipates the arguments that Horkheimer and Adorno would develop two decades later in *Dialectic of Enlightenment*, and it may be summarized in the claim that the various forms of mystifications that converged in Gundolf's book were symptomatic of deficiencies in the theoretical and historical implementations of the Enlightenment project. It is this diagnostic layer of Benjamin's argument that we must now examine, and we must do so with an ultimate view towards characterizing the philosophical orientation that guides Benjamin's marking of a caesura in Goethe's novel.

Central to Benjamin's diagnosis of a failed Enlightenment is the affinity he discerns between Goethe's novel and Kant's critical grounding of Enlightenment rationality. Kant's critical system is almost certainly one of the philosophical conceptions that Benjamin has in mind when he claims that the enigma of a self-obscuring work such as *Elective Affinities* can only be disclosed by way of a detour, namely, a consideration of its "siblings in the realm of philosophy."[1] In a first approach, the elective affinity with Kantian critical philosophy would appear to be a simple matter of historical proximity. For, as Benjamin writes, "at the exact moment when Kant's work was completed and a map through the bare woods of reality was sketched, the Goethean quest for the seeds of eternal growth began" ("GEA" 298).

Benjamin's subsequent argument about Kant takes its point of departure from the latter's pedantic definition of marriage as a type of contractual agreement in which the parties consent to "lifelong mutual possession of their sexual organs" ("GEA" 299). Strikingly, Benjamin stipulates that "the subject of *Elective Affinities* is not marriage" ("GEA" 302); but this disavowal must be taken with a grain of salt, as a compensatory safeguard for the rigorous impersonality of Benjamin's approach to Goethe's novel at a time when he himself was in the throes of a marital crisis that was uncannily similar to the one portrayed by Goethe. It is nevertheless true that the problem of marriage is bound up in Benjamin's essay with a larger issue. Benjamin's prefatory remarks on the poverty of the reality inventoried by Kant suggests that he invokes Kant's legalistic definition of marriage as the exemplary manifestation of a disenchanted Enlightenment reason—one that, in Benjamin's words, declines the reassuring belief "that the most essential contents of existence are capable of stamping their imprint on the world of things" ("GEA" 298).

For a more conceptually precise account of the poverty of Kantian reason, we need to turn to Benjamin's early outline "On the Program of the Coming Philosophy" (*SW* 1:101–6). There Benjamin argued that Kant's grounding of knowledge presupposed a "shallow" form of experience limited to the verifiable and mathematizable observations of Newtonian physics, that is, "experience reduced to a nadir, to a minimum of significance." Benjamin's arguably most consequential claim, however, concerns the correlation between Kant's epistemology and his moral philosophy. The mechanistic notion of experience as a domain governed by thoroughgoing causal determinism stands, according to Benjamin, "in a peculiar correspondence" with a reductive understanding of freedom. Although no clarification of this correspondence is given, we may infer that Benjamin is thinking of the disjunction between experience construed as a system in which every occurrence is determined by antecedent causes, and freedom as the absence of such heteronomous determination. A free will, according to this view, is a will that keeps itself unsullied by temporal experience. When Benjamin writes in the Goethe essay that the rigor of Kantian philosophy demanded a refusal to believe that "the most essential contents of existence are capable of stamping their imprint on the world of things" ("GEA" 298), he may be understood as alluding to Kant's radical disjunction between the world of phenomenal experience and our sublime awareness of the freedom we possess as "intelligible" or "noumenal" beings who are not subject to time (time being the form of experience for Kant).

It should not be hard to see why this way of thinking about free agency raises the specter of arbitrariness. A total absence of antecedent grounds would seem to result in that liberty of indifference whose impasse is epitomized by that hypothetical scenario commonly attributed to the Scholastic philosopher John Buridan: namely, the predicament of a donkey that starves to death because it has no reason to choose either of two equidistant heaps of straw. Although Kant believed he had averted this threat by defining the positive concept of freedom as rational self-legislation, Benjamin holds, as we shall see, that a form of freedom premised on our ability to transcend temporal experience is bound to result in a state of indecision, leaving us defenseless against arbitrary choices and irrational compulsions. This would seem to be the upshot of the quote from Klopstock that serves as the motto of the first part of the essay on *Elective Affinities*: "Whoever chooses blindly is struck in the eyes by the smoke of sacrifice" ("GEA" 297). This motto encapsulates Benjamin's version of the long-standing objection of formalism that Schiller and Hegel leveled against Kant's moral philosophy.

For the purposes of my reconstruction of the dialogue between Benjamin and Adorno, it seems important to note here that the ethical problematic broached by Benjamin will also motivate Adorno's reflections on ethics. In his *Adorno: Disenchantment and Ethics*, J. M. Bernstein has reconstructed this problematic in terms that are equally relevant to Benjamin's essay on Elective Affinities. According to Bernstein's Weberian interpretation of Adorno, a fundamental effect of the disenchantment wrought by the Enlightenment is the destruction of what Bernstein terms the "complex concept."[2] Responsive to the auratic individuality of objects and persons, the "complex concept" fused the archaic naming power of language with its communicative function. It thus acknowledged a basic passivity toward the world that is a hallmark of experience in the emphatic sense. Experience in this sense is simultaneously cognitive and ethical. To know an object in terms of the complex concept that underwrites untrammeled experience is to be disposed to the right practical engagement with it. To quote Bernstein's example, "one possesses the concept of tomato not only when one can distinguish tomatoes from apples, but when one knows and obeys the proprieties of action in relation to them (tending, picking, eating, etc.)."[3] Similarly, in my experiential relation to another person, to know the other's situation in terms of the complex concept is to be moved to perform the right act: the other is in pain, hence I must come to his help.

As the Enlightenment extended the reign of abstract concepts subservient to scientific-technical rationality, the world—to quote Bernstein's formulation—"lost its 'magic' in the simple sense that the concrete objects of experience lost their axiological colors."[4] Scientific reason excises the moments of particularity, novelty, practical relevance, and transformative significance from experience. Experience is thus reduced to a series of mathematizable data about the causal mechanisms of nature. Grasped by a disengaged subject, the invariant laws of the empirical world so understood enable technical-scientific mastery over it. As Bernstein puts it, the ideal motivating scientific reason is "a world in which nothing would or could matter to an individual, in which the course of events was neutral with respect to subjectivity, in which subjects were beyond meaningful change or transformation . . . the image of life without history."[5] Instances of experience are thus "no longer spaces of hope or despair, promises made, disasters pending."[6] No longer guided by the type of genuine experience that requires what Adorno calls "freedom toward the object," moral agency loses its former responsiveness to the plight and the singular worth of others. With freedom redefined as self-determination, the justifying ground of moral agency shifts away from the other person in his or her individuality to the self-legislated moral law, understood as the abstract form of a rationally self-determining will.[7]

The ethically disorienting situation of enlightened modernity, which Bernstein takes to be the principal challenge to which Adorno sought to formulate a response, equally forms the backdrop to Benjamin's ethical reflections, whose influence upon Adorno would be difficult to overestimate. To be sure, the remedy that Benjamin outlined in his essay on *Elective Affinities* is quite different from the one that Adorno would begin to adumbrate in the 1940s. Given the connection posited by Benjamin between the problematic of experience and that of freedom, the corrective he envisions would have to remedy both shortcomings. The "coming philosophy" would not only have to repeat the Kantian grounding of knowledge in reference to a more capacious conception of experience that might encompass archaic wishes, religious and erotic experiences, involuntary memories, madness, and intoxication; it would also have to submit the concept of freedom to a corresponding "decisive transformation [*eine entscheidende Umbildung*]" (*SW* 1:105). Using a key distinction drawn in the essay on *Elective Affinities*, we may take Benjamin to mean by "decisive transformation" a transformation by virtue of which the merely apparent freedom of blind choice (*Wahl*) might give way to a freedom that can actualize itself in the form of a genuine decision, or *Entscheidung* ("GEA" 346). The connection that Benjamin establishes between *Elective Affinities* and Kant's critical philosophy is thus more than just a heuristically useful parallel. Benjamin's redemptive critique of the novel is, I claim, the closest he comes to elaborating the decisive transformation of the Kantian critique that he declared to be of paramount importance in his early program. Indeed, the essay might be described—with a nod to Hamann and Herder—as a metacritique of Kant's critical philosophy.[8]

The two post-Kantian problems of freedom and experience converge in the conceptual crux of the essay, a passage in which Benjamin aligns two dichotomies: that of arbirary "choice" (*Wahl*) versus "decision" (*Entscheidung*) and that of lived experience (*Erlebnis*) versus integral experience (*Erfahrung*). Perhaps because the latter distinction will receive rich elaborations in Benjamin's later writings, its pertinence to the *Elective Affinities* essay has tended to escape notice in the existing scholarship. Yet already in "On the Program of the Coming Philosophy" and in the Goethe essay, the contours begin to emerge of what the later writings will envision under the heading of *Erfahrung*, namely, a continually growing repository of enduring, shareable, and ethically binding significance whose integration is the continuous work of forgetting and remembering, wishing and storytelling. Integral experience in this specific sense is gradually displaced in modernity by the isolated, and in principle mathematizable, impingements of lived experience—a transformation that Benjamin defiantly affirms in some of his writings, and soberly registers in others with a view to the aesthetic compensations devised by

Baudelaire and Proust.[9] Whereas Benjamin's later writings will attribute this transformation to the atomizing forces of capitalism and the discontinuous temporality of urban modernity, the essay on *Elective Affinities* is concerned with less historically proximate and more rarefied causes of this transformation, which have to do with deficiencies in the theoretical articulation and historical actualization of Enlightenment reason. Moreover, unlike in later writings that comment on the modern disintegration of experience, Benjamin's argument in the Goethe essay is mainly concerned with the loss of ethical orientation that results from these shortcomings.

The line of ethical reflection that runs through Benjamin's essay has not received the amount of attention warranted by its centrality to the text. The tendency to steer clear of this strand in the essay is to a certain extent understandable. Most scholars seem to find Benjamin's intense concern with "fidelity" so embarrassingly quaint that—as Sigrid Weigel notes—they typically give the relevant passages a wide berth.[10] Yet the line of thought animated by this concern arrives at a conclusion that is as disarmingly forthright as it is unsettling. Its upshot is a summary repudiation of bourgeois decorum:

> For what the author shrouds in silence a hundred times can be seen quite simply enough from the course of things as a whole: that, according to ethical laws, passion loses all its rights and happiness when it seeks a pact with the bourgeois [*bürgerlichen*], affluent, secure life. This is the chasm across which the author intends, in vain, to have his figures stride with somnambulistic sureness upon the narrow path of pure human civility. That noble curbing and controlling is unable to replace the clarity that the author certainly knew just how to remove from himself, as well as from them. (In this, Stifter is his perfect epigone.) In the mute constraint that encloses these human beings in the circle of human custom, indeed of bourgeois custom, hoping there to salvage for them the life of passion, lies the dark transgression which demands its dark expiation. ("GEA" 343)

The ethical alternative to this complacent civility is indicated early on in the essay: "Less hesitation might produce freedom, less silence clarity, less leniency the decision. Thus, cultivation [*Bildung*] keeps its value only where it is free to manifest itself" ("GEA" 302). Crucially, however, Benjamin's plea for decisiveness is not a lapse into crude vitalistic decisionism. This much should be clear from his emphatic distinction between mere "choice" (*Wahl*) and a "decision" (*Entscheidung*) that establishes fidelity by acknowledging an "affinity" between two individuals. The central claim of Benjamin's ethical reflection concerns the "unambiguous and rigorous" criterion upon which such a decision must be based: to wit, "the character of the experience [*Erfahrung*] preceding the decision." For, as Benjamin asserts, "only this experience is able to sustain the decision that, beyond all later occurrences and comparisons, reveals itself to the experiencing agent as essentially singular and unique, whereas every attempt by upright human beings to found decision on lived experience [*Erlebnis*] sooner or later fails" ("GEA" 347). Because it is prone to the blind compulsions, mechanically recurrent patterns, and demonic ambiguities of mere natural life, the immediacy of lived experience cannot serve as the basis for a decision. A new and binding beginning must be guided, instead, by experience mediated and integrated through remembrance.

What this frequently overlooked line of thought in Benjamin's essay gestures toward is, then, an ethics of remembrance.[11] Its most direct statement can be found in Benjamin's reflections on Ottilie's diary. The diary is interpreted by Benjamin as the site of a vigilant but sterile self-reflection that mutely registers experiences and thereby lays them to rest, stifling their slow and subliminal maturation toward a decision that might find expression in clear speech:

> For if it is the danger of the diary as such to lay bare prematurely the germs of memory in the soul and prevent the ripening of its fruits, the danger must necessarily become fatal when the spiritual life expresses itself only in the diary. Yet all the power of internalized existence stems finally from memory [*Erinnerung*]. It alone guarantees love a soul. It breathes in that Goethean recollection: "Oh, you were in times lived through / My sister or my wife." ("GEA" 338)

That this ethical conception borders on aesthetics becomes clear when Benjamin proceeds to link Goethean recollection to the Platonic doctrine, expounded in the *Phaedrus*, that earthly beauty prompts an anamnesis of our prenatal contemplation of the very form of beauty. Later in this chapter, I will return to this point of perilous proximity between ethics and aesthetics in order to clarify how Benjamin avoids a conflation between the two domains; and in chapter 4, I will have more to say about what the Benjaminian ethics of remembrance implies for the plot of Goethe's novel.

For now, the key point to be underscored is that the linkage between decision and integral experience enables Benjamin to embed his ethical argument in a more comprehensive critique of Kantian enlightenment. Kantian reason privileges the "naked, primitive, self-evident experience" of sense perception that furnishes data for the modern natural sciences founded by Bacon, Galileo, and Newton. Even in the context of everyday life and practical agency, Kantian enlightenment tends to be oblivious to the larger structures of significance that emerge through the workings of remembrance, and only recognizes the immediacy of lived experience. The power to reach decisions based on integral experience thus gives way to a stunted practical self-understanding that construes agency as a matter of making choices between alternate courses of action in a world charted through scientifically regimented experience. Kant's moral philosophy is accordingly addressed to the standpoint of an agent who deliberates in order to choose the maxim of action that is in conformity with pure reason. However, as Horkheimer and Adorno will argue in their recasting of a Hegelian objection, the formalism of a pure reason unsullied by empirical inclinations underdetermines agency (*DE* 70); and it is indeed easy enough to see why the purely rational principle of noncontradiction is of little avail in a marital crisis such as the one portrayed in *Elective Affinities*.[12]

Since pure reason cannot furnish sufficient grounds for a decision, and recourse to integral experience is blocked, the Kantian agent faced with such a crisis has only three options, each of which ends up delivering him over to myth. First, our agent may choose a course of action on the basis of sensible impulses or inclinations, which amounts to surrendering to natural compulsion. To mention an example from *Elective Affinities*, this is how the parties would have to decide whether they should renew or terminate a marriage after five years, according to the scheme outlined by the Count visiting the protagonists (*EA* 67). Second, an agent may choose a course of action arbitrarily, undetermined by anything. Thus, in the conversation between the spouses with which the novel opens, Eduard proposes to draw lots to determine whether or not to invite Ottilie and the captain; and similarly, Mittler declines the spouses' request for advice with the exasperated words: "Do as you like: it's all the same. Have your friends here, or leave them where they are: all one" (*EA* 16). The problem is that even if one's choice itself is arbitrary in this sense, in order to implement it in the empirical world, the agent will need to draw on capacities he possesses as an embodied natural being, and in doing so he will become, once again, subject to natural compulsions.[13] Third and finally, our agent may try to salvage his sense of freedom by sacrificing natural gratifications and acting against his inclinations in the name of duty. Such a negatively defined motive cannot prevail for long in the face of the persistent natural compulsions that shape our embodied lives. That Benjamin views the predicament of the characters in light of this last option emerges most clearly in his remarks to the effect that the characters of the novel act out of a "chimerical striving for freedom," and indeed out of a striving for "a falsely conceived freedom," which "draws down fate" upon them ("GEA" 332).

What this means is spelled out by Benjamin in terms that are, again, broadly consonant with Schiller's and Hegel's critiques of Kantian formalism. Benjamin's remarks on the characters' commitment to the restraining of passions through "cultivation" (*Bildung*) and to emancipation from tradition only serve to highlight the affinity of their ethical stance with the Kantian understanding of freedom as spontaneous choice that is not determined by antecedent causes ("GEA" 302–3). Because the characters construe freedom in such reductive terms, again and again they find themselves powerless in the face of those aspects of nature that elude rational control, which thus take on the menacing character of mythic necessity. Myth is a register of experience in which the world appears as an opaque realm of demonic energies whose vexing ambiguity defies reason's demand for clear distinctions, a realm governed by the ineluctable necessity of guilt and sacrifice ("GEA" 307–8). This was indeed—or so Benjamin argues—the dominant register in Goethe's own experience of nature as a "chaos of symbols," which informs the literary imagination at work in *Elective Affinities*.[14]

In the novel, mythic necessity surfaces in the form of the quasi-chemical attractions that govern the characters' passions. The demonic ambiguity of these attractions proves intractable when the spouses are prompted by adulterous desire to make love to each other and beget a child who will end up resembling the absent objects of their fantasies. Mythic necessity finally triumphs in the blind stipulations of a "right" (*Recht*) to which the characters cling in their futile effort to assert their power of self-determination, and which condemns all living beings to guilt and penance. What it would take to find release from the mythic forces unleashed by an incompletely realized enlightenment should be clear by now. Release from myth would require a change in the characters' understanding of experience, and together with it a "decisive transformation" of the relation between experience and free agency.

The Ideal of the Problem

Myth in the sense just outlined constitutes what Benjamin terms the "material content" of *Elective Affinities*, by which he means its time-bound, historically specific substance. Although the social world portrayed by Goethe remains captive to the mythic recurrences of mere natural life, foreclosing a genuinely historical temporality in which a free decision might establish a new order, nevertheless this way of living beneath the threshold of historical time is itself characteristic of a historically specific social world. The deep structure of this social world is defined, as we have seen, by a reductive understanding of experience and a concomitant loss of ethical orientation that leaves us defenseless against the compulsions and ambiguities of the natural domain. Benjamin's exposition of the workings of myth as the historically specific material content of the novel is, however, only the first step in his argument. This step is accomplished through a procedure he calls "commentary" ("GEA" 297). Commentary in Benjamin's sense combines philological scrutiny of the lifeworld portrayed in the novel with a type of historical and intellectual-historical contextualization that abstains from reductive forms of biographical explanation. The detour through the Kantian variant of the Enlightenment project contributes to this strand of commentary.

The ultimate aim of Benjamin's essay is, however, to bring philosophical insight to bear upon the material content that has been inventoried through commentary. Unlike the time-bound particulars of the material content, what Benjamin calls the "truth content" of the work is something that outlives the historical moment of the work's genesis ("GEA" 298). Indeed, it can only be determined from the standpoint of a posterity no longer directly enmeshed in the historical reality from which the material content derives. Establishing this truth content requires an act of construction that sheds new light on the minutiae uncovered through commentary. As Benjamin came to see things through his reworking of the early Romantic theory of criticism, significant works of art owe their internal organization to the interminable movement of self-reflection animating their linguistic medium. The task of criticism is to extend this immanent self-reflection of the literary work. Such a procedure must be destructive insofar as it mobilizes energies latent in the work that burst the semblance of closed totality conjured up by aesthetic form. To the extent that it throws into relief a philosophical truth, however, criticism also has a productive yield.

In the most general form, Benjamin's understanding of the philosophical truth at issue is outlined in the well-known opening argument of the essay, which distinguishes critique proper, interested in the truth content of the work, from the antecedent labors of commentary upon its material content. The upshot of these remarks is that the truth content and the material content are intimately bound up in every significant work. Indeed, Benjamin suggests that commentary and critique converge, since "achieved insight into the material content of subsisting things finally coincides with insight into their truth content. The truth content emerges as that of the material content" ("GEA" 300). The distinction between the two is nevertheless decisive, indeed literally so, for the critical judgment regarding the work's stature. In the historical moment that gave rise to a significant work, its truth content and material content existed in a symbolic fusion with one another, making the two indistinguishable in the eyes of contemporaries. In the eyes of later generations of readers, however, the material contents begin to stand out as the increasingly dated and opaque trappings of a bygone era, which call for commentary. Although the truth content of the work remains latent throughout this process, for that very reason it increasingly separates from the newly conspicuous material contents. What was initially a symbolic fusion between truth content and material content thus gradually gives way in the course of reception history to an allegorical juxtaposition between the two, in a process that Benjamin compares to the separation of wood into ash and fire. It is this separation effected by reception history that permits us to pose the critical question regarding the work's stature, namely, the question of "whether the semblance/luster [*Schein*] of the truth content is due to the material content, or the life of the material content to the truth content" ("GEA" 298). Whereas works exhibiting the former relation are merely ephemeral exercises in false profundity, the latter relation is the hallmark of truly significant artworks.

Now, the distance of roughly 110 years from which Benjamin approaches Goethe's novel is not so large that we should expect to find a wide gulf separating the material content described in his commentary from the correlative truth content. And yet, when later on in the essay Benjamin returns to the concept of truth content, what he has to say about it sounds curiously abstract and remote from the ethical concerns foregrounded in the exposition of myth as the material content of the novel. In light of these later comments, in fact, the truth content appears as a highly rarefied and esoteric affair. For these comments associate the truth content of artworks with a meta-philosophical problematic that has to do with the systematic aspiration and the self-reflexive character of philosophy, a problematic that Benjamin discusses under the heading of "the ideal of the problem" ("GEA" 333). By this locution Benjamin means the question regarding the ground of the systematic interconnection of all philosophical questions. So understood, the ideal of the problem identifies the ultimate desideratum of a fully achieved enlightenment: namely, the establishment of a foundational principle that would enable us to understand all the disparate lines of inquiry pursued by philosophical thought as expressions of a systematically elaborated, unitary rationality. Yet Benjamin's conception of the ideal of the problem also points to the aporia that bedevils this project of Enlightenment reason. Put simply, the question concerning the ground of unity of all philosophical questions is itself a philosophical one. Indeed, it is *the* eminently philosophical question: ever since its beginnings in Plato's dialogues, philosophy has been anxiously preoccupied with its own identity and unity as an epistemic practice.

This concern moved to the forefront of philosophical speculation in post-Kantian idealism, which took its guidance from an extremely demanding ideal of systematic unity in tackling particular philosophical questions. Fichte thought he could establish such a system on the basis of a self-evident unconditional principle, whereas Hegel claimed to have achieved systematicity by demonstrating the dialectical interdependence among moments of the Notion. Because of his broadly Kantian orientation, Benjamin is barred from pursuing either of these strategies. Consequently, he holds that the ground of the unity of all philosophical questions entails an endlessly recursive progression. Every putative formulation of the question designated by the ideal of the problem would merely yield a new totality of philosophical questions, requiring us to formulate the question concerning their ground of unity anew, and so on ad infinitum.[15] It follows from this infinite recursiveness, moreover, that the ideal of the problem cannot be spelled out in the form of a question that one might actually pose, let alone answer. At most, the ideal of the problem can be given a presentation that highlights its problematic character. This, however, is not something that philosophy can achieve. Rather, philosophy must here become criticism of art and look to art for presentations that have an affinity with the ideal of the problem.

I quote the key passage in which Benjamin equates the truth content of works of art with the ideal of the problem:

> The ideal of the problem . . . lies buried in a manifold of works, and its excavation is the business of critique. The latter allows the ideal of the problem to appear in the work of art in one of its manifestations. For critique ultimately shows in the work of art the virtual possibility of formulating the work's truth content as the highest philosophical problem. ("GEA" 334)

Paul North has given an illuminating explication of this key juncture.[16] As North argues, the kinship between the problematic systematic ideal of philosophy and the work of art is fundamentally a matter of appearing. Philosophy consists of an open-ended body of questions, a system whose perpetual expansion is driven by the ideal of a rational totality; however, this ideal underwriting all lines of philosophical questioning must remain virtual and unactualized, forever threatening philosophy with illusoriness. Artworks, by contrast, are actual constructs of semblance that appear as strongly unified. "Not analogous to philosophical systems, with no rational correspondence," as North concludes, "artworks nevertheless 'let' the ideal of philosophy's problem appear, as *apparance* [*sic*]. Actual apparitions, they lend truth to philosophy's fantasy."[17]

We might add that the works of art that appear most strongly unified are the ones we call beautiful. Benjamin's claim that the ideal of the problem finds indirect exhibition in significant works of art must therefore be understood in conjunction with the dense remarks on beauty that occur later on in the essay. If, as the Kantian doctrine of aesthetic ideas suggests, a beautiful appearance is one characterized by a certain imaginative inexhaustibility, then the work of art may be thought of as a finite, unified object that contains within itself just such an aesthetic infinity.[18] However, the way in which this infinity appears in art is characterized by an "apparance" (to use North's neologism) that is akin to the one attaching to the virtual, forever deferred, idea of totality animating philosophy. For Benjamin suggests that the beguiling plenitude of beautiful semblance also hints at something that must remain latent in it: it is "the veil thrown over that which is necessarily most veiled" ("GEA" 351). Constitutive of beautiful semblance is something that "remains essentially identical to itself only when veiled," and which would be "transformed in the unveiling." Indeed, once unveiled, this latent kernel would become—in Benjamin's deliberately ambiguous word—"*unscheinbar*," which is to say both non-apparent and unremarkable.

Although Benjamin calls this latent kernel of beautiful semblance a "secret," it should not be construed as some sort of esoteric wisdom. Jan Urbich has given a rigorous elucidation of Benjamin's understanding of the secret shrouded by beautiful semblance, which brings to light a surprising affinity between the Benjaminian theory and the Hegelian logic of essence.[19] In what follows I adopt Urbich's reconstruction, interlacing it with certain Kantian motifs that I take to be relevant to Benjamin's conception.

While Urbich takes his point of departure from the phenomenology of the beautiful, his argument quickly takes a speculative turn. To every beautiful object as such belongs lively semblance. Such lively semblance exists only in relation to an appreciating subject's embodied life—or as Kant puts it, to the "enlivening" of the subject's faculties in conjunction with the body.[20] Thus partaking of life, beautiful semblance is inherently ephemeral. However, the essence that appears in beautiful semblance—that of which it is the semblance—is something enduring. Whether legitimate or spurious, a *claim* to represent some such timeless essence is implicit in the semblance belonging to every beautiful object as such. That claim announces itself in the sense of fulfillment and self-sufficiency characteristic of aesthetic pleasure, as well as in its self-perpetuating dynamic, a feature central to Kant's aesthetics.[21] The semblance involved in beauty is thus dialectical: it is the positive, symbolic actualization of a timeless essence; however, since all semblance as such is ephemeral, the semblance belonging to the beautiful is also the opposite of this timeless essence, and hence at most an illusory evocation of it. The essence of the beautiful is therefore something that actualizes itself through its veiling. As Benjamin puts it, beauty is "essence—one which . . . remains essentially identical to itself only when veiled" ("GEA" 351).

Benjamin holds, of course, that in the case of significant works of art this index inscribed in beautiful semblance to something constitutively veiled is not just a mirage but the mark of a genuine truth content. Moreover, Benjamin takes that truth content to be convergent with the ideal of the problem, as it has been previously defined. To make sense of this connection, the concept of "apparence" developed by North and Urbich's Hegelian interpretation of the dialectic of beauty need to be complemented with a Kantian argument. For, in asserting a connection between the artwork and the systematic ideal of philosophy, Benjamin's thinking seems broadly in line with the linkage established by Kant between "aesthetic ideas" and ideas of reason. In the *Critique of the Power of Judgment*, Kant argues that beautiful works of art present aesthetic ideas, that is, richly patterned sensible manifolds that elicit in the viewer's mind a pleasurable and hence potentially interminable proliferation of associations that no finite concept can subsume; and Kant argues, furthermore, that the way in which such a sensible manifold eludes subsumption under finite concepts can evoke a rational idea of totality that transcends experience.[22] This evocation occurs by a kind of inverse analogy: a sensible manifold that *eludes subsumption* under finite concepts calls forth a rational idea of infinitude that *transcends instantiation* in any sensible object subsumable under finite concepts. This Kantian doctrine may be understood as a technically elaborate equivalent to North's gloss on Benjamin's thought, namely, that artworks "'let' the ideal of philosophy's problem appear, as *apparance*."[23]

The "apparence" in question, it must be stressed, is not a straightforward appearance. The imaginative inexhaustibility of the beautiful artwork can only evoke the rational idea of totality by an inverse analogy, but it cannot give a positive exhibition of that rational idea. We can rephrase this point in terms of the Hegelian dialectic of semblance elucidated by Urbich. When the beautiful semblance of the artwork engages and enlivens the viewer's mind and calls forth a rational idea of totality, it thereby renders that otherwise elusive, transcendent idea effectively actual (*wirklich*). However, precisely because this actualization occurs in the temporal and noncommittal register of aesthetic play, it also creates a veil of beguilingly lively semblance. This lively semblance obscures the true character of the transcendent idea of reason, namely, the fact that this idea is the virtual projection of a binding totality that is immune to time. What all this implies for criticism is above all a forceful repudiation of the view—a piece of "philosophical barbarism," according to Benjamin—that beauty is truth become visible:

> The task of art criticism is not to lift the veil but rather, through the most precise knowledge of it as a veil, to raise itself for the first time to the true view of the beautiful . . . to the view of the beautiful as that which is secret. Never yet has a true work of art been grasped other than where it ineluctably represented itself as a secret. ("GEA" 351)

In art criticism, aesthetic contemplation of beauty is not just a source of disinterested pleasure taken in the free play of our faculties, but a necessary preliminary to recognizing the artwork as an intimation of that systematic ideal of rationality which stands in the vanishing point of every philosophical inquiry and eludes positive representation. The task incumbent on art criticism of the Benjaminian sort, then, is not to derive from the work of art the answer to a particular question but to draw attention to a fundamental questionableness, a semblance engendered by something that constantly withdraws from appearing, which the work of art has in common with the open-ended totality of philosophy. The task, in other words, is to intimate a question at the heart of the work that cannot be formulated.

There is, to be sure, something puzzling about Benjamin's exceedingly abstract determination of the truth content of art in terms of the open-ended totality of philosophy. Read in isolation, his hermetic pronouncements on this matter might easily be misconstrued as implying that the truth content of all works of art is the same empty placeholder for a question that cannot be formulated. Such a reading would attribute to Benjamin a position reminiscent of Heidegger at his most obscurantist and reductive—the Heidegger who sees every artwork, whether by Hölderlin, Van Gogh, or Trakl, as a pious gesture toward the ineffable question of Being.[24] As we have seen, the opening argument of Benjamin's essay runs counter to this sort of fixation upon an empty depth. For there Benjamin contends that the truth content of every significant work is "inconspicuously and intimately" "bound up" with its material content, such that the truth content of the work endows its material content with "life" ("GEA" 297–98). Our problem now is that it is not immediately clear how Benjamin's interpretation of *Elective Affinities* conforms to this general scheme. Why should the question of the problematic unity of philosophy be thought to be bound up with the historically specific predicament of an incomplete enlightenment turned mythic, the latter being the putative material content of *Elective Affinities*? And if Benjamin is right that the truth content of great works enlivens their material content, in what sense is it the philosophical problematic of systematicity that endows Goethe's portrayal of the mythic predicament with "life"?

To answer this question, we need to recall that release from myth, according to Benjamin, would consist in a "decisive transformation" of the relation between experience and freedom. Under the aegis of an incomplete enlightenment, we are in thrall to the freedom of choice—a "falsely understood freedom" that we seek to actualize by choosing either on the basis of lived experience or against it—and hence we remain susceptible to the dark promptings of a nature that lies beyond the reach of our narrowly conceived reason. The alternative to this mythic captivity would be the ability to make genuinely binding decisions on the basis of integral, that is to say remembered, experience. We can now see that the decisive transformation envisioned by Benjamin has everything to do with the unformulable question concerning the unity of philosophy. To notice the connection, all we have to do is remember that the concept of experience and the question of what constitutes free agency stand in the center, respectively, of theoretical and practical philosophy—these two being the branches of philosophy whose problematic relation poses the greatest challenge to the Kantian aspiration for a philosophical system. The ideal of free choice upheld by Kantian enlightenment is "a falsely understood freedom," one that requires insulation from temporal experience; and with the inevitable failure of this "chimerical striving for freedom," we are bound to revert to making choices that obey natural inclinations akin to the affinities between chemical elements. Resurfacing as the decay product of a failed enlightenment, myth assimilates free agency to the deterministic realm of nature and thereby erases the distinction between the respective domains of practical and theoretical philosophy. Decision based on integral experience would restore the connection between the two domains without obliterating their difference.

Here it is helpful to turn, however briefly, to a sketch titled "The Theory of Criticism" from 1919–20 in which Benjamin first outlined his theory of the ideal of the problem. In this sketch, unlike in the essay on *Elective Affinities*, Benjamin offers an explanation for the claim that the ideal of the problem finds its presentation in a multiplicity of artworks. The reason for this correspondence is that each philosophical question constitutes a unique locus within the forever emergent system of philosophy, a point of departure from which our pursuit of increasingly fundamental questions can approach the elusive ultimate question concerning the ground of the unity of the projected systematic totality (*SW* 1:218). Accordingly, there can be diverse artistic manifestations of the ideal of the problem, depending on the specific philosophical issue that the work of art relates to the ideal of the problem, that ideal being the common vanishing point of every line of philosophical inquiry. Hence, each philosophical problem may be correlated with a significant work of art. Conversely, Benjamin holds the rather counterintuitive view that the complete set of significant works of art constitutes a "harmonious" order that is homologous with the philosophical system. Let us now recall, furthermore, the related point that philosophical questions arise within a potentially endless historical process animated by the dream of systematic totality, such that each philosophical question bears an index to a unique historical moment.[25] It should now be clear that the relation between particular philosophical problems and the ideal of the problem maps onto the relation between the historically specific material content and the abiding truth content of the work of art.

Let us now see how this scheme is implemented in Benjamin's interpretation of *Elective Affinities*. One of the abiding problems of philosophy is that of the relation between theoretical and practical philosophy, or experience and freedom. In Goethe's novel, this problem appears on the level of material content, in the historically specific form of myth born of incomplete enlightenment. Myth, in this sense, involves a calamitous conflation between experience and freedom that will tend to occur in the midst of a supposedly enlightened social world whose deficient rationality seeks in vain to keep the two domains apart by severing their connection. Goethe's novel does not simply illustrate this disastrous dynamic. Rather, Goethe's oppressive depiction of the characters' mythic entrapment is at least intermittently enlivened and transfigured by intimations of the elusive, forever problematic ideal of systematicity that might, were it attained, hold the key to solving this predicament. In a manner that broadly parallels Kant's interpretation of aesthetic experience as the intimation of the undemonstrable unity of theoretical and practical philosophy, Benjamin construes *Elective Affinities* as an artistic adumbration of the problematic ideal of systematicity that would settle the relation between these two branches of philosophy.

Ethical Ambiguity and Ambiguous Beauty

It is important to remember here that the ideal in question is a regulative one that cannot be attained. The system that would integrate experience and freedom remains a problematic ideal for Benjamin, one whose indirect exhibition in art must take the form of a beautiful semblance that simultaneously veils and indicates a constitutively hidden "secret." This is in keeping with

Benjamin's stipulation in the outline "On the Program of the Coming Philosophy": "no matter how necessary and inevitable it may be to reconstruct, on the basis of a new transcendental logic, the realm of dialectics, the realm of the transition between the theory of experience and the theory of freedom, it is just as imperative that this transformation not end up in a confounding of freedom and experience" (*SW* 1:106, translation modified). Benjamin's assertion that the criterion of decision lies in the integral experience preceding the decision should not be misconstrued as a theorem that actually secures the linkage between experience and freedom once and for all. This assertion does not solve the familiar problem of the relation between theoretical and practical philosophy so much as it offers a more acute and truthful formulation of that problem.

To treat the assertion as a theorem identifying the solution would be to misunderstand it as meaning that the integral experience preceding the decision unequivocally prescribes a motive to act in a certain way. In this misguided view, an agent can arrive at the right course of action by something like straightforward deductive inference from their antecedent experience—as though the criterion of experience might yield ascertainable knowledge of what is morally right. As Winfried Menninghaus has pointed out, however, Benjamin rejects the idea that moral action is explicable in terms of motives that might be integrated into the order of objective knowledge.[26] Ethically relevant subjective states—of which hope and conviction are of particular interest to Benjamin—may of course provide agency with a certain measure of guidance. What they cannot do is unequivocally prescribe for each situation an appropriate course of action. For, as Benjamin stipulates, "the empirical realization [*Vollzug*] of ethics [*Sittlichkeit*] is never specified in the ethical [*sittlichen*] norm."[27]

The impossibility of deducing an ethical decision from experience should also be clear from the fact that it is integral, rather than lived, experience that is ethically relevant. Unlike the regimented experience that serves natural-scientific knowledge, integral experience is formed through an interplay of forgetting and remembrance that is mediated by such cultural practices as storytelling. It is an open-ended process rather than a rule-governed procedure for arriving at a cognitive judgment. As Benjamin will write in his essay on Leskov, the counsel of experience conveyed by a storyteller is "less an answer to a question than a proposal concerning the continuation of a story which is in the process of unfolding" (*SW* 3:144–45). There is, of course, more than one way of continuing a story, and the continuation one chooses can retroactively alter the meaning of what came before. In making an ethical decision on the basis of prior integral experience, one also decides on a certain interpretation of that experience.

Already in its opening chapter, *Elective Affinities* offers an illustration of just how inconclusive the criterion of integral experience can be. When Eduard insists that the spouses should invite the captain to their estate,

Charlotte, who claims as a woman to be especially attuned to how things "hang together" in life, declares: "my feelings are against the idea. I have a presentiment [*Ahnung*] that nothing good will come of it" (*EA* 8). In reply to Eduard's accusation that she is being superstitious, she explains:

> "I am not superstitious," Charlotte replied, "and attach no importance to these vague promptings [*dunklen Anregungen*]—if they were only that. But they are most often unconscious memories of fortunate and unfortunate consequences which, in our experience, have resulted from our own or other people's actions [*unbewußte Erinnerungen glücklicher und unglücklicher Folgen, die wir an eigenen oder fremden Handlungen erlebt haben*]. And in any situation nothing is more significant than the intervention of a third party. I have seen friends, brothers and sisters, married couples, and couples in love whose relationships have been wholly altered and their circumstances entirely reshaped by the fortuitous or chosen advent of somebody new." "That might happen," said Eduard in reply, "when people go blindly about their lives, but not if experience has already brought them some enlightenment and are more conscious of what they are doing [*die schon durch Erfahrung aufgeklärt, sich mehr bewußt sind*]." "Consciousness, my dear," said Charlotte to this, "is an inadequate weapon, and may indeed be a dangerous one for whoever wields it." (*EA* 8)

The next chapter of the novel shows, however, that such an enlightened consciousness of the limits of consciousness is insufficient for telling true premonitions from false ones. Arguing against the plan to invite the captain and Ottilie, Charlotte voices the worry that the two might end up falling in love with each other—but withholds from Eduard a crucial piece of information, noted only by the narrator, that suggests a different reason for her unease. Before their belated marriage, when Charlotte had already "ceased to think of herself in relation to Eduard," she introduced Ottilie to Eduard with the secret intention to arrange a marriage between the two—a scheme that fell through because "Eduard had his earlier love for Charlotte obstinately in mind" (*EA* 13–14). In light of this prehistory, we might reasonably suspect that the idea of inviting Ottilie to the estate—which Charlotte half-heartedly suppresses at first but eventually divulges to Eduard—stems from Charlotte's vague intimation that her belated marriage to Eduard was after all a mistake and Ottilie had all along been the right match for him. If this is the case, then Charlotte heeds a truthful premonition rooted in integral experience, not when she initially rejects Eduard's plan, but when she finally consents to it; and conversely, her previously voiced misgivings must be chalked up to a reluctance to acknowledge doubts about the belatedly fulfilled bond between Eduard and herself.

The questions surrounding the backstory of the novelistic plot are central to Benjamin's interpretation of the novel and will be addressed in more detail in chapter 4.[28] For the present purposes, the key point illustrated by Charlotte's wavering is that integral experience cannot become the secure possession of a self-transparent subject. As an ethical criterion, it is indispensable yet equivocal. This is another way of saying that the transition from experience to action is not continuous but requires an act, precisely, of decision. One who is about to make a decision must take her guidance, on the one hand, from an anterior ethical orientation such as hope or conviction, and on the other, from the integral experience preceding the decision. However, neither the one nor the other unequivocally prescribes the course of action that one must adopt. Nor is there a generalizable method for determinining what an agent's preceding experience, interpreted in light of her ethical orientation, dictates vis-à-vis the singular situation at issue. The connection between theoretical and practical philosophy must therefore remain a problematic one.

This is the consideration that I take to motivate Benjamin's claim that the project of reestablishing the connection between experience and freedom cannot result in a confounding of the two domains. Accordingly, in the outline "On the Program of the Coming Philosophy," Benjamin asserts that the "world-historical superiority" of the Kantian system lies in its tripartite division into epistemology, moral philosophy, and aesthetics, which in turn rests on the triad of relational categories established by Kant (*SW* 1:106). The coming philosophy envisioned by Benjamin would therefore have to preserve this systematic "typology" (*Typik*). Benjamin's highly compressed remarks imply, moreover, that the post-Kantian idealists erred in not basing the progression from a thesis through an antithesis to a synthesis on the Kantian categories of relation. Crucially, however, Benjamin does not aim to remedy this mistake by recasting the post-Kantian progression in terms of the relational categories identified by Kant. The project he outlines refuses to conform to the progression from thesis through antithesis to synthesis that is often viewed as the template for dialectical thinking. For, as Benjamin declares, "beside the concept of synthesis, another concept, that of a certain nonsynthesis of two concepts in another, will become very important systematically, since another relation between thesis and antithesis is possible besides synthesis" (*SW* 1:106). This key remark suggests that Benjamin intends to rethink aesthetics—the systematically central third domain between epistemology and morality—as the domain of a "nonsynthesis" between theoretical and practical philosophy, experience and freedom.

What could this possibly mean? To answer this question, we must return to the previously noted point of perilous proximity between ethics and aesthetics. As we have seen, the ethics of remembrance that establishes a problematic, fallible linkage between experience and freedom borders in Benjamin's conception on a Platonic aesthetics of erotic anamnesis. In order to found fidelity in love, a decision must take its guidance from the commanding power of beauty interiorized through remembrance, rather than from the erratic lived experience of passion ignited by the immediate and necessarily ephemeral presence of beauty ("GEA" 344). At the heart of Benjamin's critique of *Elective Affinities* is, however, an insight into the vexing ambiguity of beauty. This ambiguity may be viewed as the aesthetic flip side, as it were, of the equivocity that plagues the ethical criterion of integral experience so long as the ideal of systematic totality remains a merely virtual projection.

We have already seen that Benjamin's thinking takes up Platonic and Kantian themes in construing beauty as an intimation of philosophical systematicity, and in particular of the connection between experience and free agency, truth and goodness. For beautiful semblance unquestionably appears in experience, and it has the power to instill aspirations and command actions. As Plato warned, however, the same seductive force with which a beautiful human shape can impel the lover to embark on the long stepwise ascent toward the universal form of beauty may also arrest him in the preliminary stage of erotic obsession, leaving him defenseless in the face of sexual compulsion. A few years before Benjamin wrote his essay, this danger inherent in Platonic eros found expression in the final thoughts addressed to Phaedrus by the love-struck and mortally ill writer-protagonist of Thomas Mann's *Death in Venice*.[29] The Platonic proviso that "beauty is inessential without memory" ("GEA" 338) can only caution against this pitfall but does not provide a definitive safeguard.

Much the same applies to the modern equivalent of the Platonic proviso, which can be found in a seemingly technical detail of Kant's account of aesthetic pleasure. When Kant describes our delight in the beautiful as a state of free harmonious play involving a sensuous element and a conceptual one, the sensuous element he identifies is not simply the passively received data of the senses, but that sense data as it has been worked upon by the reproductive imagination, the latter being a technical term for that basic function of memory which is at work in all perception.[30] The pure judgment of taste can maintain its essential disinterestedness—which, according to Kant's strikingly counterintuitive definition, consists in its lack of dependence on the existence of the beautiful object—only to the extent that the object's immediate presence to the senses has been mediated, interiorized, and hence superseded, by memory. Even so, Kant stresses that the pure judgment of taste can always surreptitiously slip into an impure, because merely appetitive, type of delight in something "agreeable" given to the senses.[31]

Benjamin complicates this ancient Platonic problematic, however, by embedding his relevant reflections in a dialectical conception of myth. The lapse into animality that Plato cautions against is not the only pitfall associated with beauty—though Benjamin's emphasis on the demonic ambiguity of sexual phenomena certainly betrays that Platonic worry ("GEA" 335). There is also a more subtle danger lurking here. The very immediacy that accounts for the power of beauty over us can also induce us to mistake the intimation of a systematic totality for its actual givenness. We may thus succumb to the illusion that the beautiful object or person we admire somehow embodies in a self-evident and harmonious form everything we could possibly need to know, for the purposes of practice as well as theory. In Kantian parlance, this illusion might be described as the mistaking of a regulative idea for a constitutive concept that can be instantiated in experience. The seductiveness of this illusion is at least partly due to the fact that it induces us to believe that totality is something we might actually possess in the form of the beautiful person or object, rather than an ideal projection. If, moreover, the ideal unity intimated by beautiful semblance appeals to us because it promises release from myth, and we mistake this intimation for an achieved transcendence of myth, then in fact our enchantment by beauty has left us utterly defenseless in the face of myth and thus delivered us over to the most insidious mythic enchantment.

It is then one of Benjamin's most important claims about Goethe that, not being "proof against the power of living beauty" ("GEA" 349), he was uniquely vulnerable to the delusion just described. Of course, this claim about the empirical author would be uninteresting if Goethe's enchantment by beauty did not surface in his works. Benjamin argues, however, that it very much does, and that it surfaces in a particularly virulent way in the beautiful semblance that suffuses *Elective Affinities*. This beautiful semblance emanates from a single character, namely, Ottilie, whom Benjamin describes as the center of the novel. Her central position is due to the fact that her erotic-aesthetic appeal is not limited to the other characters but also casts a spell upon the narrator, and indeed, crucially, upon the empirical author Goethe as well. It would, of course, be imprecise to say that Goethe was in thrall to a fictional character of his own invention—though in a statement cited by Benjamin, Goethe himself all but admitted as much ("GEA" 354). What enthralled Goethe, leaving him defenseless in his art as well as in his life, was "the power of living beauty" in all its forms ("GEA" 349).

Ottilie is thus not simply a character whom Goethe portrays as beautiful. Rather, Goethe's imagining and portrayal of Ottilie is the fullest manifestation of an authorial stance in which sovereign artistic activity becomes compromised by the passivity of erotic captivation. Goethe's passionate investment in Ottilie "removes" her, as Benjamin puts it, "from the epic plane in which the writer reigns, and . . . transmit[s] a foreign animation [*fremde Lebendigkeit*] to her for which he is not responsible" ("GEA" 338, translation modified). As a consequence, in Goethe's portrayal of Ottilie artistic shaping gives way to what Benjamin calls "conjuration." The archaic echoes of that term are apt, for the activity so designated by Benjamin amounts to a regression from the sovereign authority that the modern institution of autonomous art confers upon the artist. Whereas autonomous art imposes form upon the pre-rational chaos of life, conjuration uses "formulas," such as the admiring epithets that the narrator bestows on Ottilie, in order to combine elements of that chaos into potent symbols, all the while pretending to be creating something out of nothing ("GEA" 319, 338, 340). One of the reasons, then, why Benjamin chose *Elective Affinities* as the object of his "exemplary criticism" is that its mode of narration, perilously poised on the boundary between art and conjuration, compels a rigorous reckoning with the question of what art is in the first place, and hence a demarcation of art from non-art.[32]

Whenever Goethe transgresses the confines of art in evoking Ottilie's beauty, he succumbs to the same mythic powers that doom his characters. This verdict is supported by the observation that Goethe's conjuration makes Ottilie's beauty inseparable from her "plant-like muteness," the fact that she "vegetates without decision," as well as from a virginal innocence whose spuriousness is evident from the erotic appeal it holds, attesting to the demonic ambiguity endemic to the mythic sphere ("GEA" 335–37). The mythic evocation of Ottilie's beauty finally reaches its apotheosis in her portrayal as an innocent martyr who is fated to incur guilt but whose sacrificial death atones the transgressions of the others and thereby affords reconciliation ("GEA" 309). Hence the deeply morbid character of the "foreign animation" that Goethe's conjuration imparts to the figure of Ottilie, and by way of her to the novel as an aesthetic totality.

Yet this unsparing criticism leveled at Goethe on interrelated ethical and aesthetic grounds combines in the essay with Benjamin's tribute to a powerful countervailing impulse at work in Goethe's novel. *Elective Affinities* thus becomes in Benjamin's interpretation a monument, not to a heroic triumph—as Gundolf and other conservative critics would have us believe—but to an inner struggle that remains undecided. According to Benjamin's interpretation, the novel lodges a rebellious "protest" in the medium of art against the mythic powers that engulf the narrative and to which Goethe submitted in his life ("GEA" 326–27). This struggle reaches the highest pitch of intensity in the portrayal of Ottilie, whose figure simultaneously epitomizes a captivation by myth and a saving impulse on Goethe's part. "For what is clear in all of this," asks Benjamin as he approaches the conclusion of his essay, "if not one thing: that it is the figure—indeed the name—of Ottilie which spellbound Goethe to this world, so that he could truly rescue someone perishing, could redeem in her a loved one?" ("GEA" 354).

The reference to Ottilie's name is decisive. Earlier in the essay Benjamin alluded to a passing comment made by Goethe in *Poetry and Truth*, which makes clear that he had borrowed the name Ottilie from the legendary figure whose blindness was healed through baptism and who subsequently became the patroness saint of good eyesight.[33] This circumstance, along with a constellation of textual details that Benjamin assembles with considerable philological ingenuity, lend support to his claim that Ottilie embodies the very principle of "gentle veiled beauty" ("GEA" 344). It is because Ottilie embodies a gentle kind of beautiful semblance that this beauty appears—but merely appears—to afford a reconciliation that requires no conflict and whose characteristic affect is a kind of complacent sentimentality (*Rührung*). However, the emphasis on Ottilie's name helps Benjamin establish the key point that Goethe went beyond conjuring up the semblance emanating from Ottilie and took care to identify her *as* a figure epitomizing beautiful semblance. Goethe did so, moreover, because even as he was writing in thrall to the beautiful semblance that he was conjuring up, he also struggled "to rescue what is essential in it" ("GEA" 349). Based on the line of thought explicated earlier, we can guess what Benjamin means by this: namely, the "secret" that "remains essentially identical to itself only when veiled" ("GEA" 351). Goethe rescues this non-apparent, essential dimension of beauty by showing the beautiful semblance emanating from Ottilie to be at its most intense when it is in the process of extinguishing as Ottilie starves to death ("GEA" 349, 354). By this means the novel counters the alluring illusion of achieved totality that arises from beautiful semblance and acknowledges that the essence of beautiful semblance is something that cannot itself appear. An exemplary manifestation of Goethe's unresolved struggle against myth, *Elective Affinities* is, in Benjamin's interpretation, a deeply equivocal construct that simultaneously engenders and dispels the illusion that beauty actually instantiates a systematic synthesis of experience and freedom.

The Expressionless

Although the self-critique on Goethe's part that emerges from this interpretation of Ottilie's extinguishing beauty is a remarkable finding, it is still a purely negative one. In terms of the systematic project of "On the Program of the Coming Philosophy," one might say that Ottilie's extinguishing beauty can be understood as showing that beauty is not the achieved synthesis between experience and freedom; but it does not yet establish a determinate relation of "nonsynthesis" between the two domains. In no way can Ottilie's slow expiration be understood as a manifestation of the sort of truth content that Benjamin is after. According to a particularly intriguing yet opaque doctrine of Kant's third *Critique*, the human shape constitutes the archetypical "ideal of beauty" that serves as the ultimate yardstick for aesthetic judging, including of artworks.[34] Yet if there is a non-apparent secret underlying human beauty it is personhood, and not the ideal of the problem that Benjamin identifies as the truth content of art. From the lover's point of view, to be sure, the beautiful human being may come to symbolize the projected systematic totality that would integrate experience with freedom. However, only a beautiful work of art can by means of its material content thematize a specific philosophical problem with a view toward the projected totality of philosophy. Truth content pertains to works of art alone, not to human persons.

The spell cast by beauty is equally perilous in both cases, however. If Goethe had to murder Ottilie (as he bitterly remarked) in order to rescue what was essential in her beauty, Benjamin will have to exercise a certain measure of critical violence to salvage the truth content hidden beneath the spurious beauty permeating *Elective Affinities*. As he asserts, "only an incorruptible rationality, under whose protection the heart might abandon itself to the prodigious, magical beauty [*der ungeheueren, beschwornen Schönheit*] of this work, is able to cope with it" ("GEA" 339–40). In order to examine how this critical rationality vindicates the philosophical truth content of the novel, we must shift our attention from Ottilie's beauty to the beauty that suffuses the novel as an aesthetic artifact. Of course, the distinction between the two is merely heuristic, for the beauty that spreads over the novel emanates from Ottilie as the focal point of Goethe's enchanted-enchanting conjuration. Still, it is on the level of the artwork as a constructed whole that beauty can intimate the problematic ideal of the philosophical system; and it is also on this level that beauty threatens to be mistaken for the achieved actuality of that ideal.

The difficult key passage to which we must turn now describes a constituent of significant artworks that preempts this very mistake:

> Artistic creation neither "makes" anything out of chaos nor permeates it; and one would be just as unable to engender semblance, as conjuration truly does, from elements of that chaos. This is what the formula produces. Form, however, enchants chaos momentarily into world. Therefore, no work of art may seem wholly alive, in a manner free of spell-like enchantment [*ungebannt lebendig*], without becoming mere semblance and ceasing to be a work of art. The life undulating in it must appear petrified and as if spellbound in a single moment. That which in it has being is mere beauty, mere harmony, which floods through the chaos (and, in truth, through this only and not the world) but, in this flooding-through, seems only to enliven it. What arrests this semblance, spellbinds the movement, and interrupts the harmony is the expressionless [*das Ausdruckslose*]. That life grounds the secret [*Geheimnis*]; this petrification grounds the content in the work. Just as interruption by the commanding word is able to bring out the truth from the evasions of a woman precisely at the point where it interrupts, the expressionless compels the trembling harmony to stop and through its objection [*Einspruch*] immortalizes its quivering. In this immortalization the beautiful must vindicate itself [*sich verantworten*], but now it appears to be interrupted precisely in its vindication, and thus it has the eternity of its content precisely by the grace of that objection. The expressionless is the critical violence which, while unable to separate semblance from essence in art, prevents them from mingling. It possesses this violence as a moral dictum. In the expressionless, the sublime violence of the true appears as that which determines the language of the real world according to the laws of the moral world. For it shatters whatever

> still survives as the legacy of chaos in all beautiful semblance: the false, errant totality—the absolute totality. Only the expressionless completes the work, by shattering it into a thing of shards, into a fragment of the true world, into the torso of a symbol. ("GEA" 340, translation modified)

While no attempt can be made here at a full elucidation of this notoriously dense passage, a few implications must be noted. The stuff of works of art is drawn from the pre-conceptual stratum of experience, a stratum characterized by chaotic indistinction and associative fluidity. This is why the animated semblance belonging to artworks can seem to resemble the dynamism of living beings, as well as their organic unity, which eludes explanation in terms of mechanical concepts. Benjamin asserts that this semblance of life "grounds the secret [*Geheimnis*]" in works of art. This seems striking if we recall that Benjamin used the same term to designate that non-apparent moment in beauty which in works of art coincides with their truth content, that is, with the ideal of the problem. Is Benjamin now making the incongruous-sounding claim that the semblance of life grounds the non-apparent truth content of the work?

The suggestion appears less incongruous, however, if we consider both parts of the sentence: "That life grounds the secret; this petrification grounds the content in the work." The semblance of life in the work is responsible only for the way in which the artwork exceeds the reader's concepts and thereby engenders the sense of an indwelling secret. In thinking about this matter, Benjamin was likely influenced by Franz Rosenzweig's linkage between beauty and myth on the one hand, and on the other, by Novalis's and Friedrich Schlegel's tendency to use such terms as "confusion" and "artistic chaos" to designate a productive excess that can be perfected to a rational system.[35] Wherever the precise sources of this idea may lie, Benjamin suggests that there is a counterintuitive correspondence between the richly interconnected, chaotic dimension of pre-rational experience that accounts for the apparent liveliness of the artwork and the rational order of the projected philosophical system. Descended from the pre-rational chaos of experience, the undulating life of beautiful semblance eludes our concepts in a manner analogous to the perpetual withdrawal of the ideal of the problem from philosophy's attempts at formulation. This is why the unity of the artwork will tend to engender the illusion that it has actualized the virtual totality projected by the ideal of the problem. What Benjamin calls the "false, errant totality" is the illusion that the beautifully unified and alive-seeming form of the artwork actually embodies the idea of systematic totality designated by the ideal of the problem.

The expressionless destroys this illusion. By disrupting the self-communing wholeness of beautiful semblance, it marks the unbridgeable distance between an aesthetic unity descended from the chaos of pre-rational experience and the higher, though merely virtual, rational totality projected by the ideal of the problem. However, the marking of that distance also makes it possible for us to recognize aesthetic unity as a true intimation of philosophical totality, one that does not falsely claim to actualize the latter. If the undulating life of beautiful semblance grounds the enigmatic elusiveness of the work, the expressionless interruption of that life confers the status of truth content upon this secret. In Benjamin's formulation, beautiful semblance "has the eternity of its content precisely by the grace of that objection."

In these difficult pronouncements on the expressionless, Benjamin outlines an answer to the question of how, as Eli Friedlander puts it, "content that is utterly determinate can ever emerge from the deferral and ambiguity essential to the form of the work of art."[36] The solution to this quandary that Benjamin proposes is clearly indebted to the Schlegelian idea that great works of art are self-reflective. Yet whereas Schlegel conceives of this self-reflection in positive terms, as a raising of artistic presentation to a higher power, Benjamin construes it as a negative agency. In particular, the determinate content imposed upon the undulating ambiguity of beautiful semblance embodies a definite kind of negativity—a negation, that is, of the illusory totality engendered by the unity of aesthetic form, coupled with a determinate recognition of the virtual totality projected by the ideal of the problem *as* distantly analogous to the unity of aesthetic form.

In his remarks on the expressionless, Benjamin takes up some of the most resonant theoretical constructs of modern aesthetics and gives them a new inflection. For this reason, the best way to highlight the specificity of his theory is to contrast it with the relevant precursor theories. In the remainder of this section I will attempt just such a contrastive characterization by drawing on Jan Urbich's philosophically nuanced interpretation. Although I largely agree with Urbich's construal of the Benjaminian expressionless, I will take issue with his characterization of Kant's and Nietzsche's conceptions, and hence arrive at a different assessment of Benjamin's position vis-à-vis these two precursors.

Urbich develops his interpretation in response to an influential essay on the expressionless by Winfried Menninghaus, which focuses on the connections to Kant. According to Menninghaus, the work of art appears in the light of Benjamin's remarks as a construct involving two oppositional moments: much as the sublime complements the beautiful in Kant's aesthetics, the Benjaminian expressionless disrupts in the name of philosophical reason the false semblance of totality engendered by beauty.[37] In a corrective to this dualistic interpretation, Urbich convincingly argues that the relation between beauty and the expressionless is not one of external opposition. Rather, the expressionless is a moment internal to the beautiful as such.[38] The claim inherent in the beautiful to present an eternally valid essence is qualified by an immanent objection against the medium of ephemeral life in which that essence actualizes itself.

Urbich spells out the speculative logic of the expressionless in terms of Benjamin's definition of the beautiful as an essence necessarily veiled by semblance. Although semblance actualizes essence by making the latter manifest and effective (*wirklich*), it thereby also threatens to supersede essence. As Urbich points out, Benjamin's worry about the ever-present danger of losing sight of essence in one's fascination with semblance is an aesthetic ramification of his comprehensive critique of the "instrumental grasp of 'cognition,'" that is, of the ideology that knowledge consists in a relation of possession by a subject.[39] In order to preserve the distinction between semblance and essence, there must be something in semblance that reminds us of the noncoincidence of essence with semblance. More precisely, that aspect of essence which remains unexpressed in semblance must itself appear—but appear precisely as the trace of something unexpressed. Urbich accordingly defines the expressionless as a moment that marks essence's difference from semblance even in the latter's actualization of the former. The expressionless is "the expressed inexpressibility of essence," and hence "not just the simple negation of expression but expressions's absolute negation *as* expression."[40] Construed as "essence's exteriority within essence," this reminder of what remains unexpressed in semblance ensures that essence can appear in semblance without becoming entirely superseded by the latter.

In Urbich's interpretation, then, the expressionless has the function of introducing a rational distinction within beauty and thus endowing it with the power to refer to a true essence. The external difference between semblance and essence is prefigured by an analogous difference internal to essence—between, on the one hand, essence insofar as it lends itself to expression in semblance and, on the other hand, the expressionless as the exteriority of that moment in essence which eludes such expression. The speculative movement of actualization through exteriorization that occurs when essence appears in beautiful semblance therefore need not falsify the former, for it renders explicit, and repeats in an external form, a difference internal to essence itself. As Urbich puts it, the expressionless serves as "the bridge to that semblance into which essence must externalize itself."[41]

Still, the very fact that essence appears in semblance entails an ever-present possibility of mythic conflations between semblance and essence. If the expressionless were—as Menninghaus claims—a force extraneous to beautiful semblance, an authority anchored in some transcendent vantage point, then its intervention could definitively preempt such conflations. Crucially, however, Benjamin denies this: "The expressionless is the critical violence which, while unable to separate semblance from essence in art, prevents them from mingling" ("GEA" 340). Because the expressionless is a moment internal to beauty, its marking of the distinction between essence and semblance creates merely the possibility of true appearing, but it does not free true appearing from its entanglement in potentially false semblance.

Translated into the phenomenology of the beautiful, this speculative conception suggests that beautiful semblance intrinsically points beyond itself by marking its own failure to be adequate to the truth that it portends. However, this moment of transcendence is not an external corrective, but a tendency proper to beautiful presentation as such. Beautiful presentation "extends itself" through a "critical self-negation" that breaks open the immanence of semblance, without altogether abandoning it.[42] Beautiful semblance can point beyond itself to its hidden ground in essence insofar as it consists of what Urbich calls a "referential nexus of thoroughly-formed disturbance," and elsewhere, a "critically effective disappearance on the surface of beautiful semblance."[43] The principal effect of the expressionless is thus to preempt any claim made on behalf of beautiful semblance to embody an actually achieved totality. By shattering the work "into a fragment of the true world, into the torso of a symbol"—to quote Benjamin's formulation—the expressionless turns it into an allegory that calls for critical interpretation. Such critical interpretation, however, merely extends the self-critical moment constitutive of the beautiful artwork as such.

Benjamin's emphasis on the disruptive character of the expressionless lends his formulations a distinctly modernist accent. Yet Urbich is right to make the somewhat surprising suggestion that the basic structure of Benjamin's conception is classical.[44] For this conception turns the negative dynamic of transcendence that Kant treated under the heading of the sublime (i.e., "the expressionless") into a moment internal to beautiful semblance. Countering Menninghaus's dualistic interpretation, Urbich concludes that this feature of Benjamin's conception represents a departure from the external opposition established by Kant between the beautiful and the sublime.[45]

A closer look at the Kantian framework suggests, however, that the contrast between the two thinkers' accounts is even stronger than Urbich claims. Far from treating the dichotomy of the beautiful and the sublime as a merely external opposition, Kant too ends up relativizing the dichotomy—but he does so by arguably granting a certain primacy to the other pole, that of the sublime. Admittedly, the "Analytic" of the "Critique of the Aesthetic Power of Judgment" discusses beauty and sublimity under separate headings. Yet once Kant turns his attention from nature to art, the line separating the two modalities of aesthetic experience becomes blurred. Indeed, Kant comes close to identifying a sublime moment that is essential to the beautiful. For Kant explains the beauty of the artwork in terms of its presentation of an "aesthetic idea"—a richly patterned sensible manifold that "stimulates so much thinking that it can never be grasped in a determinate concept"—and maintains that the aesthetic idea so understood affords an inverse, negative presentation of a transcendent idea of reason that cannot be exhibited in experience.[46] The structure of the experience that Kant associates with the beautiful artwork precisely corresponds to that of the sublime. Thus, whereas Benjamin construes the sublime as a moment internal to the beautiful, Kant all but suggests that beauty—at least in art—is a species of sublimity. This difference notwithstanding, the Kantian doctrine of aesthetic ideas remains relevant to Benjamin's conception, for it offers the most plausible model for making sense of Benjamin's identification of the truth content veiled by the beauty of the artwork with the ideal of the problem. In this way, the Kantian doctrine allows us to construe the beautiful semblance belonging to the artwork and the sublime moment of self-critique through the expressionless as dialectically related aspects of art's intimation of a transcendent philosophical truth.

While Urbich underplays the difference between Benjamin's and Kant's conceptions, if anything he overstates the contrast to Nietzsche's theory of tragedy. Against Menninghaus's emphasis on the affinity between Nietzsche's and Benjamin's conceptions, Urbich argues that Benjamin's understanding of the expressionless as a self-critique of the beautiful sharply contrasts with what Urbich takes to be a merely external opposition between the Dionysian and the Apolline in Nietzsche's framework.[47] However, contrary to Urbich's assumption, the opposition between the Dionysian and the Apolline is not external either. Nietzsche consistently describes Apolline semblance as a "discharge" that relieves the excess of the Dionysian ground. Conversely, when Nietzsche declares dreaming to be the paradigmatic psychological expression of the Apolline principle, he does so in view of the paradoxical phenomenon of lucid dreaming ("It is a dream! I will dream on"), thereby making self-critique essential to Apolline art—as it must be, if indeed Apolline individuation is premised on self-knowledge and respect for boundaries.[48] Accordingly, in the meditation on the third act of *Tristan and Isolde* that arguably constitutes the hidden center of *The Birth of Tragedy*, Nietzsche interprets the work's climax in the heroine's ecstatic death as a puncturing of Apolline semblance from within. "Thereby," Nietzsche writes, "Apolline deception is revealed for what it is: a persistent veiling, for the duration of the tragedy, of the true Dionysiac effect, an effect so powerful, however, that it finally drives the Apolline drama itself into a sphere where it begins to speak with Dionysiac wisdom and where it negates itself and its Apolline visibility."[49] Nietzsche writes in this connection of a "breaking and bending-back of the point of Apollo [*Umbrechen der apollinischen Spitze*]," whereby Dionysian musical inspiration "leads the world of appearances to its limits where it negates itself and seeks to flee back into the womb of the one, true reality."[50] The self-negation of the Apolline, in which "Apollo speaks [the language] of Dionysos," corresponds precisely to the self-critique of the beautiful in the Benjaminian expressionless.[51] To be sure, this structural homology between Nietzsche's and Benjamin's conceptions should not make us overlook the fact that, on the level of phenomenological content, Benjamin inverts the Nietzschean model: whereas in Nietzsche's conception appearances characterized by individuation, stability, and intelligibility emanate from a contradictory metaphysical ground, Benjamin claims that an equivocal, "undulating" surface semblance portends an elusive rational truth.

The key lesson that emerges from these comparisons is that beauty cannot simply be aligned with myth in Benjamin's conception. This point is all the more important because Benjamin posits a relation of "mutual exclusion" between myth and truth ("GEA" 326); if beauty were fundamentally mythic, it would have no part in truth. As far as the relation between myth and truth is concerned, Menninghaus is right to note a difference between Benjamin's thinking in the essay on *Elective Affinities* and the successor conception that Horkheimer and Adorno will develop some twenty years later in *Dialectic of Enlightenment*.[52] Although Benjamin's essay clearly influenced Horkheimer and Adorno's argument that an incomplete enlightenment tends to regress to myth, the reverse claim advanced by the later authors—namely, that myth in its archaic forms already gestures toward enlightenment—appears only on the margins of Benjamin's writings.

To be sure, that counterpart thesis is not entirely absent from Benjamin's thinking. It will suffice to recall his often-quoted assertion to Scholem in a conversation about the outline "On the Program of the Coming Philosophy." "A philosophy that does not include the possibility of soothsaying from coffee grounds and cannot explicate it," Benjamin declared to Scholem, "cannot be a true philosophy."[53] In the essay on *Elective Affinities*, the latency of truth in the mythic realm may be inferred from the idea I outlined in explicating the passage on the expressionless: namely, that the symbolic interconnectedness characteristic of the pre-rational, chaotic stratum of experience anticipates the unity of the projected philosophical system. The work of art appears animated and its effect enlivens the viewer's mind insofar as the work presents a sensible manifold drawn from this archaic and chaotic dimension of experience. The tendency of this animated semblance to usurp the place of the essence it displays is checked by the self-critique of semblance through the expressionless—in other words, by traces within semblance of what remains unexpressed in it. In order to constitute the beautiful form of an artwork, the animation (or "undulation") of semblance must be arrested—or, as Benjamin puts it, "spellbound"—by the expressionless. The expressionless is thus responsible for the freezing of animated semblance to beautiful form, as well as for the moment of sublime transcendence in beauty. It accounts for the closure of aesthetic form as well as for its disruption by traces of a transcendent truth.

Hölderlin

This coincidence between formal closure and formal disruption receives a more concrete articulation in the essay when Benjamin invokes Hölderlin's concept of caesura in order to characterize the textual juncture at which the expressionless intervenes. To be sure, Benjamin's recourse to the Hölderlinian model hardly simplifies matters. By quoting from Hölderlin's "Annotations to Oedipus," Benjamin introduces into his essay an idiosyncratic reworking of a concept that was never straightforward to begin with.

The protean character of the concept of caesura does not seem entirely surprising in view of its etymological derivation from an elementary verb, the Latin caedere, which means "to cut" or "to hew." Even in the prosodic analysis of verse—the native terrain of the concept of caesura—a stable consensus regarding its meaning took a long time to emerge.[54] In the tradition traceable to antiquity, the term referred to a break marked by a word boundary or a syntactical juncture at or around the middle of a verse composed in regular meter (for instance, hexameter or alexandrine). What determines the placement of the caesura in a given line remains a point of contention to this day, around which a large body of highly technical scholarship has accumulated. These technical issues are bound up with the question, which has provoked a fair amount of speculation, as to why certain forms of verse call for caesuras in the first place. In a 1919 article on the Homeric caesura, the Homerist Samuel Bassett sums up this tangled knot of conjectures and controversies by stating that "there are few questions in classical scholarship about which there is more confusion, or wider difference of opinion."[55]

Whereas in classical prosody the concept of caesura refers to a cut that structures the individual poetic verse, Hölderlin adapts the concept to designate an interruption that confers formal structure upon the large-scale diachronic process of tragedy. The need for such a repurposing of the concept arises from Hölderlin's attempt to translate *Oedipus the King* and *Antigone* with a view toward the exigencies of modernity. Hölderlin's sense of these exigencies stems from his conviction that art must first achieve the opposite of one's innate temperament and only then, following the initial detour of foreignness, hazard an artistic rendering of one's ownmost nature. Since, according to Hölderlin, the formal sobriety of ancient tragedy and its harsh lessons of finitude were premised on a fiery natural temper that strove for ecstatic union with the divine, and this artistic sobriety in its turn became the ground of our ownmost nature—that of reflective modern subjects who accept the constraints of finitude—we no longer partake of the dynamic that animated ancient tragedy.[56] In transposing the tragedies of Sophocles into a "Hesperian" register, therefore, Hölderlin's aim is twofold. First, he means to make these works accessible to aspiring modern poets and modern audiences by bringing out the repudiated passion that had to remain hidden beneath the formal discipline of ancient tragedy, and which is the proper artistic inverse of our sober nature.[57] Second, he wants to preserve the "lawful calculus" (*gesezliche Kalkul*) of ancient tragedy, so that it might serve as a model for that difficult artistic appropriation of our sober nature which we will have to undertake once we have completed the necessary detour of a passionate art.[58]

It is in his remarks on this latter aspect, the "lawful calculus" of tragedy, that Hölderlin uses the prosodic term "caesura" to name a constitutive feature of large-scale tragic form. In *Antigone* as well as in *Oedipus the King*,

Tiresias's speech marks a caesura, inasmuch as the words of the blind seer tear the destiny that stands in the forefront of the dramatic plot out of its human context and refer that destiny to "the excentric sphere of the dead."[59] Hölderlin claims that the placement of this interruption of the dramatic plot is determined in each play with a view to counteracting an imbalance that results from the changing intensity of "tragic transport" in the course of the dramatic process. To that extent, the caesura that interrupts the succession of dramatic representations also ensures the formal "equipoise" (*Gleichgewicht*) of each play. At the same time, this balancing interruption also brings to light the otherwise hidden ground of the tragic process. For, as Hölderlin suggests elsewhere, the constitutively hidden absolute ground of temporal change can only become manifest in a moment of blockage that arrests the "tearing" rhythm of the process and through this sudden suspension makes us feel the underlying principle of change.[60] The caesura is thus the point at which a catastrophic dynamic of diachronic succession is stabilized by a synchronic dynamic, affording the contemplative distance needed to grasp the tragic process as a formally balanced, necessary whole.[61]

The passage in which Benjamin quotes Hölderlin's definition of the caesura calls for extensive quotation:

> As a category of language and art and not of the work or of the genres, the expressionless can be no more rigorously defined than through a passage in Hölderlin's "Anmerkungen zum Ödipus" ["Annotations to Oedipus"], whose fundamental significance for the theory of art in general, beyond serving as the basis for a theory of tragedy, seems not yet to have been recognized. The passage reads: "For the tragic transport is actually empty, and the least restrained.—Thereby, in the rhythmic sequence of the representations wherein the transport presents itself, there becomes necessary what in poetic meter is called caesura, the pure word, the counter-rhythmic rupture—namely, in order to meet the onrushing change of representations at its highest point, in such a manner that not the change of representation but the representation itself very soon appears." The "occidental Junoian sobriety"—which Hölderlin, several years before he wrote this, conceived as the almost unattainable goal of all German artistic practice—is only another name for that caesura, in which, along with harmony, every expression simultaneously comes to a standstill, in order to give free rein to an expressionless power inside all artistic media. Such power has rarely become clearer than in Greek tragedy, on the one hand, and in Hölderlin's hymnic poetry, on the other. [It is] perceptible in tragedy as the falling silent of the hero, and in the rhythm of the hymn as objection. Indeed, one could not characterize this rhythm any more aptly than by asserting that something beyond the poet interrupts the language of the poetry. Here lies "the reason a

> hymn will seldom (and with complete justification perhaps never) be called 'beautiful.'" If in that lyric it is the expressionless, in Goethe's it is the beautiful that comes forth to the limit of what can be grasped in the work of art. What stirs beyond this limit is, in one direction, the offspring of madness, and, in the other, the conjured appearance. ("GEA" 340–41)

Benjamin's appropriation of the Hölderlinian model involves three modifications. First, he recasts the concept of caesura, originally introduced for the restricted purposes of theorizing tragedy, as a fundamental category of all art. What this means is perhaps most clearly stated in a fragment from the period of Benjamin's work on the essay, which correlates the "messianic" content in the work of art with a formal moment of retardation in which "perception is dammed up [*sich staut*], and this is what is essential to its form."[62] Second, whereas Hölderlin is mainly interested in the variable *placement* of the caesura within the tragic process, Benjamin draws attention to the variable *intensity* of the expressionless interruption relative to the intensity of the interrupted beautiful semblance. In this respect, Benjamin posits a spectrum whose opposite extremes are reached in Goethe's and Hölderlin's poetry, the former being the epitome of beauty that is nearly unadulterated by expressionless self-critique (bordering on "conjuration"), and the latter epitomizing a maximally disruptive self-critique with a minimum of beautiful semblance (bordering on "madness").

Third, and most important for our purposes, although Benjamin's generalized conception of the caesura retains the paradigmatic status of ancient tragedy, it shifts the placement of the caesura within the tragic work. For Hölderlin, in *Antigone* as well as in *Oedipus*, it was the prophetic intervention of Tiresias that marked the caesura of a "pure word" in which "representation represents itself as represention."[63] Benjamin's comments on tragedy, however, shift the caesura to "the falling silent of the hero."[64] When, moreover, Benjamin applies this understanding of the tragic caesura to Goethe's novel, it is not the hero but the narrator whose falling silent is construed as the object of a quasi-dramatic presentation that interrupts narration. Thus, whereas Hölderlin located the caesura in an instance of speech that interrupts dramatic action, Benjamin redefines it as a silent spectacle that arrests the flow of narrative discourse. In the transferral of the category from dramatic to narrative literature, an inversion has occurred, with the unexpected result that ancient tragedy and modern novel now appear as mirror images of one another.

Hope, like a Star That Falls from Heaven

Benjamin's conception of the philosophical truth content of the work of art thus turns on a latent self-critical moment in the work, which critique must amplify to a caesura. In order to see how this amplification is achieved in Benjamin's reading of *Elective Affinities*, we now need to turn to the sentence interpolated by Goethe's narrator that Benjamin identifies as the caesura of the novel. That sentence occurs near the end of the novel, in a scene in which Eduard and Ottilie embrace for the first time in rapturous anticipation of a happy resolution. Although they are oblivious to the impending disaster, the narrator does not lose sight of the implacable logic that governs the course of the narrated events:

> Hope, like a star falling from heaven, soared above their heads and away [*Die Hoffnung fuhr wie ein Stern, der vom Himmel fällt, über ihre Häupter weg*]. It seemed to them they belonged to one another, they believed it; for the first time ever they gave and received kisses that were sure and free [*entschiedene, freie Küsse*], and when they parted it was like an act of violence and they suffered pain. (*EA* 207)

And now let us review Benjamin's comments on this passage:

> . . . in the symbol of the star, the hope that Goethe had to conceive for the lovers had once appeared to him. That sentence, which to speak with Hölderlin contains the caesura of the work and in which, while the embracing lovers seal their fate, everything pauses, reads: "Hope, like a star that falls from heaven, soared above their heads and away." They are unaware of it, of course, and it could not be said any more clearly that the last hope is never such to him who cherishes it but is the last only to those for whom it is cherished. With this comes to light the innermost basis for the "narrator's stance." It is he alone who, in the feeling of hope, can fulfill the meaning of the event. ("GEA" 354–55, translation modified)

The difficulty of this passage is only partly due to the extreme compression of meaning achieved by Benjamin. A more basic puzzle is posed by Goethe's ambiguous evocation of the apparition of hope. The sentence highlighted by Benjamin does not simply compare hope to a shooting star; rather, the sentence actually makes hope shooting star-like by imputing movement to it. The movement at issue is described in paradoxically equivocal terms. Used in reference to a natural phenomenon that folk superstition would decipher as a portent of fulfillment, the image of the "star that falls from heaven" simultaneously hints at the loss of a promise, a disaster in the literal sense of an ill-starred event, and, echoing the idiomatic expression "vom Himmel fallen," the near-miraculous fulfillment of a wish. Moreover, the very direction of the movement indicated by the sentence undergoes a swerve in the final adverb "away" (weg): whereas a shooting star would burn up in its fall, the hope likened to the apparition at issue here is said to be speeding along past the characters on an infinite trajectory.[65] This paradoxical conjunction of evanescence and persistence finds an echo in Benjamin's crucial but initially enigmatic claim that "the last hope is never such to him who cherishes it but is the last only to those for whom it is cherished" ("GEA" 355). This assertion in its turn anticipates the essay's famous closing sentence: "Only for the sake of the hopeless ones have we been given hope" ("GEA" 356). Both formulations hint at the way in which the narrator's stance toward the characters registers the peculiar persistence of hope at the very moment when all hope is about to be lost for them.

In what sense is it the case, however, that "the last hope is never such to him who cherishes it"? The following gloss on this pronouncement suggests itself. Being hopeful is never just a matter of having arrived by objective reasoning at an optimistic assessment of the prospects of fulfilling a particular aspiration. Rather, hope is a subjective stance that enables one to project oneself into the future, an orientation that defines the very perspective from which one sees the world and assesses particular situations. Exceeding every finite project or aspiration, hope is, in Kantian parlance, more of a transcendental apriori than a prognostic belief justified by an empirical warrant. Playing a variation on Wittgenstein's dictum about language, one might say that the limits of my hope are the limits of my world.[66] Although one who hopes must keep oneself open to the possibility of disappointment, the definitive annihilation of one's hope is not a possibility that can register on the hopeful person's own horizon of expectation.[67] Because of this aprioristic character of hope, the notion that one's hope might founder is inconceivable from the first-personal point of view of the hopeful person. It is then no more possible for the hopeful person to feel that her hope is the "last" hope of which she is capable than it is to assess in advance how much disappointment she could take before her hope would be crushed. So long as one hopes, one must, at least on some visceral level, hold hope to be inextinguishable even in the face of possible disappointments. Consequently, when I speak of "my last hope," the last hope I thus assert must be one that I harbor on behalf of someone else, not for myself. In those rare instances in which I speak of my last hope for myself, the one on the verge of hopelessness must be my self as an object of estranged self-reflection, not I as a subject animated by hope.

How is this transcendence of hope borne out by the event that registers in the sentence from *Elective Affinities* that Benjamin marks as a caesura? The event is said to occur "above their heads" because Eduard and Ottilie do not know that their hopes are about to be dashed. The narrator knows this, however, and does not heighten suspense by withholding this knowledge from the reader. The oppressive air of doom is not allowed to lift for even a single passing moment. Yet, paradoxically, it is precisely the narrator's foreknowledge of impending doom that brings to light a transcendent surplus in his hoping over and above the characters' hopes. Because the characters do not know that their ardent desire for a resolution is doomed, they cannot see beyond this limited objective. Their single-minded preoccupation with this purpose blocks their view, leaving them oblivious to the larger stakes involved in their predicament. It is otherwise with the narrator. His hopeful investment in the protagonists' fate is fueled by a hope that reaches beyond Eduard and Ottilie to encompass all humanity.

Adopting the philosophical framework outlined by Benjamin, we might think of Goethe's narrator as harboring a hope for redemption from myth; that is, for a transformation that would inaugurate an order of things in which genuine decisions founded on integral experience would finally be possible. The object of this hope may of course be defined in the narrow terms of the characters' aspirations or, alternatively, from the more comprehensive perspective of the narrator, which encompasses but also extends beyond Eduard's and Ottilie's limited desires. Viewed from the former standpoint, the hope that flashes up in this critical moment is indeed the last one, akin to a shooting star that burns up. However, it is precisely the defeat of the characters' desires that allows for the emergence to light of a hope invested in the characters whose scope extends beyond their narrow conception of happiness and hence outlives them. Viewed from this more comprehensive vantage point, the star to which hope is likened evokes a comet, an enduring celestial body that appears periodically and speeds above our heads and away—in a horizontal movement whose momentum parallels that of reading—rather than a meteor burning up in its fall. We can now see that Benjamin invokes the Kantian concept of the sublime advisedly in relation to the symbol of the star ("GEA" 354). For the apparition of hope evoked in the caesura of *Elective Affinities* closely follows the logic of the Kantian sublime—sublimity being an experience in which the finite need of a lower faculty must be frustrated in order for reason's infinite aspiration to come to light. Similarly, it is the defeat of the protagonists' narrowly defined desires that brings to light a hope that requires to be understood in more comprehensive terms.

This way of thinking about the narrator's hope can help clarify how Benjamin's theory of the expressionless finds application in his reflection on the narrator's remarks. As we have seen, the narrator's enchantment by the beautiful semblance conjured up in the figure of Ottilie is bound up with his sentimental investment in the false idea of reconciliation symbolized by her gentle beauty. Based on the argument developed earlier in this chapter, we can understand the narrator's enthrallment to beautiful semblance as a captivity to the seductive illusion that the harmonious unity of beautiful semblance does not merely intimate but actually instantiates the philosophical ideal of a systematic totality integrating experience with freedom. This illusion holds the false promise of a peaceable reconciliation and reaches its point of greatest intensity when Ottilie and Eduard embrace in eager anticipation of the resolution, just before that false promise is destroyed. At this critical point, however, the narrator's stance is marked by a paradoxically split consciousness that we may understand as a literary manifestation of

Goethe's unresolved inner struggle against myth. In recounting the protagonists' embrace, the narrator is in thrall to the enchanting power of beautiful semblance and its spurious, sentimental promise of reconciliation. And yet, in that very same moment the narrator also has a lucid foreknowledge of the impending disillusionment. This surplus of disenchanted insight is the negative correlate of a strongly counterfactual hope whose upsurge at this moment reasserts the merely ideal, projected character of the systematic totality that would make a true reconciliation possible. The true idea of reconciliation that is at play here includes within its purview the characters along with the narrator—as well as, crucially, the author—and at the same time exceeds all of them. Since the upsurge of this counterfactual hope compels the understanding that the rational order required for reconciliation must for the time being remain unrealized and indeterminate, it leaves the mark of something expressionless on the narrative.

We can now also begin to see the pertinence of the formulations by Hölderlin that Benjamin cites in his general definition of the caesura. In the caesura, the expressionless is said by Hölderlin to interrupt beautiful semblance as "the pure word, the counter-rhythmic rupture—namely, in order to meet the onrushing change of representations at its highest point, in such a manner that not the change of representation but the representation itself very soon appears" ("GEA" 340). As interpreted by Benjamin, the word "hope" in the key remark by Goethe's narrator is indeed a pure word, inasmuch as the hope at issue here is not limited by any empirically defined aim. For the ultimate "object" of this hope is, as we have seen, not an object at all but the ideal of a fully actualized rationality that would resolve the problematic relation between experience and freedom, along with all other philosophical problems. With Goethe's acknowledgment of this hope, "the change of representation" gives way to "representation itself" in the sense that the process of narration, animated thus far by the lure of a beautiful semblance that falsely purports to instantiate a systematic totality, here becomes interrupted by a recognition of the counterfactual character of the underlying systematic ideal.

Now, one might object that hope is hardly the only attitude with the power to dispel the false promise of totality. Wishing, for instance, may be thought to have the same power to reassert the counterfactual character of the systematic ideal. If, however, our non-attainment of that ideal primarily surfaces in our historical lifeworld as a lack of connection between predominant modes of experience and the socially prevalent understanding of freedom, then it makes sense that hope should be our characteristic orientation toward that unattained ideal. For being hopeful determines the affective coloring that suffuses our experience of the world, and it does so in a way that can energize us to seize free agency; since, however, hope as a motive to act does not suffice for prescribing a determinate course of action, this connection between experience and freedom remains indeterminate and hence problematic. Through its very structure, so to speak, hoping registers both the mythic diremption that severs freedom from experience and the virtual ideal of a system that would resolve this predicament. Otherwise put, hope reminds us of the authority of that ideal as well as of its unattained, virtual character. In terms of the recasting of the Kantian system envisioned in "On the Program of the Coming Philosophy," hope exhibits a determinate relation of "nonsynthesis" between experience and freedom.[68]

The Sole Justification of the Faith in Immortality

In view of the Christian motifs that abound in the concluding chapters of *Elective Affinities*, one cannot help being reminded of two passages from the New Testament whose faint echo reverberates in Goethe's sentence. The suggestion of a comet evokes the moving star that guided the Magi to Bethlehem, which commentators since Origen have assumed to be a comet—an allusion whose irony is hard to miss in light of the impending death of the child. The parallel suggestion of a falling star, however, recalls Revelation 8:10–11:

> 10. Then the third angel sounded: And a great star fell from heaven, burning like a torch, and it fell on a third of the rivers and on the springs of water.
> 11. The name of the star is Wormwood. A third of the waters became wormwood, and many men died from the water, because it was made bitter.[69]

By subtly referencing two passages that bookend the New Testament from opposite ends, Goethe's sentence conjoins the promise of redemption with apocalyptic fulfillment. An avid reader of Franz Baader, Benjamin was too well-versed in Christian theology to have missed this resonance in Goethe's sentence. Indeed, the resonance is amplified by the epigraph that Benjamin chose for the second part of his essay, namely, the opening plea for "innocent water" from Hölderlin's "Patmos" ("GEA" 320). For a central concern of Hölderlin's great hymn is precisely the eschatological connection posited by Pietists between the promise associated with Christ's birth and its apocalyptic fulfillment as envisioned in the book of Revelation. This connection is epitomized by the piece of theological dogma that Hölderlin was tasked with vindicating in his hymn, namely, the putative identity of John the Apostle, John the Evangelist, and the John who wrote the book of Revelation on the island of Patmos.[70] When Hölderlin invokes "innocent water" in the verses cited by Benjamin, he is calling upon the hermetic element of spiritual mediation to aid the imaginary journey to Patmos through which he unfolds his heterodox poetic pneumatology; and this innocent element finds its apocalyptic counterpart in the waters made lethal by the falling star of Revelation 8:11. Thus, not only does the epigraph from "Patmos" prefigure the contrast that Benjamin will draw between the "death-dealing power of the still waters" in *Elective Affinities* and the redemptive, "living current" of the river in the embedded novella ("GEA" 332), it also suggests that disaster and redemption stand in a necessary correlation.[71]

Unlike Hölderlin's hymn, however, Goethe's novel can invoke no theological warrant for the conjunction between shooting star and comet, disaster and redemptive promise. Indeed, the guarantor of the hope that Benjamin holds up at the end of his essay is nothing beyond the " 'the narrator's stance.' It is he alone," writes Benjamin, "who, in the feeling of hope, can fulfill the meaning of the event—quite as Dante assumes in himself the hopelessness of the lovers, when, after the words of Francesca da Rimini, he falls 'as if a corpse fell' " ("GEA" 355). We have already seen how the Goethean narrator's readiness to absorb and be shattered by the hopelessness of the lovers at the same time permits him to conceive a more comprehensive and enduring, transcendent hope. This hope, however, is one harbored "for all the dead," and it is said to constitute "the sole justification of the faith in immortality, which must never be kindled from one's own existence" ("GEA" 355). It persists in the narrator's stance toward characters that are doomed.

This connection between narration, death, and hope can be further elaborated in the terms of Benjamin's meditation on the "physiognomy" of the narrator in his late essay on Leskov, titled simply "The Storyteller." Especially pertinent are Benjamin's remarks on the reader's investment in a novel:

> The nature of characters in a novel cannot be presented any better than it is in this statement, which says that the "meaning" of their life is revealed only in their death. But the reader of a novel in fact looks for human beings, from whom he derives the "meaning of life." Thus, he has to realize in advance, no matter what, that he will share their experience of death: if need be, their figurative death (the end of the novel), but preferably their actual one. How do the characters make him understand that death is already waiting for them—a very definite death, at a very definite place? This is the question which feeds the reader's consuming interest in the events of the novel.
>
> The novel is significant, therefore, not because it presents someone else's fate to us, perhaps didactically, but because this stranger's fate, by virtue of the flame which consumes it, yields to us the warmth which we never draw from our own fate. What draws the reader to a novel is the hope of warming his shivering life with a death he reads about. (*SW* 3:156)

These remarks open up a perspective that seems missing from Heidegger's well-known pronouncements on "being-toward-death," with their unrelenting solipsism.[72] Mortality is a condition that is shared in a more emphatic sense than are other limitations that humans have in common. Far from it being the case that our own death constitutes the ultimate horizon of our projections of meaning, we can relate to our own death only by imaginatively assuming the perspective of another, or by analogy to another's death. In isolation from others, my self-consciousness would be powerless to assume the weight and pathos of mortality, since it cannot look back upon itself from beyond its own cessation. Such investment in one's own life *as* mortal is possible only through the detour of analogy with another person's mortality. Narrative fiction is a particularly apt medium for fostering such understanding. Since in the process of reading fiction our access to the life and death of another person is focalized through the vantage point of a knowing narrator, I can contemplate the course of that person's life in light of its inevitable and poignantly specific ending. "A man who dies at the age of thirty-five," as Benjamin quotes Moritz Heimann, "is at every point in his life a man who dies at the age of thirty-five" (*SW* 3:156). I can care for that foreign, and indeed fictional, life *as* a mortal life with a type of pathos that I cannot muster in caring for my own life. This is presumably what Benjamin has in mind when he claims that the experience of reading about the hero's death can transmit "warmth" to one's own "shivering" life.

Yet the warmth gained through the reading of narrative fiction cannot stem from the chilling lesson of mortality alone. It thus seems important that the warmth to be gained from reading a literary narrative is said to be the object of a hope ("the hope of warming his shivering life with a death he reads about"), rather than a matter of ethical duty or calling (say, the calling to live resolutely in the face of own's mortality). The nature of this hope is adumbrated in Benjamin's thoroughly un-ironic invocation of the clichéd phrase "the meaning of life." It is worth pausing to ask, then, what the problem of meaning might have to do with the connection between mortality, narration, and the transcendence of hoping that emerges from Benjamin's interpretation of the caesura of *Elective Affinities*.

Benjamin's marking of the caesura suggests that the reader of Goethe's novel gains more than just a clear understanding of his mortality. Rather, thanks to the narrator's stance, the reader may also gain an indirect, analogical access to a hope invested in him that exceeds his own life—a hope with a universal scope that is usually occluded by narrowly self-regarding concerns, and which is directly available only to another person who can reflect on the meaning of one's life in the wake of one's death. The reader's "hope of warming his shivering life with a death he reads about" (*SW* 3:156) may thus be understood as a kind of second-order hope: a hope for access to a utopian hope that might encompass but transcend the reader's life as well as the lives of the characters. Nothing but the narrator's stance underwrites "the hope of redemption that we nourish for all the dead. This hope," Benjamin adds, "is the sole justification of the faith in immortality, which must never be kindled from one's own existence ("GEA" 355). Something like immortality—not one's own, but that of remembered others—becomes possible through narrative memory, inasmuch as narration can register a hope whose power to endure is at its most striking when it outlives and overshoots the defeated aspirations of the dead. If literary narration has the "weak messianic power" (*SW* 4:390) to restitute meaning to failed lives by registering such hope, then we might think of Benjamin's essay as an attempt at amplifying precisely this weak power.

Benjamin's remarks on the paradoxical hope for the sake of the hopeless that surfaces in *Elective Affinities* also suggest a gloss on a key passage in the later essay on Leskov that comments on the reader's "burning interest" in the fate of the novelistic hero. Benjamin revives the dead metaphor buried in that cliché and unfolds it to an allegory: the reader, as Benjamin writes, "destroys, swallows up the material as a fire devours logs in the fireplace. The suspense which permeates the novel is very much like the draft of air which fans the flame in the fireplace and enlivens its play" (*SW* 3:156). If the source of this suspense is the peculiar hope for hope that I just described, then the fire in this allegory corresponds to the hope itself that might warm our shivering lives, that is, the utopian hope that projects a larger framework of meaning. It is then a testimony to the cogency of Benjamin's allegorical imagination that this fire, decipherable as hope, so closely resembles the one he evoked in the famous opening argument of the Goethe essay under the heading of truth content: "Thus, the critic inquires into the truth, whose living flame continues to burn over the heavy logs of what is past and the light ashes of what has been experienced" (*SW* 1:298). The convergence between the two passages seems apt. For—to hazard a schematic summary of Benjamin's conception—if the doctrine of the ideal of the problem gives an objective specification of the truth content that interests the philosophical critic, then hope is its subjective correlate, the appropriate attitude towards the ideal of the problem.

Something beyond the Poet Interrupts

Having noted the relevance of Benjamin's essay on Leskov to the matter of narrative stance in Goethe's *Elective Affinities*, we would do well to linger a little longer in Russia. Around the same time that Benjamin wrote his Goethe essay, the young Mikhail Bakhtin was filling a series of school notebooks with the emergent text of a major treatise titled "Author and Hero in Aesthetic Activity."[73] Similarly to Benjamin, Bakhtin in his early works was deeply indebted to Hermann Cohen's neo-Kantianism, and in this particular treatise he addresses issues adjacent to the ones that surfaced apropos of Benjamin's caesura marking. For this reason, Bakhtin's treatise offers a contrastive foil against which we can highlight some of the philosophical commitments underyling Benjamin's thinking about narrative stance and authorship.

Under the evident influence of Cohen, Bakhtin is principally concerned with the activity by which an author achieves an "aesthetic consummation" of the hero, that is, bestows formal unity upon the hero's life. Bakhtin's thinking about this problem follows the same Aristotelian axiom that Benjamin would assert in his essay on Leskov: "The nature of characters in a novel cannot be presented any better," as Benjamin declares in 1936, "than it is in this statement, which says that the 'meaning' of their life is revealed only in their death" (*SW* 3:156). In Bakhtin's conception, death is one of the two "outer boundaries of inner life."[74] In death, inner life is "turned outward," for it can now be remembered by others as a completed whole with a determinate meaning. Moreover, since I am not the hero of my own life but its author, it is only through the form-giving activity of another person contemplating my life "under the token of death" that my life can acquire an aesthetic form.[75] A principal effect of such an "aesthetic consummation" lies, according to Bakhtin, in the establishment of a "rhythm" that patterns the hero's life. What determines this rhythm, as Bakhtin understands it, is not the author's reaction to the objects or situations confronting the hero, but a reaction on the author's part to the hero's reactions to the objects of lived experience. Its pattern "presupposes a certain predeterminedness of striving, experiencing, action (a certain hopelessness with respect to meaning)."[76] There can thus be no place in rhythm for that "extrarhythmic" moment, marked by discontinuity and a dissonant co-presence of alternate possibilities, in which I have to make a decision about a genuinely open future.

For the purposes of the contrast with Benjamin, Bakhtin's most intriguing claim is that the memory involved in the aesthetic shaping of a dead person's life must be "without hope from the standpoint of the meaning that keeps it in motion."[77] Even the author's tendency to hope vicariously on behalf of the hero must be held in check by a lucid awareness of the futility of the hero's life. In a remarkable passage that needs to be quoted in full, Bakhtin claims that aesthetic rhythm requires a "kind, cherishing hopelessness":

> The aesthetic approach to another's interior being requires first of all that we should not put our faith and hope in that other, but that we should accept and receive him axiologically apart from this faith and hope, i.e., that we should be outside of him, and not with him and in him. . . . The aesthetic embodiment of the inner man anticipates from the very outset the hero's hopelessness with respect to meaning. . . . In this sense, we could say that death is the form of the aesthetic consummation of an individual. Death as a want of success and justification with respect to meaning settles the accounts as regards meaning, sets a task, and provides the methods for an *aesthetic* justification, i.e., a justification independent of meaning. The deeper and the more perfect the embodiment, the more distinctly do we hear in it the definitive completion of death and at the same time the aesthetic victory over death—the contention of memory against death (memory in the sense of a certain value-related act of exerting,

> fixating, and accepting independently of meaning). Throughout the entire course of an embodied hero's life, one can hear the tones of a requiem. Hence that distinctive hopelessness of rhythm as well as its sorrowfully joyful lightness, that is, its relievedness of the pressure exerted by the irresolvable seriousness of meaning. Rhythm takes possession of a life that has been lived: the requiem tones at the end were already heard in the cradle song at the beginning. In art, however, this lived-out life is saved, justified, and consummated in eternal memory; hence the kind, cherishing hopelessness of rhythm.[78]

In keeping with this line of thought, Bakhtin considers it a failure of aesthetic consummation when an author writes about a hero with an investment of hope.

If we now return to Benjamin's characterization of the narrator of *Elective Affinities*, it is immediately clear that this figure violates Bakhtin's stipulation of thoroughgoing hopelessness on two levels. First, Benjamin's interpretation of the sentence that he marks as the caesura of *Elective Affinities* presumes that Goethe's narrator is not from the outset hopeless vis-à-vis the characters. By means of the analogy to Dante's shocked loss of consciousness, Benjamin interprets that sentence as the discursive rehearsal of a momentary loss of discursive control which registers a suddenly dawning, terrible sense of futility. Second, the loss of a sympathetic hope that has up until now resonated with the limited aspirations of the characters opens up the narrator's horizon and creates the space needed for a utopian hoping that encompasses the narrowly defined hopes of the characters, but also exceeds and outlasts them. The simultaneity of these two events—marked by the equivocal image of a star that falls and at the same time continues on its path "away"—cannot be accommodated within the type of predetermined rhythm that allows narration to effect an aesthetic consummation of the hero. The moment of this caesura is akin to a syncope, both in being "extrarhythmic" in the Bakhtinian sense—not to be conflated with the Hölderlinian idea of "counter-rhythmic rupture"—and in the medical sense suggested by the analogy to Dante's loss of consciousness.

This contrast between Bakhtin's and Benjamin's conceptions of narration is indicative of a more comprehensive difference between their ways of taking up the Kantian legacy mediated by Hermann Cohen. The architectonic order of Kant's philosophical system requires a strict demarcation of distinct types of normativity from one another, ensuring that none of them encroaches on the territory of another. However, although separation among the respective domains of the three *Critiques* is central to Kant's project, he is equally invested in the idea of a unitary rationality common to the three branches of philosophy.[79] Bakhtin and Benjamin inherit this problematic in divergent ways.

Bakhtin follows Kant in positing a sharp separation among the three normative domains, namely, scientific knowledge, art, and ethical life. In particular, Bakhtin's entire thinking about authorship is governed by a strict disjunction between ethical concern and aesthetic activity: "When a human being is in art," writes Bakhtin, "he is not in life, and conversely. There is no unity between them and no inner interpenetration within the unity of an individual person."[80] This is why Bakhtin claims that literary narration must be without hope, hope being an attitude proper to the still-unfinished, ethically responsible act of living. To be sure, Bakhtin does not elide the question of the connection between art and life. When he does pose that question, however, the answer he proposes—which turns, precisely, on the notion of answering—is not a systematic one: "what guarantees the inner connection of the constituent elements of a person? Only the unity of answerability. I have to answer with my own life for what I have experienced and understood in art, so that everything I have experienced and understood would not remain ineffectual in my life."[81] For Bakhtin, then, unlike for Kant, the task of unifying the three domains of life is not a theoretical but an ethical one, to be accomplished within one of the three domains whose unification poses a problem.

In contrast to Bakhtin, and arguably in greater proximity to the Kantian conception, the early Benjamin holds on to the idea of a philosophical system that might unify disparate domains, and in particular the domain of knowledge and that of ethical action. This theoretical orientation explains Benjamin's interest in "the realm of the transition between the theory of experience and the theory of freedom" (*SW* 1:106, translation modified), as well as his claim that the beautiful artwork intimates the ideal of the problem that would hold the key to that transition. And it is because Benjamin refuses to treat the act of literary narration as wholly separable from the ethical act of living that he devotes his exemplary criticism to a novel whose narrator at a key juncture abandons that "kind, cherishing hopelessness" which Bakhtin takes to be the prerequisite of aesthetically successful narration.

This observation about the philosophical orientation underlying Benjamin's essay is related to a terminological point. In comparing Benjamin's conception with Bakhtin's, it may have appeared as though my entire discussion was based on a category error. After all, the reflections by Benjamin that I examined in the previous section concern the stance of the narrator as a textual function, and the significance of that stance for the reader. Bakhtin's study, by contrast, deals with the creative activity of the author as an empirical person. Why should the latter be directly relevant to the former? The short answer to this question is that it is a central, although frequently overlooked, fact about Benjamin's interpretation of *Elective Affinities* that it refuses to divorce considerations regarding the narrator from conjectures about the empirical author.

We can spell out this claim by specifying the moment of "the expressionless" in Goethe's sentence. The first and most obvious sense in which the sentence signals something that remains expressionless is that the characters are oblivious to the hope that the narrator cherishes for them. A second and less obvious form of expressionlessness pertains to the perspective of the narrator. In part this has to do with the notion, central to Benjamin's thinking and lucidly developed by Winfried Menninghaus, that fundamental ethical orientations such as hope can never be explained in terms of rationally knowable motives that prescribe a definite course of action.[82] The "moral word" in which such an orientation expresses itself must be clear as to the course of action to which one commits oneself, but that word is nevertheless pregnant with a silence about the ultimate motive for the decision that has been made. As I argued, this impossibility of translating ethical commitment into knowledge is ultimately due to the merely virtual, problematic character of the ideal of systematic rationality. In the case of the narrator's sentence that Benjamin singles out as the caesura of *Elective Affinities*, however, the problematic character of that systematic ideal is relevant in a further sense as well. Not only does it explain the absence of an expressible ground for the hope voiced by the narrator, an absence typical of every hope as such; rather, in the case of this particular, utopian hope, the ideal of a systematicity that might reconcile experience with freedom also constitutes the object of hoping.

Notice, however, that everything that has been said thus far about the narrator applies with equal force to the empirical author Goethe. The third and most important form of expressionlessness is therefore the one reflected in Benjamin's claim that in the caesura "something beyond the poet interrupts the language of the poetry" ("GEA" 341). At this point, then, the text is no longer expressive of a subjective intent or emotion that the author may have harbored when writing the novel. The precise sense in which this assertion holds true for the narrator's sentence in *Elective Affinities* comes into view as soon as the sentence is considered against the backdrop of the biographical considerations introduced by Benjamin. As we have seen, these considerations revolve around Goethe's portrayal of Ottilie as indicative, on the one hand, of his mythic enchantment by beautiful semblance, and on the other, of his struggle to wrest himself free from this spell and salvage what is essential in beautiful semblance. This critical focus on the juncture between ethics and aesthetics, or life and art—which contrasts sharply with Bakhtin's categorical insistence on the need to keep the two spheres apart—lends weight to Benjamin's recourse to biographical evidence towards the end of the essay. These remarks, which set the stage for his marking of the caesura, call for a closer examination.

Benjamin begins by quoting a passage from Sulpiz Boisserée's account of a conversation he had during an evening walk with the aged Goethe, and then adds his own reflection:

> "During the journey, we came to speak of *Elective Affinities*. He emphasized how rapidly and irresistibly he had brought on the catastrophe. The stars had risen; he spoke of his relation to Ottilie, of

> how he had loved her and how she had made him unhappy. At the end, his speeches became almost mysteriously full of foreboding.—In between, he would recite light-hearted verse. Thus, weary, stimulated, half-full of foreboding, half-asleep, we arrived in Heidelberg in the most beautiful starlight." If it did not escape this reporter how, with the rising of the stars, Goethe's thoughts steered themselves toward his work, Goethe himself was quite probably hardly aware—a fact to which his language attests—how sublimely elevated over every mood [*über Stimmung erhaben*] the moment was and how clear the warning of the stars. In such admonition, what had long ago faded away as lived experience [*Erlebnis*] persisted as integral experience [*Erfahrung*]. For in the symbol of the star, the hope that Goethe had to conceive for the lovers had once appeared to him. ("GEA" 354, translation modified)

The circumstances of a confession made by Goethe thus cast a retrospective light on the sentence in his novel that Benjamin is about to mark as the novel's caesura. In light of the episode recounted by Boisserée, the sentence in the novel begins to resonate with the problematic of beautiful semblance that caused Goethe so much vexation throughout his life.[83] In the narrator's fleeting acknowledgment of an enduring hope, the masterfully controlled narration of a course of events unfolding with inexorable mythic necessity becomes unsettled by Goethe's own unresolved struggle with the powers of myth; and conversely, the interference from this passage in the novel charges the scene of Goethe's personal confession with an excess of significance.

"What had long ago faded away as lived experience [*Erlebnis*] persisted as integral experience [*Erfahrung*]"—thus Benjamin summarizes the constellation that he has established between the caesura of the novel and the biographical episode recounted by Boisserée. By marking the caesura of the novel, Benjamin releases an integral experience buried beneath an aesthetic totality that critics such as Gundolf have tended to construe in the reductive terms of lived experience. To characterize the episode recounted by Boisserée as an instance of integral experience is to suggest that its significance is not exhausted by what Goethe actually lived through during that evening walk. For the full meaning of that experience to emerge, it had to be mediated, first by a witness who noticed the simultaneity between the natural phenomenon and the personal confession, and then by a critic who had the acuity to correlate this moment of meaningful coincidence with a juncture in the novel. It is as if Goethe himself had become a character in a story that has gained in complexity and resonance through the process of its transmission and therefore calls for an attentive reader.

What we have here, then, is a model case of Benjamin's understanding of the relation between author and work. Against the reductive procedures of biographical criticism, Benjamin holds that an author's works cannot be deduced from his personality, for it is precisely in and through his works that an author's personality is decided in the first place and hence acquires a determinate shape ("GEA" 321). Yet to acknowledge this is not to deny that consideration of the author's life as determined by his works can yield a more nuanced understanding of those works—precisely *as* determinants of life, or otherwise put, as attempts to wrest a determinate meaning from the vexing ambiguities of lived experience. In this case, the biographical episode recounted by Boisserée, whose meaning can be deciphered from a symbol buried in the novel, also in its turn sheds light upon the work. What it shows is that the symbol of the star registers a hope that held sway over Goethe's life and work and fueled his secret, artistically sublimated rebellion against myth. This hope is "something beyond the poet" in three related senses: first, because its surfacing in the text is unintended; second, because its scope exceeds the poet's life, being a hope that encompasses others; and third, because the integral experience of hoping establishes a pattern of significance that only becomes legible to an external witness.

It should be clear by now that Benjamin could not have recognized the sentence in the novel in which this hope surfaces if his argument had respected the limits imposed by a strictly immanent interpretation of the novel. Indeed, from the latter point of view, Benjamin's interpretation of the narrator's sentence as a caesura is bound to appear as an arbitrary, "erratic accent."[84] In order to charge the narrator's sentence with such decisive significance, Benjamin must connect it to a later, similarly fleeting episode in Goethe's own life and establish a constellation between the two moments—indeed, a constellation in a literal sense of the term, for (to anticipate the point that I will address next) the correspondence being established is one between two stellar phenomena. This procedure violates the aesthetic integrity traditionally attributed to consummate works of art.[85] It does so deliberately, however, and in keeping with Benjamin's critical project. For what tradition has enshrined as the consummate work of a semidivine author is in this case a "false, errant totality" ("GEA" 340), a document of mythic enchantment in which truth content survives only as an expressionless trace that must be deciphered in the light of extraliterary biographical evidence. The ambiguous genitival construction of the essay's title acknowledges precisely this need to violate the putatively sacrosanct boundary between the work and its author.

Saving the Phenomenon

It might seem odd that Benjamin's interpretation of *Elective Affinities* should turn on the marking of a caesura in which "something beyond the poet" interrupts "the language of the poetry" ("GEA" 341). Why assume that a term native to the prosodic analysis of poetry, which Hölderlin adapted for his theory of tragedy, might be instructively applied to a work of narrative fiction? But the impression of incongruity vanishes when we turn to Benjamin's remarks on the conjunction in *Elective Affinities* among the three major literary forms, and specifically on the lyrical aspect of the novel. Following Hermann Cohen, Benjamin claims that *Elective Affinities* owes its unity to a pervasive lyrical mood, a kind of sentimental emotion (*Rührung*), which stems from Goethe's enchantment with the beautiful semblance that condenses around the figure of Ottilie. What counteracts this unifying lyrical mood is the caesura of the expressionless, which Benjamin finally identifies as a kind of mystery play:

> The mystery [*Mysterium*] is, on the dramatic level, that moment in which [the work] juts out of the domain of language proper to it into a higher one unattainable for it. Therefore, this moment can never be expressed in words but is expressible solely in representation [*Darstellung*]: it is the "dramatic" in the strictest sense. An analogous moment of representation in *Elective Affinities* is the falling star. The novel's epic basis in the mythic, its lyrical breadth in passion and affection [*Neigung*], is joined by its dramatic crowning in the mystery [*Mysterium*] of hope. ("GEA" 355)

We will have to return to this claim about the dramatic character of the caesura when we consider Adorno's argument about the caesura of the *Odyssey*.

Related to this construal of hope as a silent dramatic spectacle is another important point, which will also prove relevant to the examination of Adorno's caesura marking in the next chapter. I am thinking of the retort to Plato's denunciation of semblance that emerges from Benjamin's account of the mystery play of hope:

> That most paradoxical, most fleeting hope finally emerges from the semblance of reconciliation, just as, at twilight, as the sun is extinguished, rises the evening star which outlasts the night. Its glimmer, of course, is imparted by Venus. And upon the slightest such glimmer all hope rests; even the richest hope comes only from it. Thus, at the end, hope justifies the semblance of reconciliation, and Plato's tenet that it is absurd to desire the semblance of the good suffers its one exception. For one is permitted to desire the semblance of reconciliation—indeed, it must be desired: it alone is the house of the most extreme hope. ("GEA" 355)

This passage adds a key nuance to the connection between the characters' defeated desires and the hope that registers in the narrator's comment. Although the characters' aspirations must be doomed in order for the transcendence of hope to emerge, the mystery play that dramatizes this transcendence nevertheless does require the fleeting illusion that reconciliation is possible. This is so even though the semblance at issue is emphatically and perniciously false. The idea of reconciliation that underwrites Ottilie's and Eduard's hopes as they embrace is premised on an ethics of restraint, consideration, and sacrifice. This ethical outlook precludes decisive agency and finally delivers the characters over to a guilt-laden natural realm subject to the blind stipulations of right. The sentimental mood suffusing the scene signals the narrator's, and indeed Goethe's, entanglement in this mythic delusion. Yet this very entanglement also makes possible the critical moment in which mythic semblance is punctured from within. The dormant utopian hope harbored by the narrator could not surge to the surface of the narrative if it did not find a transient object of investment in the scene in which Eduard and Ottilie "for the first time ever exchanged resolute and free kisses" (GHA 6:456).

At various points in his intellectual trajectory, Benjamin invokes the ancient idea of "saving phenomena." In his early writings, in particular, the formula stands for the task of rescuing experience from the contingency and worthlessness to which it was consigned when Kant divorced knowledge from experience.[86] How the essay on *Elective Affinities* contributes to this undertaking should by now be clear. In the *Arcades Project* that occupied Benjamin during the final period of his life, however, he gives the ancient formula a twist that suggests another perspective on the Goethe essay, and especially on the marking of the caesura:

> What are phenomena saved from? Not only, and not in the main, from the discredit and neglect into which they have fallen, but from the catastrophe represented very often by a certain strain in their transmission, their "enshrinement [*Würdigung*] as heritage."—They are saved through the exhibition of the fissure [*Sprung*] within them.—There is a transmission that is a catastrophe.[87]

We might say, then, that in the case of *Elective Affinities* the catastrophe is what Benjamin describes as a "hundred-year tradition [that] has done its work and almost buried the possibility of original understanding," a tradition whose mystifications are epitomized by Gundolf's book ("GEA" 311). By marking a caesura in the novel, Benjamin intervenes to rescue the work from this catastrophic transmission.

There is a sense, however, in which the object of the rescue undertaken by Benjamin is both more specific and more general than Goethe's novel. For the essay also performs a saving of the phenomenon in the sense that it reinstates a sphere of integral experience that is not limited to appearance (*Erscheinung*)—that is, to phenomenal experience conducive to natural-scientific knowledge—but also encompasses false semblance (*Schein*). What Benjamin saves by noting an exception to the Platonic repudiation of semblance is the *mere* semblance of reconciliation, which constitutes the prerequisite for the mystery play of utopian hope: "Upon the slightest such glimmer all hope rests; even the richest hope comes only from it" ("GEA" 355). This glimmer is what connects the aged Goethe's confession to Boisserée, subliminally prompted by the rising stars, and the novelistic narrator's recording of a hope akin to a falling star.

The astral imagery foregrounded by this philological constellation is not fortuitous. It was, in fact, in the astronomical context that the imperative to save phenomena first acquired epochal significance. Here it is important to point out that although Benjamin consistently associates the principle of saving phenomena with Plato, the formula does not actually occur anywhere in the Platonic corpus.[88] Benjamin's misattribution is nevertheless telling. We may infer from it that he probably knew Pierre Duhem's very influential 1908 study, which is premised on precisely this misattribution.[89] For the astronomers discussed by Duhem, the formula expressed a commitment to explaining the seemingly erratic motions of heavenly bodies in terms of simple rational laws, such as that of circular movement. The crucial point stressed by Duhem is that the formula did not require astronomers to believe that such explanations captured the true nature of celestial reality—which Christian theology, after all, had placed beyond the reach of human understanding. Rather, saving the phenomena merely required that explanations based on formalistic hypotheses "worked" in the heuristic, predictive sense.[90]

Here it is worth pausing to note, following Roland Reuss, that the formula of "saving the phenomena" in the original Greek includes the verb *sózó* ("to redeem"), which implies a telos of integration, closure, and restitution, and not the verb *rhuomai* ("to save"), which designates a swift removal from danger.[91] "Redeeming phenomena" would therefore be a more accurate translation of the ancient formula. The heuristic formalism of astronomical explanation heals the wound created by the erratic movement of celestial bodies, in that it integrates that movement into an intelligible, albeit hypothetical, order. By contrast, a saving of the phenomena in the negative sense would be an interpretation that tears the phenomena out of their all-too intelligible terrestrial context and refers them to a postulated higher order that eludes our understanding. In the images we make of such saving acts, stars may stand for the uncertain destination of rescue, rather than for the phenomena that require to be saved. A poignant example of such saving of the phenomena can be found in Nietzsche's *The Gay Science*. In one of his countless attempts to come to terms with the vexing memory of his friendship and falling-out with Richard Wagner, Nietzsche undertakes a saving of the phenomenon by envisioning a "Star friendship" corresponding to the estranged friends' enmity here on earth:

> That we had become estranged is the law *above* us; through it we should come to have more respect for each other—and the thought of our former friendship should become more sacred! There is probably

> a tremendous invisible curve and stellar orbit in which our different ways and goals may be *included* as small stretches—let us rise to this thought! But our life is too short and our vision too meagre for us to be more than friends in the sense of that sublime possibility [*erhabenen Möglichkeit*].—Let us then *believe* in our star friendship even if we must be earth enemies.[92]

The abiding utopian hope that "saves" the false semblance of reconciliation in *Elective Affinities*, as Benjamin understands it, is a sublime hypothesis in precisely this negative sense. It is an act of anagogical interpretation—to use the Scholastic term for the hermeneutic ascent to spiritual meaning, itself an offspring of the pneumatic allegoresis inaugurated by the Hellenistic-era Jewish thinker Philo of Alexandria. Such an interpretation leads our gaze upward without actually achieving integration into an intelligible order.[93]

As already noted, Duhem argued that the principle of "saving" astronomical phenomena merely required that the formal explanation worked and entailed no knowledge claim about the true nature of reality. While current historical research suggests that this interpretation does not really hold true for every author discussed by Duhem, his account does capture the intentions of an especially influential group of authors—namely, the early apologists for Copernicus's heliocentric model. These advocates repeatedly tried to underplay the subversive potential of Copernicus's proposal by insisting that its sole purpose was to save the phenomena and not to uncover the true nature of the underlying reality.[94] This early modern deployment of the ancient formula is very much relevant to Benjamin's invocations of the latter. For, in a distant homage to Kant, Benjamin turned the figure of the Copernican revolution into a pivot for his own thinking. In the *Arcades Project*, he would envision "a Copernican revolution in historical perception," in whose wake the fixed point is no longer the facticity of the past—to which historical knowledge in the present must passively conform, according to historicism—but the eminently political act of awakening from mythic delusion, which has the power to alter the past by releasing hitherto suppressed meanings.[95] To the extent that Benjamin's marking of a caesura in *Elective Affinities* represents an attempt to awaken the work from the mythic spell cast by a catastrophic tradition, the wager of the essay already presupposes something like a Copernican revolution of historical awareness. Only through a critical awakening in the sense of that later theory can Benjamin arrive at the hope that the dead lovers will "awaken, if ever, not to a beautiful world but to a blessed one" ("GEA" 355).

Much depends, of course, on how the astronomical metaphor is understood. The scientific revolution ushered in by Copernicus did, as a matter of historical fact, go beyond a saving of the phenomena in the Duhemian sense espoused by Copernicus's early apologists. Yet we have no reason to assume that the same is true of the revolution of historical awareness advocated by

Benjamin. It certainly does not seem to be the case in the essay on *Elective Affinities*, which salvages the work by breaking it open and referring it to a projected ideal of rational totality that eludes positive representation. Benjamin's meditation upon the semblance of reconciliation that flashes up in its vanishing, like a shooting star, is indeed a bid to save a phenomenon. According to the historical heuristics that underwrites Benjamin's argument, this false and fugitive semblance finds its justification in the utopian hope that it inspires in the narrator. Such semblance cannot, however, in its turn demonstrate the rightness of the utopian projection. Nothing can vindicate the latter, other than—in the best of cases—the historical experience that it works.

Chapter 2

✦

Adorno's Hard Caesura

The Impassive Homeric Narrator

Outis and *Ott-* : Epic and Novel

Walter Benjamin, as we have seen, marks a caesura at a juncture in *Elective Affinities* at which Goethe's mythically occluded portrayal of a social world is punctured by an experience of utopian hope that transcends his characters', the narrator's, and even Goethe's own limited consciousness. Responding to a self-critical moment immanent to the novel, Benjamin's caesura marking completes and amplifies this self-critique. Benjamin thus intervenes to decide a struggle between mythic forces and saving impulses that otherwise remains unresolved in the novel, a struggle that manifests itself not in terms of the plot so much as on the formal-aesthetic plane. This intervention takes its guidance from Benjamin's urgent sense of mythic tendencies that conspire to obstruct insight into the work and threaten to vitiate every possibility of human fulfillment.

If we now turn to Theodor W. Adorno's passing and elliptical remarks on an "expressionless" moment and a "caesura" in book 22 of the *Odyssey*, we might be forgiven for thinking at first that his use of these concepts borrowed from Benjamin's essay on *Elective Affinities* is a simple matter of terminological convenience. Nor can we decide the question of the significance of this borrowing by simply noting the fact—which is worth pointing out here—that the Benjaminian caesura model exerted a pervasive influence on Adorno's thinking about art, and especially on his thinking about music. This influence can be traced back to conversations that took place after Adorno and Benjamin attended a performance of the opera *Wozzeck* by Adorno's mentor Alban Berg in December 1925, only a few months after the publication of the essay on *Elective Affinities*. As Benjamin was to remark later, this was the sole occasion on which an intense discussion between the two was sparked by music, an art form that otherwise remained curiously marginal to Benjamin's thinking.[1] In the wake of these conversations, the concept of caesura became central to Adorno's reflections on *Wozzeck* and also found its way into his writings about Schoenberg and Beethoven, the latter being the composer to whose works Adorno's musicological reflections were most powerfully drawn. As if to leave no doubt about the provenance of this term, in his posthumously published *Aesthetic Theory* Adorno invokes the sentence that Benjamin identified as the caesura of *Elective Affinities* as an analogue for certain musical phrases in Beethoven.[2]

Again, however, the breadth of Adorno's reliance on the Benjaminian category does not alone prove that his remarks at the end of the excursus on Odysseus reflect a substantial engagement with the Benjaminian model in all its complexity. After all, in most passages in which Adorno uses the category of caesura, his choice of the term does not appear to be motivated by any elaborate consideration beyond a generalized modernist fascination with moments of rupture and fragmentation in art.[3] In the excursus on Odysseus, however, Adorno's engagement with the Benjaminian caesura model runs deep—or so I will argue in this chapter. Of all the texts by Adorno that invoke the Benjaminian category of caesura, it is in fact the excursus on Odysseus—Adorno's earliest application of that model to literature—that involves by far the most nuanced and consequential reworking of the model borrowed from the essay on *Elective Affinities*.

Even in a first approach, the hypothesis of a merely superficial terminological borrowing must appear somewhat improbable in light of certain connections between the literary works with which Benjamin's and Adorno's critical texts are respectively concerned. A Homeric subtext runs through *Elective Affinities*, and once we become attentive to it, Adorno's recourse, in reflecting on the *Odyssey*, to a critical model originally developed in relation to that novel appears anything but arbitrary. A first, schematic indication of this Homeric subtext can be found in the faint echo of Odysseus's cunning reference to himself as "nobody" (outis) in Goethe's unsettling games with the root "ott-" contained in the names of the four main characters (Eduard Otto, Charlotte, Otto, Ottilie). Although Horkheimer and Adorno claim that "Enlightenment as a nominalist tendency stops short before the *nomen*, the non-extensive, restricted concept, the proper name" (*DE* 17), even this last bastion of non-interchangeability appears to have fallen in a fictional world whose narrative representation begins with the proposal "Eduard—let that be the name we give to a wealthy baron in the best years of his life . . ." (*EA* 3), and in which the character so named is said to have ceded his middle name (Otto) first to his friend and then to his (or should one say their?) child.

There is, moreover, a key juncture in the novel at which the narrow focus of the narration suddenly widens to encompass Homeric vistas. At the very end of part 1, which is to say at the midpoint of the novel, Goethe briefly opens up the otherwise hermetically closed chamber in which his novelistic experiment unfolds to admit a glimpse of large-scale historical forces that would seem to call for epic portrayal. In the fit of despair induced by Charlotte's pregnancy, Eduard leaves the estate to throw himself into a military campaign prompted by the "renewal of the war" (EA 115). This reference can only be to the post-Revolutionary Coalition Wars, the first of which had already received neo-Homeric treatment at Goethe's hands in the hexameters of the epic poem *Hermann and Dorothea* (1797). That Goethe meant to highlight the epic potential of this juncture is clear from the fact that following the break between part 1 and part 2, the narration resumes with an authorial reflection on how in "in ordinary life as in an epic poem [*Epopöe*] . . . when the principal characters withdraw, remove themselves from view, become inactive, at once some second or third and until then scarcely noticed person takes their place" (*EA* 117). After his homecoming, Eduard himself offers an explanation for his military adventure that turns the equivocity of names, and the interchangeability of their bearers, into the basis for an undertaking that echoes both of the Homeric epics:

> A glass marked with our initials thrown into the air when the foundation stone was laid, instead of smashing to pieces it was caught and is in my hands again. "Well then," I cried to myself, having spent many uncertain hours in this solitude. "I will make myself into a sign in the place of that glass, to see whether our union shall be possible or not. I will go and seek my death, and not as a madman but as one who hopes to live. Ottilie shall be the prize I am fighting for, and she will be what I hope to win and to conquer behind the enemy lines on every battlefield and behind every fortification and in every siege. I will perform miracles, in the wish to be spared and in the intention to win Ottilie and not to lose her." These feelings guided me, they stood by me in all the dangers; but now I feel like a man arrived at his goal, all obstacles overcome and nothing now in my way. Ottilie is mine . . . (*EA* 198–99)

It is as if this modern Odysseus had fought in Troy only in order to win back his Penelope.[4] The distant land into which he ventures is thus not the place that holds the coveted prize, but merely an accidental backdrop for his trial. Attentive readers will also have noted that the superstition motivating this trial is premised on a patently willful attribution of meaning. For the initials engraved upon the glass (EO) were not those of Eduard and Ottilie but those of Eduard alone in his youth, before he ceded his middle name (Otto) to the captain (*DE* 18–19, 61).

Of course, the Homeric subtext only serves to underscore how far we are from the world of the *Iliad* and the *Odyssey*. Odysseus, as Adorno argues, "throws himself away, so to speak, in order to win himself," and his self-consciousness is forged in the face of experiences of "diversity, distraction, disintegration" (*DE* 38). No one could say the same of Eduard. The knowledge that makes up Eduard's identity remains single-mindedly focused on Ottilie—which is to say, not on the mythic Other but on the mythic Same, marked as such even by the name whose first syllable Ottilie shares with Eduard (who was originally named Otto). One would look in vain for such an incorrigibly self-absorbed hero in the Homeric corpus. Although Eduard stylizes his military enterprise into a grand trial, Goethe's narrator gives a markedly more prosaic account of Eduard's departure: he is said to revert to "old habits and old inclinations . . . to kill time and to fill the space of life [*Lebensraum*] up with something. Hunting and war are one such recourse a nobleman always has at his disposal" (*EA* 115, translation modified).

Despite all the perils that Eduard will undergo abroad, this portion of dead, spatialized time will fail to introduce an element of genuine transformative experience into the artificial experiment of elective affinities staged by Goethe. We do not learn anything about Eduard's vicissitudes, just as he for his part appears not to have learned anything new from them. This adventure constitutes an excursus in the literal sense, one whose formal significance lies in what it fails to bring about—and, as we will see in chapter 4, in the narrative space that it allows for the introduction of other sources of meaning from without. It is precisely because Eduard's adventures fail to make a difference, and because the social world portrayed in the novel occludes every possibility of transformative experience, that his homecoming results in a disaster, one that is less gruesome but no less devastating than the revenge of Odysseus.

The reason I dwelled on the Homeric subtext of *Elective Affinities* is that it anticipates, albeit in an inverse form, a striking feature of the chapter titled "Excursus I: Odysseus or Myth and Enlightenment" in *Dialectic of Enlightenment*. Originally written by Theodor W. Adorno in 1942–43 and revised for publication by Adorno and Max Horkheimer, the excursus focuses on one side of the dialectic named in the title of the book to reconstruct the emergence of the rational bourgeois subject from the mythic universe of the *Odyssey*. To put the matter in this way is, on the face of it, merely to state well-known facts. Yet readers who have struggled with the argument of the essay will likely take issue with the imputation of a reconstructive intent to Adorno. And they will be right to do so, for Adorno's thesis that "the hero of the adventures turns out to be the prototype of the bourgeois individual" is clearly not a claim about how things really were in the twelfth century BC or how the Homeric poems would have been received by the audience of an archaic-era bard. Anachronism is, in fact, essential to the theory of history that Horkheimer and Adorno develop in their joint work. Examples abound already in the dense opening essay of the book, such as the assertion that the natural-scientific reduction of the world to "a gigantic analytical judgment" is "of the same kind" as the myth of Persephone, or the description of the fettered Odysseus listening to the sirens as a modern concertgoer (*DE* 20, 27).

In the excursus on Odysseus, this sort of provocative anachronism most often takes the form of invocations of the quintessentially modern genre of the novel. Occurring as they do in the opening and the concluding pages of the essay, Adorno's references to the novel establish a conceptual frame for his argument that everywhere informs the substantive claims he is advancing. The casual remark toward the end of the excursus that Homer's listeners are "really readers" (*DE* 62) is only a particularly glaring sign of the curious supposition that informs Adorno's entire argument. Even more strikingly, it is with an assertion about the novel's historical relation to two other narrative genres that the essay comes to a close: "Only as novel is the epic transmuted into fairy tale" (*DE* 62, translation modified). Yet the pertinence of this cryptic statement to the *Odyssey* is far from obvious.

If, however, we recall the Homeric subtext of *Elective Affinities*, a hint at the likely rationale for Adorno's anachronistic treatment of the *Odyssey* as a novel may be discerned in his conceptual borrowing from Benjamin's essay on Goethe's novel. Presenting certain junctures of novelistic narration in an epic light was an ironic device that enabled Goethe to underscore the difference of the social world he was portraying from the Homeric universe. By reversing Goethe's ironic anachronism and reading the *Odyssey* through a novelistic lens, Adorno takes issue with this suggestion of a radical dissimilarity between the ancient epic and the modern novel.

Even before we can say anything determinate about Adorno's thinking about the relation between antiquity and modernity, it should be clear that his interest in this relation is not purely historiographical. In view of the fact that Adorno draws on the Benjaminian caesura model a mere two years after Benjamin's death, it seems natural to suppose that he is mindful of the critique that Benjamin leveled against historicism in the text that is often seen as his testament. In the theses "On the Concept of History," posthumously published with the help of Adorno and Horkheimer in the same year in which Adorno began writing about the *Odyssey*, Benjamin called for a writing of history that might capture "an irretrievable image of the past which threatens to disappear in any present that does not recognize itself as intended in that image" (*SW* 4:390). To recognize our present in the *Odyssey* is to remember that the Homeric epic is not just a literary document from a remote past but a canonical classic, a work that has become constitutive of who we are and how we understand ourselves. In particular, much of the sedimented substance that formed the bedrock of the cultural identity of Wilhelmine Germany's educated bourgeoisie was the result of successive appropriations of Homer, and especially of the story of Odysseus's homecoming.[5] Following Benjamin's injunction, Adorno turns to the *Odyssey* to discern in a germinal form the defining tendencies and aporias of modernity. It is thus not with the *Odyssey* that his allegorical reading is principally concerned, but with the culture that owes its very shape to the *Odyssey*.

Yet the proposal to read the *Odyssey* as a novel would seem to call for specifically literary arguments in its support, and this expectation remains frustrated by the sketchiness of Adorno's pertinent comments. The resultant lacuna is all the more striking because Adorno's attribution of "novel-like features" (*romanähnlichen Züge*) to the *Odyssey* seems to fly in the face of an imposing body of theoretical reflections. Although the genealogy of the novel has often been traced back to antiquity, Lukács, Bakhtin, and Benjamin all concur in opposing the novel to the epic as the modern counterpart of the latter. Of the relevant texts by the theorists just mentioned, Bakhtin's "Epic and Novel" from 1941 cannot have been known to Adorno, even though, as I will suggest, its central idea can be of help in understanding Adorno's argument. As for Lukács, signs of an intermittent engagement with his treatment of the epic will soon come into view. More importantly, however, a profound and sustained engagement with Benjamin's thinking runs through the excursus on Odysseus.

Since, however, this dialogue with the legacy of Adorno's late friend occurs beneath the surface of the excursus, it only emerges against the backdrop of the overt polemical agenda that governs Adorno's anachronistic conceptual framing. This agenda is less clearly discernible in the final text included in *Dialectic of Enlightenment* than in the early draft of the excursus written in 1942–43, which was not published until 1998.[6] Presumably because of its specifically German context, this polemical strand ended up being curtailed in the final version, whose publication in exile and subsequent republication in the immediate wake of Germany's "Hour Zero" must have made that context appear less topical. Since, however, the polemic in question is directly relevant to Adorno's novelistic reading of the *Odyssey* and to his dialogue with Benjamin in the excursus, it cannot be bypassed here.

Countering *Kulturphilosophie*

The draft version of the excursus outlines two distinct approaches to Greek antiquity that emerged in Germany during the last decades of the nineteenth century. Paradigmatic for the split between them is the polemic that unfolded in the 1870s, when the young Ulrich Wilamowitz-Möllendorf invoked the claims of philological rigor to rebuke Nietzsche for his idiosyncratic reimagining of Greek tragedy in line with the Wagnerian program of cultural-political renewal. The historical positivism of the philological school of which Wilamowitz would eventually become the most prominent figure tended to abstain from anthropological speculations about the archaic, primitive thinking deposited in the mythic and religious contents of literary works. Instead, German philologists typically focused on the rationally intelligible aspects of ancient works, as well as on the available archaeological evidence regarding their contexts ("GE" 37–38). Such abstinence from mythological interpretation left the field open for ideologically driven appropriations that paid no heed to the protocols of scholarly argumentation. A complementary tradition thus emerged, one of vitalist *Kulturphilosophie*. Its glorification of the archaic stratum sidelined by Wilamowitz and his ilk drew inspiration from Nietzsche's philosophy of the Dionysian and, to a lesser extent, from Bachofen's primitivism.

The hermeneutic energies animating the latter approach were greatly enhanced by the antimodernist turn of the educated bourgeoisie (*Bildungsbürgertum*) in Wilhelmine Germany.[7] This class, whose worldview was forged in humanistic *Gymnasia* that cultivated a peculiarly German devotion to Greek antiquity, began around 1900 to feel uneasy about the rapid modernization of Germany and grew increasingly averse to the reductively rational, compartmentalized, and commercial spirit of modernity. Some of the leading Weimar-era intellectuals who gave voice to this discontent—Moeller van den Bruck, Hugo von Hofmannsthal, and Thomas Mann up until 1922—advocated for a conservative revolution that would do away with the shallowness and the leveling effects of modern "civilization" and restore a *Kultur* rooted in the primordial dimensions of life. Although most of these authors hewed to an elitist aestheticism that contrasted with the emergent National Socialist glorification of the people, nevertheless, their seductive rhetoric of conservative revolution made much of the German bourgeoisie susceptible to the antimodernist, irrational appeal of National Socialism. It is the vision of Greek antiquity informed by this cultural-philosophical agenda that constitutes Adorno's primary adversary, with positivist philology as a secondary polemical target. In this regard, Adorno's representative adversary is the interwar-era conservative poet Rudolf Borchardt, whose glorification of archaic Greece underwrote a comprehensive critique of culture. This choice of polemical target marks a point of continuity with Benjamin's essay on *Elective Affinities*, in which Borchardt is mentioned in cautionary terms as a poet who has fully succumbed to that lure of artistic conjuration to which Goethe's writing is so perilously exposed ("GEA" 341).

Since it is from Borchardt that Adorno polemically appropriates the characterization of the *Odyssey* as a novel, a brief review of Borchardt's relevant ideas is in order.[8] Similarly to other proponents of conservative *Kulturkritik*, Borchardt drew heavily on the young Nietzsche's appropriation of Greek antiquity. However, whereas Nietzsche viewed the Apolline clarity of Homer's epic poetry and the Dionysian fire of Archilochus's lyric poetry as equally indispensable to the genesis of tragedy, Borchardt converts Nietzsche's assertion of the metaphysical primacy of the latter into a wholesale repudiation of the former ("GE" 38).[9] Borchardt's modified version of the Nietzschean narrative of decadence and revival deploys the peculiarly German dualism of *Kultur* and civilization: the decline of Hellenic culture is attributed to the transition from the aboriginal Doric culture of mainland Greece to a calculating merchant civilization whose center of gravity lay in the Asian colonies of Ionia. Rooted in myth, the aristocratic "poetry" of Doric culture expressed itself in a lyric "chant" whose last representative was Pindar. By contrast, in the Ionian civilization that supposedly produced Homer, the primordial vitality of poetic genius was sapped by the specious sophistication of a democratic "literature" that aimed at mere entertainment and privileged verbal narration over chant. Adorno does not mince words in summarizing the ideological thrust of this view of things: "The yellow star is attached to the mantle of the epic poet" ("GE" 39).

Of primary interest here is the generic aspect of Borchardt's argument. As Adorno writes in the early draft, "the traditional-Romantic equation between epic poetry and myth, which still underpinned Lukács's *Theory of the Novel*, was destroyed by the later Romanticism" ("GE" 42). Whereas Lukács opposed epic poetry to the novel on both formal and thematic grounds, Borchardt's considerably less fine-grained understanding of literary form underwrote a subsumption of the Homeric poems under the pejoratively applied label of the novel. In this respect as well, Borchardt takes up a motif from Nietzsche's *Birth of Tragedy*, namely, the negative valuation of the novel and the claim that this paradigmatically modern genre originated in decadent tendencies that had undone the precarious, agonistic unity of ancient tragedy.[10]

Why does Adorno adopt Borchardt's retrospective projection of novelistic features onto the *Odyssey*? Part of the answer would seem to be that such a projection is encouraged by the tributes that novelists have paid to the Homeric epic. Besides the above-mentioned Homeric echoes in *Elective Affinities* and the obvious example of Joyce's *Ulysses*, one might think here of the passage in Thomas Mann's *The Magic Mountain*—a novel to which I will return in my conclusion—in which the humanist pedagogue Settembrini admonishes the protagonist who has been seduced onto a perilous path of intellectual experimentation in the morbid world of an Alpine sanatorium: "Do not lose yourself in an alien world. Avoid that swamp, that isle of Circe—for you are not Odysseus enough to dwell there unharmed. You will walk on all fours, you are tipping down onto your front limbs already, and will soon begin to grunt–beware!"[11] Such modern invocations of the *Odyssey* suggest that there may be a kernel of truth in Borchardt's reactionary construction. Borchardt's very hostility to Enlightenment reason enabled him to ferret out its first stirrings in the depths of an archaic past; and by effectively equating world history with enlightenment, Borchardt, as Adorno puts it, paid "involuntary homage" to the latter (*DE* 37). Adorno's emphasis on the novelistic aspects of the *Odyssey* thus has the function of appropriating and redirecting an insight originally deployed in the service of a conservative agenda. As James I. Porter has shown in considerable detail, Adorno's excursus provokes, parodies, and explodes the Orientalized image of Homer. By provisionally conceding the conservative projection of the archaic Greeks as "brutish, active," and then highlighting within that regressive fantasy the "discordant traits" of rational calculation, Adorno renders "anti-Semitic Germans into ancient wayfarers and merchants, into Nobodies, that is, into Jews," and thereby creates "a double-object of hatred for his German readers, in case these had any pro-fascistic leanings."[12]

To be sure, by identifying the polemical strategy behind Adorno's procedure, we have not yet said anything about its substantive basis in the Homeric material itself. This basis will come into view later on in this chapter. For now, we must note two points of disagreement between Borchardt and Adorno. The first disagreement is due to Borchardt's blindness to the titular dialectic of Adorno and Horkheimer's book: Borchardt failed to realize that the germs of Enlightenment reason were already planted in the very mythic content whose occlusion through epic narration he deplored. For that is indeed the upshot of the programmatic introductory essay of *Dialectic of Enlightenment* that Horkheimer coauthored with Adorno. Although Enlightenment reason claims to have overcome mythic sacrifice, that very overcoming perpetuates the sacrificial logic as the mimetic tendencies of human nature are subordinated to its fearful side, defined by the drive to self-preservation (*DE* 42–43). Similarly, the eternal recurrence of the same, stipulated by the fateful necessity that permeates the mythic universe, is not only the destructive principle in the face of which the Enlightenment subject must struggle to preserve himself, but also the archetype of the self-conscious identity that the subject maintains across the totality of his nomologically unified experiences (*DE* 8).

The second, related, point of contention in Adorno's polemic against Borchardt concerns the role of narration. For not only does Adorno disagree with Borchardt in detecting the first stirrings of enlightenment in the oldest stratum of the mythic materials deposited in the *Odyssey* (*DE* 59–60), he also rejects Borchardt's view of narration as unequivocally allied with Enlightenment reason. To appreciate the rationale for this rejection, we must briefly consider a line of thought developed in the draft version of the excursus that the authors dropped from the book and which Adorno eventually published separately as a short essay on "Epic Naiveté" ("GE" 78).[13] Here Adorno argues that the dialectic of myth and Enlightenment entails an internal contradiction that vitiates all narration. By definition, the act of narration presumes that the hero has differentiated himself out of the crushing sameness of mythic nature and is to that extent "worth reporting about." However, since epic narration construes the successive adventures that this subject endures in his confrontations with mythic nature as so many vindications of his autonomous rationality, and reason in its turn has its anthropological basis in the self-preservational drive of an organism captive to the immutable laws of nature, the vindication of reason in epic narration always amounts, in the final analysis, to a recurrence of all-pervasive mythic necessity—albeit in the guise of Enlightenment. The basic posture of narration therefore stands in contradiction with its subject matter, which is the triumph of a rationality with unacknowledged roots in myth.

A corresponding dialectic becomes apparent when we approach the posture of narration towards the mythic world confronting the hero. Narrative's pretense to objective representation depends on an illusion of particularity that must be upheld even though the very act of narration effects a mediation of the represented contents by abstract universals. According to Adorno, this false semblance accounts for the "anachronistic element" attendant on all narration, a kind of willed "dumbness" that is no less evident in Goethe's and Stifter's "desperate" efforts to portray bourgeois conditions as primordial, still untouched by conceptual mediation, than in Homeric passages that petition the muse's help in portraying monstrous things. It is this pretense to epic naïveté that underwrites the prohibition on authorial reflection that Flaubert sought to observe so rigorously. And it is in protest against this "lie of presentation," as Adorno calls it, that such modernists as Proust, Mann, Gide, and Musil make reflection downright central to their novels, which to that extent perform auto-critiques of narration.[14]

The anachronism involved in the false naïveté of narration is retrogressive. It surfaces in moments when the novel reverts to epic narration, which in its turn hearkens back to pre-animistic, archaic thinking. Adorno's characterization of the *Odyssey* as a novel—my primary concern here—represents the dialectical flip side of this anachronism; and, as we shall see, it will enable him to discern in the *Odyssey* anticipations of both the Flaubertian, realist absolutization of epic naïveté and its modernist auto-critique. However, one would short-circuit the dialectic by concluding that calling the *Odyssey* a novel is just another way of locating it in a historical continuum of which the epic represents one extreme pole. For a proper understanding of Adorno's claim, it is important to recognize not only the temporal distance that separates the novel from the epic, but also the fundamental discontinuity between the two. Indeed, Adorno's constructive interpretation of the *Odyssey* culminates in the last two pages of the excursus in a reflection that establishes this very discontinuity. If this point is easy to overlook, it is because in his concluding reflections Adorno shifts to a register that recalls the most hermetic passages penned by Walter Benjamin—who is in fact Adorno's main interlocutor here, as I argue. I will now attempt to disentangle the web of allusions compressed into the highly elliptical last two pages of the essay (*DE* 60–62). My running commentary on these passages should prepare the ground for an examination of Adorno's marking of a caesura in book 22 of the *Odyssey*.

Myth versus Homeland

Adorno begins his concluding reflection by adding a qualification to the truism that Odysseus's adventures are set in motion by a yearning for the homeland: "The fact that—despite the fascist lies to the contrary—the concept of homeland is opposed to myth constitutes the innermost paradox of epic" (*DE* 60). The paradox in question is due to the disparity between the geographically specific goal that motivates Odysseus, who simply wants to return to Ithaca, and the more elusive aspiration for a homeland that registers in the *Odyssey*. Adorno's characterization of this longing is unmistakably colored by the perspective of the German Jew whose Californian exile afforded him a liberating disenchantment with Central European *Kultur*, but who would nevertheless eventually return to his war-ravaged, guilt-laden homeland, the land of his native tongue and auratic childhood memories.[15] "Precipitated in the epic," he writes, "is the memory of an historical age in which nomadism gave way to settlement, the precondition of any homeland. If the fixed order of property implicit in settlement is the source of human alienation, in which all homesickness and longing spring from a lost primal state, at the same time it is toward settlement and fixed property, on which alone the concept of homeland is based, that all longing and homesickness are directed" (*DE* 60–61). Paradoxically, then, homesickness draws its emotional energy from a longing for a lost nomadic state. Deep down, *Heimweh* is *Fernweh*, a word for which Adorno would have been unable to find a succinct translation in his American exile. The utopian homeland adumbrated in these sentences is one that unites the safety of home with the freedom of travel.

Strikingly, Adorno goes on to characterize this utopia in terms of a statement that is often taken to encapsulate the essence of Romantic theorizing: "Novalis's definition according to which all philosophy is homesickness holds good only if this longing is not dissipated in the phantasm of a lost original state, but homeland, and nature itself, are pictured as something that have had first to be wrested from myth. Homeland is a state of having escaped" (*DE* 61). Adorno knew whereof he spoke. It would have been painfully clear to him in 1942 that, were he ever to return to Germany from his exile, the place he would be returning to could never again be his homeland. Return to a narrowly defined place of origin was, of course, also not what Novalis had in mind when he wrote that "philosophy is actually homesickness—the urge to be everywhere at home."[16] By accentuating the cosmopolitan impulse of early Romanticism in his characterization of the utopian impulse evident in the *Odyssey*, Adorno counters Borchardt's call for a revival of Romantic nationalism.[17] Indeed, this polemical thrust becomes explicit as Adorno goes on to address, however obliquely, Borchardt's criticism of the Homeric poems as documents of a decadent, overrefined civilization that had become estranged from its native soil. Adorno's retort is supported by another strategically placed reference to a German Romantic poet whose work has been appropriated by conservative nationalists: "For this reason the criticism that the Homeric legends 'withdraw from the earth' is a warranty of their truth. They 'turn to men'" (*DE* 61). Freely reconfigured into a miniature emancipatory counterpart to Borchardt's "creative restoration," these embedded quotes from an elusively simple poem that Hölderlin composed after his lapse into madness are meant to convey the thought that the Homeric poems capture a truth essential to humanity precisely because they reject the regressive impulse to equate utopia with native soil.

As we will see, Adorno's argument is in fact crucially indebted to Hölderlin as the first theorist who claimed that a moment of discontinuity, or "caesura," was constitutive of significant works of art. At the very point, however, where Adorno first quotes Hölderlin, his own exposition becomes discontinuous. For the next sentence reads: "The transposition of myths into the novel, as it is completed in the narration of adventures, does not falsify them so much as drag myth into the sphere of time, exposing the abyss which separates it from homeland and reconciliation" (*DE* 61, translation modified). It is not immediately clear whether Adorno is here invoking "the novel" in a generic sense or in reference to the Homeric text. Yet the Novalis quote offers a useful hint. The aphorism by Novalis famously figures in the pathos-filled opening paragraph of Georg Lukács's *Theory of the Novel*. There the quote from Novalis prepared the ground for Lukács's claim that German Romantics had been right to see the Romantic genre par excellence in the novel (*Roman* in German), which Lukács famously characterized as "an expression of transcendental homelessness."[18] Adorno's Novalisian, Romantic construal of the utopia of the *Odyssey* might therefore warrant calling the work "novel-*like*." Yet this consideration alone hardly explains Adorno's categorical reference to that work as "the novel."

Before we can finally address this puzzle head-on, we first have to consider Adorno's ensuing remarks about a specific passage in the *Odyssey*, which is presumably invoked to illustrate "the abyss which separates [myth] from homeland and reconciliation." Adorno writes: "The vengeance wreaked by civilization on the primeval world has been terrible, and in this vengeance, the most horrifying document of which in Homer is to be found in the account of the mutilation of the goatherd Melanthios, civilization itself resembles the primeval world" (*DE* 61). The reference is to the orgy of cruelty that erupts upon Odysseus's homecoming, and specifically to the torture, mutilation, and killing of the goatherd who betrayed him. This episode drives the dialectic of enlightenment to a head: it is both a triumph of the autonomous subject who has overcome the destructive forces of myth to achieve his goal and, at the same time, a regression to the mythic violence underlying the self-preservational drive that sustains instrumental reason. As Adorno writes early on in the excursus, "ironically, it is the implacable nature that [Odysseus] now commands which triumphs on his return home as the implacable one, who as judge and avenger is heir to the very powers [*Gewalten*] he has escaped" (*DE* 38–39, translation modified). It is not hard to see why an "abyss" separates a homecoming that culminates in such violence from the utopian telos that registers in the *Odyssey*.

Song Overcome through Song

Less obvious is the sense in which narration reveals this abyss by "dragging myth into the sphere of time." Yet a clarification of this initially obscure point emerges from Adorno's next claim, which suggests that language alone prevents a calamitous conflation of the utopia that registers in the *Odyssey* with the vengeful homecoming of Odysseus: "It is not in the content of the deeds reported that civilization transcends that world. It is in the self-reflection [*Selbstbesinnung*] which causes violence to pause at the moment of narrating such deeds. Speech itself, language as opposed to mythical song, the possibility of holding fast the past atrocity through memory, is the law of Homeric escape. Not without reason is the fleeing hero repeatedly introduced as narrator" (*DE* 61). For our purposes, the crux of this passage lies in the dichotomy of mythic chant and narrative discourse, which Adorno deploys with a valuation that reverses the one underlying Borchardt's reactionary fantasies of archaic Greece. In aligning narration with self-reflection, Adorno follows the connection drawn by Benjamin between the early Romantic doctrine of prose as "the idea of poetry" and Hölderlin's conception of sobriety (*SW* 1:173–75). The latter—as Vivian Liska notes with a veiled allusion to Adorno's excursus—"corresponds to a successful disenchantment of the epic and its festive songs."[19]

In the more proximate context of *Dialectic of Enlightenment*, the dichotomy of mythic chant and narration hearkens back to Adorno's treatment of book 12 of the *Odyssey* in the opening essay of *Dialectic of Enlightenment*. It is worth revisiting here this much-discussed line of thought. In short, Adorno takes the song of the sirens to allegorize the lure of that mythic dimension in which the immutable recurrence of the same precluded any distinction between past, present, and future. For the still feeble emergent subject, the sirens' song is especially irresistible because it holds the promise of return to a familiar past. It is by cunningly exposing himself to the lure of non-differentiation and converting this exposure into an inconsequential aesthetic experience that Odysseus becomes an autonomous subject who is free from bondage to the past and hence capable of freely determining his future. The emergence of freedom in this specific sense breaks up the homogeneous expanse of mythic time into the three dimensions of historical time: "The realms of time have been separated for him like water, earth, and air. The tide of what has been has receded from the rock of the present, and the future lies veiled in cloud on the horizon" (*DE* 25). This form of self-mastery is presumably a necessary precondition for the power that Adorno will attribute to speech in his discussion of book 22, namely, the power of reflective memory to hold fast a past occurrence *as* a thing of the past. The reflective memory that articulates itself in speech (logos) stands in sharp contrast to the mythic indistinction between past and present that survives in vestigial forms in art, and especially in that fusion of perception, reminiscence, and anticipation which characterizes musical melody: "The urge to rescue the past as something living, instead of using it as the material of progress, has been satisfied only in art, in which even history, as a representation of past life, is included" (*DE* 25).

What complicates matters is the fact that the *Odyssey* is, of course, itself a work of art that was originally performed as chant rather than speech. Indeed, the performative contradiction involved in a song commemorating the overcoming of song is already acknowledged in the opening paragraph of the excursus. "To sing of the wrath of Achilles and the wanderings of Odysseus," Adorno writes there, "is already a nostalgic stylization of what can no longer be sung about" (*DE* 35, translation modified). Thus, in the passages excised from the excursus that he eventually published in the essay on epic naïveté, Adorno once again takes up the acoustic metaphor and the metaphor of the elements that he first introduced in reference to the sirens episode. This time, however, he focuses on the experience of the audience of the poem, not on that of Odysseus. The *Odyssey* is described as "the attempt to listen to the forever renewed crashing of the sea upon the rocky coast, to retrace patiently how the water inundates the cliffs and then rushes back again with a roar, letting the solid land light up in deeper colors. Such roaring [*Rauschen*] is the sound of epic speech. It is the sound in which what is univocal and solid encounters that which is equivocal and fluid, precisely in order then to separate from the latter" ("GE" 78). Paraphrasing this image in terms of the distinction between song and speech, one might say that the *Odyssey* is a work in which articulate speech consolidates itself through being haunted by the seductive indistinction of song.

This line of thought bears on an important question that has been raised by Albrecht Wellmer apropos of Adorno's famous interpretation of the sirens episode as an allegory of the origin of aesthetic subjectivity.[20] As Wellmer points out, if Odysseus needs to remain tied to the mast in order to survive the irresistible lure of regression to unmediated wholeness, then clearly "the song has not really become an object of aesthetic contemplation for him." But then, asks Wellmer, "*when* would it have been 'reduced' to such an object of contemplation?" Wellmer's first answer is that this reduction evidently happened "at the moment when Odysseus had stopped trying to untie himself and had begun to lose himself in the song of the Sirens." This creative extension of the allegory does identify an outwardly observable indication that something like a reflective self has appeared on the stage. Having renounced the regressive desire for undifferentiated wholeness and learned to endure otherness both outside and within the self, this reflective self has discovered "the possibilities of an adult human happiness as well as the exciting new pleasures of aesthetic contemplation."[21] However, the difficult question concerns the specific practices or mechanisms that make such an aesthetic education possible.[22] And it is precisely at the end of the excursus, in the very passages we are concerned with here, that at least the vague outlines of an answer first begin to emerge. For Adorno's emphasis on the liberating power of speech suggests that, as Wellmer puts it, "the transformation of the Sirens' song into a work of art does not really occur aboard Odysseus's ship, but through the very epic 'song' which sings about the Sirens's song and Odysseus's overcoming of its irresistible power."[23]

Wellmer's paradoxical-sounding proposal to the effect that song is overcome through song only underscores the need to pursue the line of questioning initiated by him further in more concrete terms. Let us return, then, to the suggestion that transpires from the excised passages on epic naïveté, the suggestion that, in the *Odyssey*, articulate speech encounters the indistinction of chant in order to separate from it. This curious notion begins to ring true as soon as one considers the *Odyssey* not as an artifact frozen in time but as an object with an immanent historical animation—as a work, that is, whose genesis recapitulates on another level the narrative of emergence that it recounts, at least according to Adorno's reading. If we consider the process by which centuries of oral transmission gave way to the first written records in the eighth century BC, and then to the editorial efforts undertaken in the sixth and the third century BC, then we can see that this process corresponds to the emergence of the modern subject who in reading the *Odyssey* no longer surrenders to an alluring song, but understands a logos premised on the differentiation of past, present, and future.

Even early readers of the *Odyssey* would have known better than to succumb, except intermittently, to the realistic illusion conjured up by epic naïveté; they would have known that the narrated adventures were, by then, already a thing of the past. Readers occupying a vantage point of more advanced modernity would also be aware, moreover, of the meta-level difference between their silent reading of the Homeric poem and the experience of ninth-century listeners of an anonymous Ionian bard. When Adorno claims that the memory preserved in "language as opposed to mythical song" affords a reflective transcendence of the mythic violence that erupts in the vengeance exacted by the homecoming Odysseus, he is presupposing the standpoint of a modern reader who encounters the *Odyssey* as a canonical written text. Adorno's initially baffling characterization of the *Odyssey* as a novel is just a hyperbolic expression of this presupposition.

Having established this point, we can finally turn to the critical passage concluding the excursus, which may be said to complete Adorno's transformation of the *Odyssey* into a novel. Adorno writes:

> The cold detachment of narrative, which describes even the horrible as if for entertainment, for the first time reveals in all its clarity the horror which is in song solemnly confounded into fate. But the pausing of speech is the caesura that allows the events narrated to be transformed into something long past, and causes to flash up a semblance of freedom that civilization has been unable wholly to extinguish ever since. Book 22 of the *Odyssey* describes the punishment meted out by the son of the island's king to the faithless maidservants who have sunk back into harlotry. With an unmoved composure comparable in its inhumanity only to the *impassibilité* of the greatest narrative writers of the nineteenth century, the fate of the hanged victims is described and expressionlessly compared to the death of birds in a trap, with that silence whose arrest is the true remainder in all speech. (*DE* 61, translation modified)

In considering this passage, we would do well to bear in mind the previously introduced dichotomy of song and speech, for Adorno's argument trades on characteristics of speech that are thrown into relief by the contrast with song. Since no elaboration of the dichotomy is offered, however, it is up to us to lend phenomenological texture to the two terms. We might say, then, that song creates a false impression of fateful necessity in two respects. First, because it indiscriminately celebrates everything it sings about;[24] and second, because the continuum of melody, in which every moment is shadowed by what Husserl called retention and protention, represents a vestige of nonlinear, not-yet-articulated mythic time.[25] By contrast, speech for the first time allows room for the rudiments of freedom. It does so in a synchronic respect to the extent that the signifying relation between the self-conscious linguistic subject and the intentional object establishes a minimal distance from reality (*DE* 5, 11). Moreover, and crucially for Adorno's argument, speech allows for freedom in a diachronic respect inasmuch as it differentiates between tenses, and because the silences that articulate discourse grant the space in which a word can stand on its own, freed from its enchainment to the preceding one, allowing for a syntax expressive of logical relations and, by extension, for a rational mastery over nature. The key point remains, however, that the dichotomy of song and speech can only be made from the vantage point of a culture in which the *Odyssey* is already available in the medium of writing as opposed to orality. It is only to a later reader who encounters the poem as a narrative marked by "cold detachment" that the terrible semblance of fatefulness permeating the Homeric song is revealed.

The True Remainder in All Speech

Having highlighted this general connection between narration and reflection, Adorno turns to a passage in book 22 of the *Odyssey* in which narration is checked by reflection. This passage, which relates the gruesome punishment of the maids who slept with the suitors, needs to be quoted in full:

> Showing initiative, Telemachus insisted,
> "I refuse to grant these girls
> a clean death, since they poured down shame on me
> and Mother, when they lay beside the suitors."
> At that, he wound a piece of sailor's rope
> round the rotunda and round the mighty pillar,
> stretched up so high no foot could touch the ground.
> As doves or thrushes spread their wings to fly
> home to their nests, but someone sets a trap—
> they crash into a net, a bitter bedtime;

> just so the girls, their heads all in a row,
> were strung up with the noose around their necks
> to make their death an agony. They gasped,
> feet twitching for a while, but not for long.[26]

It is after the last clause that Adorno posits a pause in narration that he terms a "caesura." Having thus arrived at the key juncture that prompted this study, we can now zero in on Adorno's difficult comments on the passage. Although the concept of caesura suggests a sharp incision, the interruption that Adorno claims to discern in book 22 of the *Odyssey* turns out to be a complex movement. He begins to track this movement by noting an "expressionless" silence that intrudes upon the comparison of the maids hanged by Telemachus to trapped birds in lines 468–472. He writes:

> Book 22 of the *Odyssey* describes the punishment meted out by the son of the island's king to the faithless maidservants who have sunk back into harlotry [*den treulosen Mägden, den Hetärentum Zurückgefallenen*]. With an unmoved composure comparable in its inhumanity only to the *impassibilité* of the greatest narrative writers of the nineteenth century, the fate of the hanged victims is described and expressionlessly [*ausdruckslos*] compared to the death of birds in a trap, with that silence whose arrest [*Erstarrung*] is the true remainder in all speech. (*DE* 61, translation modified)

The meaning of this silence appears to be threefold. In terms of the narrated events, it is the silence of death. The analogy to the trapped birds associates this silence, moreover, with the muteness of humans who have been reduced to mere animal nature, or, as Adorno goes on to write, "thrust down into the realm from which Odysseus the judge has escaped" (*DE* 61–62), an allusion presumably to the Circe episode. Finally, since the word "expressionlessly" is an adverb modifying "compared," we are also given to understand that a silence weighs upon the narration itself insofar as it abstains from all reference to the agony of the maids and restricts itself to a precise statement of observable facts, resulting in a clinically cold description that feels all the more jarring for the beguiling lyricism of the simile of birds.

Strikingly, Adorno call this silence of the nature-bound mortal creature, which the narrative acknowledges only by keeping silent about it, "the true remainder in all speech [*der wahre Rest aller Rede*]." The silence that makes speech possible by articulating its strings of sounds—so we may unpack Adorno's formulation—bears witness to that to which speech can never give full expression, namely, the sentient and mortal natural organism that sustains the rational subject with its pretensions to self-mastery. Adorno's focus on this silence in speech may be viewed as an instance of the allegorical contemplation of natural history, whose central truth Benjamin formulated as follows in a passage quoted in Adorno's 1932 lecture "The Idea of Natural History": "The greater the signification [*Bedeutung*], the greater the subjugation to death, for death digs most deeply the jagged demarcation line between physis and signification."[27] Death separates meaning kept alive by cultural transmission from the cycles of perishable natural life out of which meanings keep emerging.

Even more directly, however, Adorno's comments hearken back to the sole faint prospect that the opening essay on "The Concept of Enlightenment" still allowed for enlightening the Enlightenment about itself (to use the Hegelian locution).[28] In the opening essay, Horkheimer and Adorno assert that the rational capacity for objectifying and controlling nature originates in the self-preservational drive of the sentient natural organism that fears for its life. In its struggle to escape natural necessity, therefore, the subject is attempting to leap over its own shadow. To achieve control over external nature, it must first subjugate nature within itself. In particular, it must curtail or instrumentalize those mimetic impulses toward fearless, playful communication with the not-I whose fulfillment would constitute genuine happiness. Such mastery of the nature within the subject is, however, in the final analysis just another form of the triumph of the self-preservational drive. Every increment in humans' freedom from external nature is thus paid for by a mutilation of nature within the subject, as the intra-psychic repression and the political domination required for self-preservation override the desire for happiness through mimetic play (*DE* 42). It follows that reason cannot definitively extricate itself from the reign of natural necessity. However, Horkheimer and Adorno also suggest that the universal perspective opened up through thoroughgoing reification grants rational thought the minimal freedom needed for rising above the natural compulsion in which it originates—at least to the limited extent required for a self-reflective insight into its own captivity to nature (*DE* 29). The sole possibility of our reconciliation with nature lies precisely in the recognition that our estrangement from nature is ultimately the product of a compulsion anchored in nature itself. In such "remembrance of nature" within the rational subject—that is, in "mind's self-recognition as nature divided from itself"—lies the sole hope for a happy homecoming in which reason might prevail without violence to its natural substrate (*DE* 31–32). Registering what remains expressionless in Homer's account of the execution—namely, the agony of the maids—is a way of practicing "remembrance of nature" in this precise sense.

However, what Adorno terms "caesura" is not the expressionless silence that persists in and beneath speech, but a silence that ensues when the flow of speech is checked. And it is, according to Adorno, only in the wake of the passage just analyzed, following line 473, that the mute suffering about which lines 468–472 keep silent condenses into the actual silence of a pause in the narration. This is the juncture that prompts the remarks by Adorno with which the present chapter is centrally concerned:

> This is followed by the verse that reports about the maids lined up that "For a little while their feet kicked out, but not for very long." The exactitude of the description, which already exhibits the coldness of anatomy and vivisection, keeps a record, as in a novel [*romanmäßig*], of the twitches of the subjugated women, who, under the aegis of justice and law, are thrust down into the realm from which Odysseus the judge has escaped. As a citizen reflecting on the execution, Homer comforts himself and his listeners, who are really readers, with the assured observation that it did not last long—a moment, and all was over. But after the words "not for long" the inner flow of the narrative stands still. "Not for long?" the gesture of the narrator asks, giving the lie to his composure. In being checked by this gesture, the report is prevented from forgetting the victims of the execution and lays bare the unspeakable endless torment of the single second in which the maids fought against death. No echo remains of the words "not for long" except Cicero's *Quo usque tandem* ["How much longer (will you try our patience)?"], which later rhetoricians unwittingly desecrated by claiming that patience for themselves. (*DE* 61–62)

The caesura is described here as an effect of the narrator's brief departure from cold objectivity. Although the narrator's comforting remark about the fleetingness of the maids' agony may be thought to have the purpose of maintaining narrative momentum, it actually has the opposite significance, according to Adorno. What at first sounds like a comforting assurance can also be heard as an incredulous question that arrests the flow of narration. And what that question registers is the irrelevance of the statement, accurate though it may be in terms of measurable time, that the suffering of the maids did not last long. For the felt terror of dying, of being violently pushed to the end of time, cannot be measured in time; hence Adorno's reference to "the unspeakable endless torment of the single second." The question implied by the false comfort, followed by a silent pause, is a way of remembering that which the preceding report threatened to deliver over to oblivion.

Murray versus Wilamowitz

We are now, finally, in a position to address the conundrum outlined in the "Introduction." To recall the seemingly banal observation in which this study originated, the text of the *Odyssey* as we know it does not feature a reflective pause between lines 473 and 474. One may thus be forgiven for leaping to the conclusion that Adorno is doing violence to the text by postulating a caesura—and that this violent imposition is willful in a way that contrasts sharply with the immanently grounded "critical violence" at work in Benjamin's caesura marking.

On closer examination, however, Adorno's marking of the caesura can be shown to have a basis immanent to the material, and to be broadly in keeping with the Benjaminian conception. The philological warrant for it may be inferred from the last two footnotes of the excursus. These footnotes situate the argument vis-à-vis both Adorno's present and the remote prehistory of the Homeric texts, and thus establish a constellation between these disparate historical moments. In the penultimate footnote, a remark on the voyeuristic delight taken by Wilamowitz in Homer's unflinching portrayal of the execution of the maids serves as an occasion for a summary verdict that must have sounded particularly damning in 1943: "Wilamowitz's writings are among the most striking documents of the German intermingling of barbarism and culture, which is fundamental to modern Philhellenism" (*DE* 265). The final footnote turns to the obscure genesis of the Homeric texts, but it does so through the lens of the work of Gilbert Murray, a prominent representative of the British classical scholarship whose aid Adorno attempted to enlist in his project of "disenchanting antiquity" in order to counter the ingrained conservativism of German classical philology.[29]

Murray is, in fact, identified in the last, short, footnote of the excursus as the source of the hypothesis concerning the "consoling intention" of the line that Adorno identifies as a caesura. By comparing the earliest extant written versions of the Homeric poems, Murray concluded in the argument referenced by Adorno that the great critics of the third century BC undertook "expurgations," deleting or marking as "unworthy of Homer" several "unseemly" passages, and especially passages that described "cruel or barbarous practices."[30] In two cases noted by Murray, an evocation of barbaric cruelty was retained, but a "saving line" was inserted. This line is recognizable as a later addition because it is "inorganic," that is, it can be "added or left out with no effect upon the grammar or continuity." In both cases, the inorganic saving line identified by Murray is the same: "but not for long." It first occurs in the *Iliad*; its second occurrence is our problematic line 473 in book 22 of the *Odyssey*. On this line Murray comments in a passage that Adorno quotes in the early draft: "The torture of women," writes Murray, "was unpleasant even to an audience which approved the cruelty to the goatherd" ("GE" 88n). In other words, what Adorno terms a caesura is the trace of a literary censorship of sorts that here takes the form of a mitigating addition dictated by a change in sensibilities. The implications of Murray's argument about the civilizing tendency at work in the *Odyssey* are only thrown into sharper relief through Adorno's condemnation of Wilamowitz in the preceding footnote, which accentuates the stakes involved in the projected disenchantment of antiquity. By contrast, the virtue of Murray's scholarship, in Adorno's eyes, lies in the fact that his treatment of the *Odyssey* as a document reflecting multiple layers of redaction offers an antidote against German philologists' tendency to enshrine the Homeric poems as immutable, consummate artifacts. Murray's work suggests that the text of the *Odyssey* as we know it already incorporates a self-reflection marked by an awareness of changing audience expectations. In particular, Murray's argument about line 473 shows that a crucial result of this textual self-reflection consists in a minimal degree of readiness on the narrator's part not to withhold compassion from subsidiary characters who have fallen prey to triumphant reason—or, more precisely, to the unreason underlying reason.

The revision identified by Murray follows a logic akin to the one that a later essay by Adorno would highlight in connection with the assimilative supersession of an archaic language by a more civilized one: "Compromise as consideration for that which has been subjugated [*Ausgleich als Schonung des Unterjochten*] may well be the general definition of culture in the emphatic sense."[31] Admittedly, the compromise achieved in the narrator's perfunctory mitigating phrase must appear meagre in light of the cruelty recounted in this passage. Nevertheless, this gesture testifies to a novelistic tendency evident already in that early stage of reception history which still belongs to the genesis of the work's canonical textual form. In his reimagining of the *Odyssey*, Adorno amplifies this marginal gesture of compassion to the type of critical perspective that Benjamin envisioned under the heading of historical materialism in the seventh of his posthumously published theses in "On the Concept of History" (*SW* 4:391). That is, instead of indulging in projective identification with the victors whose perspective the tradition eternalizes, Adorno allows himself to be overwhelmed by a somatic resonance with the marginalized suffering of the vanquished. We might say, then, that it is by extrapolating from the critical, revisionary self-reflection precipitated in the text that Adorno arrives at the idea of the *Odyssey* as a novel. The excursus is thus not simply a reflection on the *Odyssey* but a rewriting of the epic as a novel, undertaken in the medium of philosophical critique. This much, in fact, is already signaled by the title of the excursus, which pointedly names the hero and not the work enshrined in the canon of Western literature.

In reading the *Odyssey* as a novel, then, Adorno pursues an agenda very much in line with the early Romantic critical program reconstructed in Benjamin's doctoral dissertation—that is, the project of continuing the interminable process of self-reflection that originates within the work (*SW* 1:151). Equally, however, Adorno's reflections on book 22 of the *Odyssey* are consonant with Benjamin's later definition of the task of criticism. As Benjamin wrote in 1931, that task is not to present a literary work in the context of its time, but rather to let the contemporary moment present itself in the time of the work's genesis.[32] Adorno's own historical situation thus becomes a key determinant of his contribution to the reception history through which the work progressively actualizes itself. His deliberate violation of the strictures of philological positivism, as well as the use he makes of Murray's genetic conjecture, show that Adorno has belatedly come around to appreciating the force of the argument that Benjamin had advanced in 1938, when he attempted to defend his theoretical approach against the harsh criticism with which Adorno explained why the Institute of Social Research rejected Benjamin's essay "The Paris of the Second Empire in Baudelaire."[33] It will suffice to quote here the passages from Benjamin's self-defense that most clearly anticipate Adorno's procedure in the excursus on Odysseus:

> Philology is the examination of a text which proceeds by details and so magically fixates the reader on it. That which Faust took home in black and white, and Grimm's devotion to little things, are closely related. They have in common that magical element whose exorcism is reserved for philosophy . . . The appearance of closed facticity which attaches to a philological investigation and places the investigator under its spell fades to the extent that the object is construed in an historical perspective. The base lines of this construction converge in our own historical experience. Thus the object constitutes itself as a monad. In the monad everything that used to lie in mythical rigidity as a textual fact comes alive . . . Therefore it seems a misjudgment of the matter to me if you find in my study a "direct inference from the wine duty to *L'Ame du Vin*." Rather, the juncture was established legitimately in the philological context—just as it would have been done in the interpretation of a writer from antiquity . . . a critique of the attitude of the philologist is an old concern of mine, and it is basically identical with my critique of myth. Yet in each case it is this critique that provokes the philological effort itself. To use the language of *Elective Affinities*, it presses for the exhibition [*Herausstellung*] of the material content in which the truth content can be historically disclosed [*entblättert*].[34]

Benjamin's reference to his Goethe essay, which Adorno had earlier praised only the more harshly to condemn Benjamin's ongoing work on Baudelaire,[35] as well as the apologetic parallel drawn to the procedures of classical philology, are both suggestive of the Benjaminian insights that Adorno appears to have taken to heart in his excursus on the *Odyssey*. For, in fact, Benjamin's essay on Goethe's novel provided Adorno with the most proximate critical model for his undertaking to counter positivistic philology and its dialectical counterpart in *Kulturphilosophie* with a reimagining of the *Odyssey* as a novel riven by a caesura.

Given Adorno's reliance on Murray's work in his pursuit of a critical agenda inspired by Benjamin, we can begin to see how Adorno's marking of a caesura in book 22 continues a movement of critical self-reflection begun in the work, and how this critical intervention is guided by Adorno's own historical horizon. Whereas the editor in the third century BC likely had every reason to think that he would be able to dispel the unease of his audience by simply inserting the inorganic "saving line," a modern reader committed to moral universalism will tend to hear that consoling observation, making light of the suffering of subjugated humans, as a self-unmasking euphemism, or as an instance of the figure of speech that ancient rhetoricians called *meiosis* or *extenuatio*. To the extent that our horrified question— "not for long?"— articulates something "in" the poem, its objective correlate is not an intention imputable to the narrator or the empirical author(s), but the poem as a linguistic construct shaped by, and bearing witness to, large-scale cultural forces that connect the poem's genesis with our own present, allowing us to discern in the poem an earlier version of ourselves.

The modern reader who responds to the saving line in this manner no longer accepts the epic narrator as an impersonal authority, but instead treats him as a textually constructed figure with definite traits and flaws, someone whose limited moral horizon cannot automatically be equated with that of the work as an aesthetic totality. In other words, at this point the modern reader will tend to attribute the voice relating the execution of the maids to an unreliable novelistic narrator whose callousness is revolting but all too familiar. Hence Adorno's initially cryptic comment: "No echo remains of the words 'not for long' except Cicero's *Quo usque tandem* ['How much longer (will you try our patience)?'], which later orators unwittingly desecrated by claiming that patience for themselves." The narrator's mitigating remark elicits from the modern reader a dismayed recoil, an outrage whose scope extends beyond particular atrocities to encompass the entire catastrophic course of history—from Catiline's scheming, which prompted Cicero's proverbial question, to the anti-Semitic diatribe in which Goebbels abused the Ciceronian formula.[36]

This interpretation of Adorno's remarks suggests that he is quite precise in ascribing the horrified question that checks the flow of narration to the "gesture" of the narrator and not to the narrator himself. For the meaning of a gesture made by someone cannot be limited to that person's subjective intentions. It is as a gesture in this sense, and as a gesture perceived from a modern vantage point, that the mitigating comment turns into an incredulous questioning of its own truth. In emphasizing this gestural aspect of the caesura, Adorno follows Benjamin's characterization of the key sentence in *Elective Affinities* as a "mystery" (*Mysterium*), defined by Benjamin as a dramatic moment that "juts out of the domain of language proper to it into a higher one unattainable for it" ("GEA" 355). When Adorno writes that at this critical point "the inner flow of narration stands still," the qualification "inner" points to the consciousness of the reader rather than to the states of mind imputable to the narrator. More specifically, Adorno's critical observation presupposes the vantage point of a reader conceived after the analogy of a dramatic spectator who responds not only to the words spoken by actors, but also to the gestural significance of their utterances.

Pausing for Breath: Luxemburg and Kraus

Not only does Adorno's marking of the caesura follow the dramatic logic of the mystery play, as elaborated by Benjamin; it also appears likely that Benjamin drew Adorno's attention to a text that would later serve as a model for Adorno's critical operation in the excursus. Towards the end of his 1931 essay on Karl Kraus, Benjamin quotes a passage from a piece by Kraus written in 1920, titled "Reply to Rosa Luxemburg from an Unsentimental Woman," which Benjamin praises as the "most powerful of postwar bourgeois [*bürgerliche*] prose" (*SW* 2/2:456). To identify the operation that appears to have made an impression on Adorno, we need to review the somewhat complicated prehistory of this piece by Kraus that Benjamin held in such high esteem. Earlier in the same year, Kraus had reprinted in *Die Fackel* a long excerpt from one of Rosa Luxemburg's letters, declaring in his prefatory remarks that the excerpt ought to be included in elementary school textbooks along with canonical works by Goethe and Matthias Claudius.[37] In the excerpt, Luxemburg offered a dramatic literalization of the German term *Unterjochung*, which uses the metaphor of yoking to denote "subjugation." Writing to Sophie Liebknecht from the Breslau prison in 1917, Luxemburg described the surge of creaturely sympathy that she felt upon encountering a tormented "brethren" in the prison courtyard: a buffalo used as a beast of burden with "gentle black eyes like a weeping child," homesick for the Romanian pastures where it was captured, and silently suffering under the savage blows of a soldier who justified his brutality with the remark "no one has pity for us humans."[38] Luxemburg wrote:

> Sonyichka, the hide of a buffalo is proverbial for its toughness and thickness, but this tough skin had been broken. During the unloading, all the animals stood there, quite still, exhausted, and the one that was bleeding kept staring into the empty space in front of him with an expression [*Ausdruck*] on his black face and in his soft, black eyes like an abused child. It was precisely the expression of a child that has been punished and doesn't know why or what for, doesn't know how to get away from this torment and raw violence . . . I stood before it, and the beast looked at me; tears were running down my face—they were his tears.[39]

The letter was first published a little over a year after Luxemburg's murder in January 1919 at the hands of far-right *Freikorps* officers, and Kraus repeatedly included it in the program of his public readings. If Luxemburg's letter was, to quote Kraus, "a unique document of humanity and poetry" that contrasted sharply with the brutality of Luxemburg's murderers, then the anonymous letter to the editor elicited by Kraus's commemorative gesture was a monument to self-satisfied stupidity and callousness. Its author, who later turned out to be an aristocratic woman by the name of Ida von Lill-Rastern von Lilienbach, mocked Luxemburg's attribution of expressive power to the animal's face. Having grown up on an estate in southern Hungary, the aristocratic woman claimed to know very well the "dull [*stumpfsinnig*, literally meaning 'obtuse-minded'] 'facial expression' " of these animals and derided Luxemburg's compassion as mere sentimentalism.

In his reply to this letter Kraus adopted his trademark polemical strategy, to which we owe some of the most blistering pages of *Die Fackel*. In the following issue, he reprinted von Lilienbach's letter, only to unleash his apocalyptic fury in the lengthy reply that he appended to it—the text that Benjamin would praise in his essay. In a vitriolic pun, Kraus compared the disdainful "scare quotes" ("*Gänsefüsse*," meaning literally "goose feet") that Lilienbach had placed around the word "facial expression" in reference to the tormented buffalo to the "kicks of a goose" (*Fusstritte einer Gans*). Raising the stakes of his polemic, Kraus drew a connection between the callousness of this aristocratic woman raised in Hungary and the barbaric atrocities perpetrated by right-wing officers following the crushing of the short-lived Hungarian Republic of Councils in 1919—and, by extension, the brutality of the officers who murdered Luxemburg.[40] Although Kraus's linguistic virtuosity was on full display throughout his diatribe, he nevertheless heaped scorn on the overvaluation of language that so often misleads humans into denying sentience to animals that lack the hackneyed "lingo" (*Kauderwelsch*) in which humans give voice to their pain. To Kraus's mind, what distinguished Luxemburg's perspective from that of von Lilienbach was precisely the former's ability to see expression where the latter saw stupor, and to decipher the language of nature where human language was absent.

This capacity for reading an apparent lack of expression as excessively expressive must be stressed because it throws into relief the key detail in this chain of texts that might have most strongly impressed Adorno—if indeed, as it seems reasonable to assume, he knew the precedents of the text that Benjamin quoted in his essay on Kraus.[41] In his preface to the reprinted excerpt from Luxemburg's letter, Kraus writes: "The entire contemporary literature of Germany cannot elicit tears like those shed by this Jewish revolutionary, nor a pause for breath [*Atempause*] like the one that follows the description of the buffalo's hide: 'and it was ripped.' "[42] This comment should serve to remind us that Kraus was not only a writer, critic, and journalist, but also a charismatic recitationist who turned public readings into dramatic performances charged with prophetic pathos. In the written remarks now at issue, Kraus's citational practice owes its force to a quasi-dramatic intervention that goes beyond faithful citation, namely, the insertion of a "pause for breath" in a textual simulation of oral performance. This artifice evokes the modulation of a vital bodily function by compassion with the bodily suffering of a fellow creature. And it seems significant that this insertion of a "pause for breath" occurs in the context of a commemoration that the ensuing polemic will amplify to an apocalyptic version, *avant la lettre*, of the Adornian remembrance of nature.

This connection would have been readily recognizable to Adorno on the basis of Benjamin's essay on Kraus, in which Benjamin was moved by Kraus's polemic on behalf of Luxemburg to evoke the vision of an elemental nature whose destructive forces have been "unfettered" to visit vengeance upon a humankind bent on domination (*SW* 2/2:456). In addition, philological conjectures, to the effect that caesuras in ancient hexameter were meant to grant the reciter a "pause for breath," might have encouraged Adorno to graft the model of the Krausian pause onto the concept of caesura.[43] Benjamin's analogies between the capacity of language to grant space for philosophical reflection and the ways in which breathing punctuates speech probably also played a role.[44] In the end, however, the precise route of influence is less important for my argument than is the deep affinity between the compassionate pause for breath that Kraus inserts into Luxemburg's letter and Adorno's postulation of a pausing that responds sympathetically to the violent throttling of the victims' breath—an *Atempause* that, contrary to the Homeric narrator's assurance, lasts forever. In a preliminary way, we might say that this affinity accentuates the centrality of nature and of somatic suffering to Adorno's marking of the caesura. Taking his guidance in this regard less from Benjamin's Goethe essay than from Kraus and from Benjamin's reflections on natural history, Adorno reinterprets the expressionless to mean a silence pregnant with the suffering to which living nature is condemned by the inhumanity of human domination.

The fact that Kraus's polemic centers on two women—one exalted for her attunement to suffering nature, the other reviled on account of her excessive interiorization of the masculine logic of domination—would have made his text particularly suggestive in Adorno's eyes. For at several key junctures, Adorno's account of the genesis of the paradigmatically masculine subject turns to the equivocal role of the feminine in the dialectic of myth and enlightenment. The execution of the maids in book 22 marks an extreme point in this dialectic, at which female characters are relegated to mere vestiges of a promiscuous "primeval world" (*DE* 61) that threatens to engulf the rational order of property and family supporting the sovereign masculine subject. Indeed, from the standpoint of patriarchal order, not only the femininity of subaltern figures such as the maids but femininity as such tends to represent a mythic vestige, one that is threatening and alluring in equal measure.[45] "The hetaera," as Adorno states in connection with the Circe episode, "both bestows joy and destroys the autonomy of its recipient" (*DE* 55). The men turned into pigs by Circe's magic obey a "mythical command" which "at the same time liberates the very nature which is suppressed in them," writes Adorno, only to add a decisive dialectical twist: "What is revoked by their relapse into myth is myth itself. The suppression of instinct which constitutes them as selves and separates them from beasts was the introverted form of the repression existing within the hopelessly closed cycle of nature, to which, according to an earlier theory, the name Circe alludes" (*DE* 55)

The cruelty with which Telemachus murders the maids can thus be understood as an external correlate of the internal violence by which man must repress his mimetic impulses in order to constitute himself as an autonomous subject. The brutality of the externalized violence manifests the hidden truth of the constitutive law of identity: namely, that it is rooted in a fear-driven compulsion to preserve oneself that perpetuates in another form the all-encompassing, immutable cycle of necessity governing the mythic realm. The logic of this compulsion is spelled out in precise terms in "Excursus II: Juliette or Enlightenment and Morality":

> Woman as an allegedly natural being is a product of history, which denatures her. But the desperate, destructive urge directed against everything which embodies the lure of nature, everything which is physiologically, biologically, nationally, or socially inferior, indicates that Christianity's attempt has failed . . . To eradicate utterly the hated but overwhelming temptation to lapse back into nature—that is the cruelty which stems from failed civilization; it is barbarism, the other side of culture . . . Women and Jews show visible evidence of not having ruled for thousands of years. They live, although they could have been eliminated, and their fear and weakness, the greater affinity to nature produced in them by perennial oppression, is the element in which they live. In the strong, who pay for their strength with their strained remoteness from nature and must forever forbid themselves fear, this incites fury. They identify themselves with nature by calling forth from their victims, multiplied a thousandfold, the cry they may not utter themselves. (*DE* 88–89)

The last sentence of this passage suggests, paradoxically, that sadism is predicated on empathy. It springs from an impulse to lend voice to a repressed internal nature by inflicting suffering upon another's body, which thus becomes a medium of vicarious self-expression. The muteness of the agony that Telemachus inflicts upon the maids in book 22 of the *Odyssey* signals an even more extreme repression, one that prohibits even this vicarious expression of repressed nature. The narrator's mitigating phrase seals this muteness.[46]

In adapting the Benjaminian caesura model, then, Adorno alters the distribution of roles between the masculine subject and its feminine other. Consider for a moment the strange lapse into banality that occurs when Benjamin evokes a melodrama of jealousy to allegorize the expressionless:

> Just as interruption by the commanding word is able to bring out the truth from the evasions of a woman precisely at the point where

> it interrupts, the expressionless compels the trembling harmony to stop and through its objection [*Einspruch*] immortalizes its quivering [*Beben*]. In this immortalization the beautiful must vindicate itself [*sich verantworten*], but now it appears to be interrupted precisely in its vindication, and thus it has the eternity of its content precisely by the grace of that objection. ("GEA" 340)

When Adorno freezes a moment of the expressionless that intrudes upon the Homeric narration, he presents a far more drastic literal variation on Benjamin's allegory. In this archaic successor scene, the man's commanding word is replaced by murderous vindictiveness. To the "trembling harmony" and "quivering" of the beautiful semblance allegorized by Benjamin's evasive woman corresponds in Adorno's caesura the final involuntary "kicking" (or "twitching") of the maids' feet; and to the eternity of the truth content that interruption by the expressionless confers upon the beautiful figure of Benjamin's allegory corresponds "the unspeakably endless torment of the single second in which the maids fought against death," a moment brought to a standstill by Adorno's critical construction (*DE* 62). It is as if Adorno took an allegory sketched out by Benjamin on the margins of his theory of the expressionless, moved it to center stage, and reworked it in a literalized form in order to highlight its overdetermined chararacter.

It does not seem all that hard to imagine an unwritten entry from *Minima Moralia* that draws a direct line from the *Odyssey* to the film "To Be or Not to Be" by Adorno's Californian fellow emigré Ernst Lubitsch, released in the same year in which Adorno began work on the excursus. We might, that is, imagine Adorno solemnly declaring that the scene in which the Jack Benny character's "commanding words" interrupt Carole Lombard's evasions is an only seemingly innocuous modern-day replaying of the gruesome Homeric execution scene. This is the sort of parody that Adorno sometimes invites by short-circuiting the connection between quotidian experience and world history. Yet the fact that Benjamin's and Adorno's caesura markings assign sharply contrasting roles to the paradigmatically masculine subject signals a genuine philosophical difference. In Benjamin's allegorical scene, the implied masculine subject stands for the sublime authority of a philosophical truth content that cannot tolerate its usurpation by the false claim to totality that emanates from beautiful form. The authoritative truth content, upheld by a masculine subject, is not the opposite of totality but the genuine, albeit merely virtual, totality of the systematic ideal—"the true world" whose "fragment" the work becomes through its fracturing by the expressionless ("GEA" 340). For Adorno, however, there is no meaningful distinction to be made between false and true totality, since totalizing thought *as such* is always false, and by definition a form of myth. In the encounter between man and woman that Adorno's caesura suspends, Telemachus figures as an agent of precisely that totalizing rationality which triumphs in Odysseus's homecoming.

In terms of Benjamin's understanding of Goethe's inner struggle, the man in Benjamin's allegory of the expressionless corresponds to Goethe's saving impulse, which led him to portray Ottilie as expiring in order to salvage what is essential in beauty. In light of the scene of masculine domination arrested by Adorno's caesura, however, what Benjamin characterizes as a redemptive moment in Goethe's art begins to look like an introversion of mythic sacrifice, whose ruthlessness may be inferred from Goethe's bitterly sarcastic remark in response to contemporaries' indignation over his pagan tendencies: "Well, I have after all executed Gretchen and starved Ottilie to death, isn't that Christian enough for people?"[47]

The correspondences and differences between the gendered scenes of arrest in which Benjamin and Adorno elaborate their respective conceptions of the expressionless thus highlight a more fundamental disagreement concerning the nexus of reason, nature, and beauty. Under the evident influence of Kant and Hermann Cohen, the early Benjamin views reason as a sublime authority whose demand for unequivocal clarity and systematic totality elevates humans above nature. According to this conception, the beautiful semblance that intimates the ideal of reason is an indispensable aid to reason and at the same time a potential usurper of its sovereignty. Adorno, by contrast, is closer to Schiller than to Kant in imagining what an unoccluded rationality would look like. From the standpoint of the Adornian utopia of a reconciliation with the nonidentical, the early Benjamin's assertion of reason's sublimity must appear as the mark of a rationality that shuts itself off from remembrance of nature in the subject, and which cannot escape the totalizing logic of myth merely by insisting that its conception of totality is virtual.

Does One Have to Make Observations about Slavery?

The question we now have to address is how the reinterpretation of the expressionless in Adorno's marking of the caesura inflects his reimagining of the *Odyssey* as a novel. The first, very simple, point to note here is that there are multiple paradigms of novelistic narration. Which of these one discerns in a given text may change from one passage to the next, and such shifts in perception prompted by the text are likely to be revealing of instabilities in one's historically conditioned aesthetic expectations. The specificity of the novelistic paradigm envisioned by Adorno comes into view most clearly in his comment that Homer's description of the execution of the maids evinces "*impassibilité*." Quoted by Adorno in the original French, this term was famously used by Flaubert in reference to the divine detachment to which he aspired. Achieving an utmost of allusive resonance through the use of a single word borrowed from another author writing in another language, Adorno establishes a constellation between his ancient material and the sordid legacy of the country in which he has recently found refuge. For the often-quoted epistolary passage in which Flaubert expounds his artistic program invokes the objectivity of ancient Greek art as an ideal yardstick and the didactic moralizing of *Uncle Tom's Cabin* as a negative foil. "Does one have to make observations [*réflexions*] about slavery?"—Flaubert asked, with palpable irritation, apropos of Beecher Stowe's novel.[48]

As it happens, Flaubert's annoyed question has a direct bearing on the passage in the *Odyssey* that Adorno is considering in the passage that is now at issue. In the introduction to her new translation of the *Odyssey*, classical scholar Emily Wilson makes a philological point that should make us question Adorno's reference to the "faithless maidservants who have sunk back into harlotry [*den treulosen Mägden, den Hetärentum Zurückgefallenen*]." As Wilson notes, such derogatory terms as "sluts" or "whores," used in most English translations of this passage in the *Odyssey*, are unwarranted by the Greek term *dmoe*, which means "domestic female slave" and implies that the maids were not free to reject the suitors' advances.[49] Perhaps Adorno was aware of this, after all. As his closing meditation tracks the progression of the narrative, he suggests that Homer—a name, we must bear in mind, that stands for a historical process rather than an individual—finds it necessary to engage in just the sort of moral reflection on slavery that Flaubert so disdained. For Homer "comforts himself and his listeners, who are really readers," with the saving line identified by Murray, which elicits from the modern reader the recoil analyzed earlier in this chapter. Pressing this point even farther, Adorno construes the saving line as a modernist violation of the Flaubertian taboo on reflection, that is, as a moment of self-reflection that interrupts the illusion nurtured by epic naïveté in a wish to break with the "lie of presentation."[50] Adorno's concluding reflection thus turns the episode in book 22 into a scene of transition from the realist aspiration for unflinchingly pitiless mirroring to a critique of that aspiration. The textual enactment of this transition presupposes a standpoint of outraged moral universalism in the face of which Flaubert's divine indifference must appear as an ideologically complicitous aestheticism. The modern reader envisioned by Adorno is one who instead concurs with Benjamin's summary verdict that "a consideration of classical antiquity that has nothing to say about slavery cannot in the end count as conclusive."[51]

The Solace of "Once upon a Time"

Following the interpretation just outlined, the caesura marked by Adorno registers a modernist critique of realism. However, the opposition between realism and modernism implicates a more fundamental historical gulf that opens up at this juncture in Adorno's meditation on Odysseus. In the last sentences of the excursus, Adorno takes up a thread begun in his earlier remark to the effect that "the pausing of speech is the caesura that allows the events narrated to be transformed into something long past." He writes:

> But in the report of the infamous deed, hope lies in the fact that it is long past. Over the entwinement of prehistory, barbarism, and culture Homer passes the soothing hand of remembrance, bringing the solace of "once upon a time." Only as novel does the epic become fairy tale.[52]

It is only in the medium of verbal narration, and not in song, that a clear distinction can be made between past, present, and future. Yet a narrative that maintains its momentum and hastily moves past the maids' agony with a mitigating reference to measurable time thereby blinds itself to the violence done to nature as mythic compulsion recurs in the guise of triumphant Enlightenment reason. The critical pause that protests against this blindness is due, as I have argued, not to a reflection on the narrator's part, but to a reflection that the modern reader cannot help but ascribe to a gestural aspect of the act of narration.

Adorno's concluding comments on the "solace of 'once upon a time'" take up a contrast, established for the first time by Goethe and Schiller, between epic poetry's portrayal of events as "completely past" and the dramatic staging of events as "completely present."[53] Only a year before Adorno began work on the excursus, Bakhtin drew the same contrast to illuminate the difference between the epic and the novel.[54] According to Bakhtin, epic narration represents events as belonging to the "utterly finished" absolute past of tradition, isolated from "new perspectives and evaluations," towards which the narrator must take up the unfree, "reverent point of view of a descendant." By contrast, the novel portrays events as occurring "on the same time-and-value plane as oneself and one's contemporaries." Although he cannot have been familiar with Bakhtin's treatment of the opposition originally established by Goethe and Schiller, Adorno significantly complicates this dichotomous view. His rewriting of the episode recounting the execution of the slave girls transforms the very act of epic narration into an object of novelistic narration: the modern reader recoils in outrage from an act of narration that is experienced as contemporaneous, seeing the latter as a sign of appalling callousness shown by a contemporary fellow human. Yet that very recoil on our part thrusts the act of narration back into a realm of archaic or indeed "absolute" pastness that "we have nothing to do with" (to borrow Bakhtin's phrase) and thereby reconstitutes narration as an object of epic memory. The act of epic narration, symptomatic of a mythic past still latent in the present, is made present only to be cast back all the more decisively into a past that is definitively closed and different from the present. In other words, when Adorno writes that, "in the report of the infamous deed, hope lies in the fact that it is long past," we should take him to assert the pastness of the report in addition to that of the reported deed.

In an apparent paradox, then, Adorno's presentist reading of the *Odyssey* as a novel has the effect of establishing a caesura between the mythic past and the enlightened present. It thus severs the continuum of a historical process in which every increment of progress is bought at the cost of regression. The indebtedness of this procedure to Benjamin's theses "On the Concept of History" is clear: by construing a fleeting moment of epic narration as a caesura, Adorno—to quote Benjamin's formulation in the theses—"make[s] the continuum of history explode" and arrests a moment in that continuum to a "now-time, which, as a model of messianic time, comprises the entire history of mankind in a tremendous abbreviation" (*SW* 4:395–96). Adorno achieves a tremendous abbreviation of this sort when he turns a juncture in narration into a moment of radical contemporaneity *and* absolute pastness at one and the same time.

The *Odyssey* becomes a novel when the modern reader, thrown back upon his moral consciousness, recoils in horror from the epic narrator and begins to perceive the latter as a character in a historical novel who embodies a long-vanished era. Moreover, it is when we read the *Odyssey* through the more compassionate generic lens of the novel, in keeping with the novelistic tendencies that already determined the genesis of the Homeric text, that our reading may turn the Homeric epic, in a second step of generic transformation, into a fairy tale—fairy tales being, as Adorno's erstwhile mentor Kracauer wrote in 1927, "not stories about miracles but rather announcements of the miraculous advent of justice."[55] For any hope for release from the mythic necessity that recurs in the vengeance exacted by Odysseus depends on our resolve to distinguish what the *Odyssey* means for us from what it might have meant during the centuries of its obscure genesis.

That difference comes to a head in connection with the question of the meaning of the revenge visited upon the maids. The Homeric text offers a straightforward motive: Telemachus murders the maids to take revenge for the shame that they brought upon him and his mother when they slept with the suitors. In Adorno's interpretation, however, Telemachus's act represents a symptomatic recurrence of mythic violence in the very triumph of the self-identical subject over mythic forces. The violence perpetrated by Telemachus is an external correlate of the introjected violence by which the subject represses mimetic tendencies stirring in the natural stratum of his life. The dispassionate stance of the Homeric narrator is premised on that introjected violence. The recoil of the modern reader postulated by Adorno responds to both forms of violence, external and internal. We are taken aback by Telemachus's cruelty; but more importantly because closer to home, what appalls us is an intra-psychic violence evident in the equanimity of the Homeric narrator, a repression of mimetic sympathy that amounts to complicity with the overt violence towards the maids.

In discerning the interiorized violence constitutive of the epic narrator's stance, we are confronted with the forgotten natural history of our own position as subjects. Adorno's marking of the caesura in book 22 of the *Odyssey* is thus a key instance of the "psychoanalytic reflection" that Seyla Benhabib describes as central to the critical project of *Dialectic of Enlightenment*:

> What is forgotten cannot be recalled at will; all forgetting originates with a trauma. The forgotten can only be recalled, made present to oneself, in the effort to relive the trauma and break the spell of the past upon the present. The access to this traumatic content brings one closer to those repressed wishes and desires whose memory is painful precisely because they had to be repressed.[56]

Through Adorno's presentist reading, the callous posture of epic narration, its lack of reflective freedom toward the narrated events, is made vividly present precisely so that the reader might recognize it as intimately familiar—and then repudiate it. A past that lingers on in a latent form is thus transformed into a past that is closed and finished, which we are no longer free to alter but which also no longer constrains us.[57]

Determinate Negation and the Prohibition of Images

It is Adorno's wager that the double negation achieved through this recoil—the recognition of our lack of freedom towards our past unfreedom—grants us for the first time the freedom to reconsider the archaic past evoked by the narrative, permitting a remembrance of nature. However, in order for the double negation just described to have such a positive yield, a key condition must be fulfilled. A dialectical reversal of unfreedom into freedom occurs only if the second negation—the banishment of epic narration to the past—is more than an empty gesture of repudiation. If critical reading, brought to bear upon a narrative that condones the silencing of nature in the interest of domination, is to afford a remembrance of nature, then the critique of narration must involve a definite recognition of that which the narrative has sidelined. Otherwise put, the caesura of silence posited by Adorno had better be a narratological variant of what Hegel terms "determinate negation." For Hegel, the negation of a given claim is determinate if the claim is shown to fall short of the truth in a definite respect, such that this critical diagnosis entails some positive determination of the truth.[58]

In order to establish whether Adorno's reading of the execution scene in book 22 of the *Odyssey* can meet the demand just outlined, we must briefly consider Adorno and Horkheimer's discussion of determinate negation in the opening essay of *Dialectic of Enlightenment*. There they suggest that a paradigmatic case of determinate negation can be found in the Judaic prohibition on graven images (*DE* 18). According to Horkheimer and Adorno, Judaic aniconism is not a wholesale and indeterminate rejection of representation as such, but a prohibition specifically on representing the absolute. Moreover, the law does not merely—and, again, indeterminately—oppose an ostensible image of the absolute to its true idea. Rather, the negation in question is supposed to be determinate in the sense that it takes the form of a "script" (*Schrift*) whose very appearance bespeaks non-resemblance to the divine and thereby conveys an "admission of falseness which cancels its powers and hands it over to truth" (*DE* 18). The argument of the opening essay suggests that an analogical affinity exists between Judaic aniconism, so understood, and the Enlightenment's repudiation of nostalgic, Rousseauian utopias of reabsorption into undifferentiated nature.[59] The authors write: "While enlightenment rightly opposes every hypostatization of utopia and unsentimentally proclaims domination as division, the split between subject and object, whose whitewashing enlightenment proscribes, becomes the index of its own untruth and of the truth."[60] The elusive truth indexed by the untruth of the subject-object divide is not a theoretical one. Rather, it is the utopia of reconciliation with nature, which cannot be hypostasized into a determinate state of affairs that we might bring about through instrumental action.

Adorno and Horkheimer's claim that the self-indicting untruth of the subject-object divide points to the counterfactual truth of utopian reconciliation—an inversion of the Spinozistic doctrine that the truth is an index both of itself and of the untruth—is crucial for the present argument.[61] In this claim advanced in the opening essay *of Dialectic of Enlightenment*, we find the warrant for Adorno's construal of the drastic reification evident in the execution of the slave girls as a cipher for the hopeful idea of reconciliation. If the determinate negation of images is paradigmatically realized in the form of "script," then Adorno's choice of the execution episode as the focal point of his redemptive critique of antiquity is anything but arbitrary. For Homer's comparison of the execution of the slave maids to bird-trapping falsely transfigures something horrendous into a bucolic image; and it was the moral indifference of epic narration, as reflected in this recourse to an aestheticized image, that prompted the anonymous editor to insert a mitigating phrase in the historical transition from chant to literary "script."

It is thus all the more troubling that the grounds for Horkheimer and Adorno's claim that the subject-object split is an index of its own untruth as well as of the truth remain obscure at best. In what I take to be the most plausible construal of the authors' pronouncement, it is inspired by Hegel's opening arguments in the "Introduction" to the *Phenomenology of Spirit*. There Hegel argues that finite models of knowledge that posit an ontological gulf between subject and object, since they *eo ipso* preclude knowledge of the absolute, condemn their proponents to epistemic frustration and thereby lay bare their own falsity.[62] Such a reading of the passage has an obvious appeal in view of Horkheimer and Adorno's citation of the Hegelian principle of determinate negation in their discussion of the Judaic prohibition on images. However, this parallel also highlights the limits of the affinity between the Hegelian argument and the claim that the split between subject and object is "the index of its untruth and of the truth." For even though the "Introduction" to the *Phenomenology* presents a succinct argument to the effect that the split between subject and object entails the untruth of finite models of knowledge, this initial negation of finite models is still indeterminate. As such, Hegel's initial diagnosis of the subject-object dichotomy is not yet an index of the truth; it certainly does not permit Hegel to arrive in one fell swoop at the absolute idealist position that can dispense with the dogmatic presupposition of such a dichotomy. The determinate negation of finite knowledge that makes possible the transition to speculative truth will require the long and circuitous path charted in the entirety of the *Phenomenology of Spirit*. If we are looking for a philosophical justification for Horkheimer and Adorno's claim that the subject-object divide is an index of its own untruth as well as of the truth, Hegel will be of no help.

A moment's reflection should suffice to reveal the implications of this problem for Horkheimer and Adorno's attempt at a Hegelian construal of the Judaic prohibition on images—whose prospects of success were always going to be rather dim in view of Hegel's ingrained anti-Judaism. The scheme of determinate negation is not applicable here. There are no philosophical grounds, Hegelian or otherwise, for supposing that the recognition of script's non-resemblance to God affords a determinate insight into divine being—any more than there are grounds for thinking that the self-indicting falsity of the opposition between subject and object yields a determinate idea of reconciliation. Indeed, the specious parallel posited by Horkheimer and Adorno between the two issues suggests that in both cases the claim regarding the positive yield of negation is underwritten by an unacknowledged theological commitment.[63]

Similarly, there is no philosophical justification for Adorno's suggestion that a remembrance of nature in the recognition of somatic suffering can evoke a determinate idea of utopia. Put simply, the imperative to prevent suffering does not suffice for defining the contours of a good life. As Rahel Jaeggi notes, it is precisely Adorno's recognition of this insufficiency that distinguishes his substantive, ethically "thick" reflections on good versus damaged life from the "liberalism of fear" advocated by Judith Shklar and Richard Rorty.[64] To illustrate Adorno's thought with an example from his work, his comments in *Minima Moralia* on the "Health Unto Death" mandated by modern capitalism point to a social pre-formation of the psyche that takes place on such a deep level as to preclude the very possibility of neurotic suffering caused by intrapsychic conflict (*MM* 58–60). While in Adorno's and our own historical present this sort of anesthesia is, as a matter of empirical fact, connected to socioeconomic structures that do inflict untold suffering on a large number of humans, nevertheless a dystopian condition of universal anesthesia—which would satisfy the imperative to avoid suffering but still fall short of every defensible idea of the good life—is unfortunately very much conceivable. Far from it being the case that a determinate idea of utopia can be derived by merely identifying shortcomings in a form of life, any diagnosis of what Adorno calls "damaged life" *as* damaged already presupposes some positive idea, however indeterminate, of a right state of affairs.[65] How such a positive idea surfaces in Adorno's excursus will be the topic of the following chapter.

Echoing the hope "for the sake of the hopeless" that Benjamin discerned in the posture of the novelistic narrator ("GEA" 356), the hope that Adorno draws from his novelistic reading of the execution episode rests on an exceedingly tenuous ground, if indeed it is not entirely groundless. Yet this finding should be considered in light of another important point of convergence with Benjamin's essay, and in particular with the saving of semblance in which it culminates. Just as Benjamin claimed that, in the case of hope, Plato's denunciation of semblance "suffers its one exception" ("GEA" 355), so Adorno now asserts that the caesura in book 22 of the *Odyssey* "causes to flash up a semblance of freedom that civilization has been unable wholly to extinguish ever since" (*DE* 61). The image of freedom that flashes up in the caesura has the status of semblance in a twofold sense: first, because it is confined to art; and second, because it depends on a critical act of retroactive construction. Adorno's claim that this semblance of freedom has proven impossible to extinguish "ever since" must therefore be understood as an expedient fiction—one that shows affinities with Plato's noble lie as well with the Kantian argument that the idea of freedom implicit in our moral consciousness proves its actuality.[66]

Chapter 3

✦

Adorno's Soft Caesura

The Immanent Utopia of Penelope's Remark

The Self-Undoing Artwork

The disenchantment of Greek antiquity that Adorno had undertaken in the first excursus of *Dialectic of Enlightenment* did not cause him to lose interest in moments of interruption in the *Odyssey*. Years after his own homecoming—such as it was—from exile, Adorno revisited the Homeric poem in a line of thought that turned, once again, on the concept of caesura. The passage in question, which occurs in the posthumously published *Aesthetic Theory*, is apt to complicate our understanding of the critical model associated with that concept. It therefore suggests a second approach to the excursus on Odysseus in *Dialectic of Enlightenment*—and by extension, as it will become clear in due course, a second approach to Benjamin's essay on *Elective Affinities* as well.

Before we can turn to the key passage that invokes the *Odyssey* in connection with a caesura, it is necessary to situate that passage within the broader context of *Aesthetic Theory*. In particular, we need to review a closely related reflection developed in the chapter titled "Art Beauty." At stake in this line of thought is the moment of "spirit" (*Geist*) in works of art. The first thing to note here is that Adorno's thinking about the spiritual moment in art sharply deviates from that of his idealist predecessors. In §49 of the *Critique of the Power of Judgment*, Kant defined the spirit of the artwork as the "material [*Stoff*] . . . which purposively sets the mental powers into motion, i.e., into a play that is self-maintaining and even strengthens the powers to that end."[1] This definition threatens to relegate the sensuous materiality of the artwork to a mere pretext for the mind's spontaneous activity. As a result, it is far from obvious that the Kantian conception can be construed in terms that allow for that receptive attunement to sensuous particulars which is so crucial to aesthetic experience. On the most general level, Adorno's determination of the spirit of artworks as "the nonfactual in their facticity" (*AT* 86) concurs with the Kantian definition. Yet Adorno radically reorients the

Kantian notion by making the moment of responsiveness to sensuous matter central to his own definition. "The spiritual element of art," he writes, "is not what idealist aesthetics calls spirit; rather, it is the mimetic impulse fixated by a spell as a totality [*der festgebannte mimetische Impuls als Totalität*]" (*AT* 90, translation modified). Since by "mimetic impulse" Adorno means a readiness for communicative engagement with and assimilative openness to that which one encounters, he may be understood here as suggesting that the spirit of art consists in its power to bring to light a layer of sensuous diversity that invites just such mimetic engagement.[2] In a social world governed by instrumental rationality, these sensuous aspects tend to get suppressed through the acts, both real and mental, that constitute the things of the world as unitary objects represented in conformity with humans' self-preservational needs. Adorno's term "the non-identical" gestures toward the dimension that remains latent in such regimented experience, and which cannot be reduced to logically ordered facts about objects of knowledge.

So understood, the spiritual dimension of art is inextricably bound up with the sensuous phenomenality of the artwork. Yet artistic attempts at doing justice to this dimension are complicated by a dialectic: "Precisely through its progressive spiritualization, through its division from nature," writes Adorno, "art wants to revoke this division from which it suffers and which inspires it" (*AT* 92). Because this dialectic cannot be stabilized, every attempt at giving aesthetic prominence to nonidentical aspects is fraught with danger. Not the least of the dangers involved is the one Adorno identifies in his critique of expressionism—a polemic that deserves attention here in view of its direct relevance to Adorno's take on the Benjaminian notion of "the expressionless." The expressionist artist presents diverse material "elements set free—colors, sounds, absolute configurations of words" in their raw immediacy, "as if they already inherently expressed something" (*AT* 91). In so doing, the expressionist overlooks the fact that "the elements become eloquent only through the context in which they occur" (*AT* 90). The result, according to Adorno, is a "spiritualization that progressively exorcises spirit" (*AT* 91), a "barbaric literalness" that turns art into "its own enemy, the direct and false continuation of purposive rationality" (*AT* 103).

Now it is not obvious why this should be so, why, in other words, elementary sensory qualities presented in their immediacy cannot in and of themselves engage our mimetic impulses in emancipatory ways. On reflection, however, we can see why Adorno's premises block this royal road to the nonidentical. It is one of Adorno's bleak insights that an innocent openness to the nonidentical is at best intermittently available to humans who have been socialized from an early age to think of themselves first and foremost as autonomous subjects. Such regimented subjects can encounter the nonidentical dimension only as a limit to their striving for cognitive and practical mastery—and indeed as a potentially lethal threat, which is why intimations of a reconciliation with the nonidentical are haunted by the fear of death felt by a subject in the grip of the drive to self-preservation. That is to say, the nonidentical can become "eloquent," to use Adorno's term, only in a context of the identitarian compulsions that it frustrates.

When Adorno defines the spirit of artworks as "the nonfactual in their facticity" (*AT* 86), he also means to capture through this formulation the context-dependence of the spiritual moment in art. The sensuous elements that contribute to the spirit of an artwork do not simply coincide with themselves but are "moments" within a "configuration" that points beyond itself and therefore has the character of "script" (*AT* 86–87). Clearly, the mode of reference characteristic of script differs from representation in a total pictorial image. Adorno accordingly insists that the formal configuration of artworks does not have the character of a closed totality. This point is effectively underscored by his observation about the paintings of (presumably) Fragonard and Watteau:

> Even the sensually most dazzling French works achieve their rank by the involuntary transformation of their sensual elements into bearers of a spirit whose experiential content is melancholic resignation to mortal, sensual existence; never do these works relish their suaveness to the full, for that suaveness is always curtailed [*beschnitten*] by the sense of form. (*AT* 87)

Mimetic pleasure taken in sensuous particulars is spoiled by the fear of a subject bent on preserving its individuated life. Fragonard's and Watteau's paintings can intimate an untrammeled mimetic openness to the nonidentical and hence point beyond the confines of a subjective standpoint that is captive to the compulsion of self-preservation; yet they evoke such a reconciled condition only as what remains unattainable to the individuated subject. This is why the promise of happiness conveyed by these paintings remains compromised by the shadow of mortality. By attributing this curtailing effect to "the sense of form," Adorno suggests that aesthetic configuration frames what is actual as broken and incomplete and precisely thereby keeps open at least the notional possibility of transcendence. This principle of configuration, the spirit of artworks, charges their sensuous elements with a reference to a "truth content" whose deciphering remains the task of critique. To use a pointed formulation, transcendence is immanent to the formal configuration of artworks.

In the effort to characterize this paradoxical moment in art, Adorno's thinking moves in striking proximity to the apologia for fleeting semblance that concluded Benjamin's meditation on the caesura in *Elective Affinities* ("GEA" 355). The proximity is evident in such passages as the following:

> The strict immanence of the spirit of artworks is contradicted on the other hand by a countertendency that is no less immanent: the

> tendency of artworks to wrest themselves free of the internal unity of their own construction, to introduce within themselves caesuras that no longer permit the totality of the appearance. Because the spirit of the works is not identical with them, spirit breaks up the objective form through which it is constituted; this rupture is the instant of apparition . . . If the spirit of artworks flashes up in their sensual appearance, it does so only as their negation: Unitary with the phenomenon, spirit is at the same time its other. (*AT* 88–89)

What this means in concrete terms had already emerged quite clearly in the important short essay "Late Style in Beethoven," published in 1937. Since in this text Adorno construes formal caesuras as moments of "the expressionless," and, moreover, he develops this idea with reference to an artistic oeuvre whose importance for him is second to none, the essay is particularly important for Adorno's reworking of the Benjaminian model.[3] At least its most directly relevant arguments must therefore be briefly recalled.

The crux of the essay is the claim that Beethoven in his late works again and again runs up against an insurmountable limit to the power of artistic subjectivity to appropriate musical materials for expressive purposes. The limit experience that cannot be adequately expressed through active shaping of musical material is none other than awareness of one's own mortality. A future reabsorption into matter over which one has no control can only be anticipated in art through a breakdown of the insistent effort to submit musical materials to expressive mastery. Adorno writes:

> The power of subjectivity in the late works of art is the irascible gesture [*die auffahrende Geste*] with which it takes leave of the works themselves. It breaks their bonds, not in order to express itself, but in order, expressionless [*ausdruckslos*], to cast off the appearance of art. Of the works themselves it leaves only fragments behind, and communicates itself, like a cipher, only through the blank spaces from which it has disengaged itself. Touched by death, the hand of the master sets free the masses of material that he used to form; its tears and fissures, witnesses to the finite powerlessness of the I confronted with that which is [*vorm Seienden*], are its final work. . . . His late work remains process, but not as development; rather as a catching fire between the extremes, which no longer allow for any secure middle ground or harmony of spontaneity. Between extremes in the most precise technical sense: on the one hand the monophony, the *unisono* of the significant mere phrase; on the other the polyphony, which rises above it without mediation. It is subjectivity that forcibly brings the extremes together in the moment, fills the dense polyphony with its tensions, breaks it apart with the *unisono*, and disengages itself, leaving the naked tone behind; that sets the mere phrase as a

> monument to what has been, marking a subjectivity turned to stone. The caesuras, the sudden discontinuities that more than anything else characterize the very late Beethoven, are those moments of breaking away; the work is silent at the instant when it is left behind, and turns its emptiness outward.[4]

Beethoven's late style thus becomes the paradigm case of a modern artistic practice that allows the spurious totality of aesthetic form to be fractured by caesuras. These moments of sudden breakdown in the artistic subject's expressive activity yield silences pregnant with the subject's dispossession as it is pushed beyond its confines.

This notion of caesura is tacitly at play in the passage from *Aesthetic Theory* to which I now want to turn. To be sure, the connection is far from obvious. For in the chapter of *Aesthetic Theory* that is now at issue, titled "Toward a Theory of the Artwork," Adorno employs the concept of caesura in a sense that at first appears diametrically opposed to the one just outlined. What the term stands for in this context is not the fracturing of aesthetic totality, but the decisive act by which the unity of aesthetic form breaks away in the first place from the undifferentiated multiplicity of the mythic, natural dimension. Apropos of this act Adorno writes: "By its opposition to the empirical world, each artwork programmatically, as it were, establishes its unity. What has passed by way of spirit determines itself in its oneness against the accidental and chaotic that are embedded in nature . . . The unity of artworks is their caesura from myth" (*AT* 186). The genesis of the artwork is thus construed by Adorno as an objective correlate of the protohistory of subjectivity charted in the excursus on Odysseus in *Dialectic of Enlightenment* (*DE* 41–42).[5] In order to exist as a distinct thing, the work of art must be constituted through mental and material acts of unification performed upon a sensuous-material manifold. The fact that art emerged as an autonomous domain to satisfy mimetic impulses that are otherwise repressed cannot entirely cancel its complicity in the logic of domination from which it offers refuge. If artworks oppose the logic of domination that prevails in the real world, they do so only by imitating it through their very constitution as unitary objects (*AT* 289).

What has emerged from the preceding discussion is that Adorno uses the concept of caesura in reference to both the making and the unmaking of the artwork. The subsumption of opposites under the same concept would seem to present a problem, inasmuch as it threatens to empty the concept of determinate meaning. On closer examination, however, the opposition between the two meanings of the term can be shown to be merely apparent. The key to the resolution can be found in Adorno's claim that the aesthetic unity forged through the caesura from myth is secretly indebted to the multiplicity that comes to light in the caesuras revealing the powerlessness of aesthetic form to fully embody spirit. "In themselves," writes Adorno, "and in accord with their immanent determination, [artworks] achieve a unity that is impressed upon the empirical objects of rational knowledge: Unity emerges from their own elements, from the multiplicity; thus they do not extirpate myth but mollify [*besänftigen*] it" (*AT* 186).

In this passage, Adorno's thinking about art moves along tracks established by Kant's epistemology. Kant argued that the component parts of the sensible manifold must exhibit a "transcendental affinity," that is, they must at the very least be amenable to the unifying activity of the understanding.[6] In the aesthetic context, the sensuous materials are not just passively accepting of formal synthesis, but they actively gesture towards it: "Dispersed multiplicity does not offer itself neutrally to aesthetic synthesis as does epistemology's chaotic material, which, devoid of quality, neither anticipates nor eludes its forming" (*AT* 186). If the formal unity of the work of art is to be more than the externally imposed schematism of conventional topoi, then aesthetic form must bring to light a tendency toward unity that inheres in the material components themselves. Just as the identical self-consciousness that triumphs over myth originates in the mythic law of the recurrence of the same—an expression of the blind drive to self-preservation that permeates nature—so the unity of aesthetic form must manifest a preexisting integrative tendency that is latent in the material. Adorno does not clarify the source of this integrative tendency. In what I take to be the most plausible construal of this element of Adorno's account, the integrative tendencies of the sensible material are due to the mimetic, communicative impulses at work in living nature. On an elementary level, these impulses manifest themselves in the self-organization of living beings. On a higher level reached in human mental life, including in artistic production, these impulses can take the form of a disposition to perceive even inert material manifolds as meaningfully interconnected—a disposition that is arguably one of the oldest wellsprings of art.

To complicate matters, Adorno inflects the broadly Kantian notion of a formal unity rooted in original affinity with a Hegelian understanding of the dialectic of identity and difference. Put simply, the constitution of an object as a self-identical unit requires its differentiation from what it is not. The integrative tendency that transforms disparate sensible materials into complex objects is, viewed from another perspective, a tendency toward separation and apartness. This is true of artworks as well as of living organisms. However, a key difference between these two classes of complex objects must also be noted. In living organisms, the dialectic of identity and difference is stabilized by the teleology of self-organization: the independent, unitary life of the organism is sustained by differences among internal organs that enjoy a degree of functional independence from one another; and the same dialectic recurs at lower levels between the organ and the living cell, as well as between the living cell and its organelles. Yet works of art, as Adorno categorically declares, are "not organisms; works of the highest rank are hostile to their organic aspect as illusory and affirmative" (*AT* 90).

What this means is that the configuration of the artwork cannot be fully understood as teleologically geared toward formal unity. To be sure, every artwork, if it is to be recognizable as such, must exhibit a minimal degree of unity. The sensuous materials gathered in the artwork are, as we have seen, not neutral toward this formal unity. However, their integrative tendency is only one side of the dialectic envisioned by Adorno: "While gazing with yearning and neediness toward the unity they could fulfill and reconcile," writes Adorno, the diverse material constituents of the artwork "always at the same time flee from it. . . . Unity is motivated not least of all by the fact that according to their own propensity the individual elements seek to escape it" (*AT* 186, translation modified).

In a first approach, the claim that the unity of the artwork must be achieved through a "caesura from myth" (*AT* 186) may be understood as encapsulating this thought. Here it is important to note, however, that Adorno's formulation in the German original introduces a dialectical ambiguity that the English translation elides. The phrase used by Adorno is not "*Zäsur vom Mythos*" ("caesura from myth") but "*Zäsur zum Mythos*," where the preposition "*zum*" carries the dual valence of "toward" and "to." A more accurate English paraphrase of Adorno's assertion would thus be "the unity of artworks is their caesura toward/to myth." The resultant ambiguity precisely captures the dialectic at the heart of Adorno's conception. The act that constitutes the artwork as a formal unity involves an act of demarcation directed against the chaotic realm of mythic nature. Yet the very same act also constitutes the artwork as just another embodiment of myth, for the unity of the emergent work realizes a tendency to merge that inheres in the sensuous manifold as a legacy of mythic chaos.

As a consequence, the paradoxical task of the artwork is to do justice to both the integrative tendencies of its sensuous materials and their nonidentical character, their "propensity . . . to escape" unity (*AT* 186). Precisely in order to preserve this refractory diversity, then, the formal unity of the artwork must stop short of organic totality and remain extraneously imposed. Aesthetic form, one might say, succeeds by failing. Instead of achieving an organic integration of the "many" into "one," the successful artwork juxtaposes the two poles and thereby presents the idea of their reconciliation as a persistent problem awaiting solution. What Adorno calls the spiritual truth content of the artwork is thus not the overarching formal principle that actually governs its constitution as a unitary object, but its power to evoke the idea of a reconciled condition in which unity would no longer demand a sacrificing of diversity. At work in the artwork is a power to intimate an undoing of power.

It is to characterize this paradoxical power that Adorno returns in this section of *Aesthetic Theory* to the *Odyssey*. Unlike in *Dialectic of Enlightenment*, however, this time it is not Odysseus but Penelope who becomes the protagonist of a philosophical allegory. Adorno writes:

> If the unity of artworks is also inescapably the violence done to multiplicity—symptomatic of which is the use in aesthetic criticism of expressions such as "mastery over the material"—multiplicity must, like the ephemeral and alluring images of nature in antiquity's myths, fear unity. The unity of logos, because it mutilates, is enmeshed in the nexus of its guilt. Homer's tale of Penelope, who in the evening unraveled what she had accomplished during the day, is an unselfconscious allegory of art: What cunning Penelope inflicts on her artifacts, art actually inflicts on itself. Ever since Homer's verses, this episode is not the addition or rudiment for which it is easily mistaken, but a constitutive category of art: Through this story, art takes into itself the impossibility of the identity of the one and the many as an element of its unity. Artworks, no less than reason, have their cunning. If the diffuseness and individual impulses of artworks were left to their own immediacy, to themselves, they would blow away without a trace. Artworks register what would otherwise vanish. Through unity the impulses forfeit their independence; it is only metaphorically that they are any longer spontaneous. This compels criticism even of very great artworks. The idea of greatness as a rule is bound up with the element of unity, sometimes at the cost of its relation to the nonidentical; for this reason the concept of greatness itself is dubious in art. (*AT* 187, translation modified)[7]

Adorno's allegorical interpretation of Penelope amplifies an aspect of the Homeric character that has been highlighted by Rebecca Comay.[8] According to Comay's suggestive reading, Penelope's faithfulness to a husband who may or may not be dead, which expresses itself in her refusal to be consoled by music and her tenacious mistrust of the man who claims to be her returned husband, attests to a "desire which refuses the consolation of every partial nourishment and thus stakes a claim on a happiness outstripping every fact." The subjectivity whose contours Comay discerns in the Homeric portrayal of Penelope belongs to "the non-place of permanent wandering, an odyssey without a final end."

In keeping with this aspect of the Homeric figure, the cunning of Penelope becomes for Adorno the feminine inverse of the power attributed to Odysseus. Cunning enabled Odysseus to turn the mythic forces of dispersal against themselves and thereby to constitute himself as an integrated, enduring, and autonomous subject. Penelope's cunning, by contrast, allegorizes the preservation of a certain heterogeneity on the side of the object. It stands for the subterfuge by which works of art salvage a diverse material manifold into a tentative and porous formal unity that does not fully level differences. We can now see why, in a passage quoted earlier, Adorno defined the "spiritual element of art" as "the mimetic impulse fixated as totality" (*AT* 90). The work of art can preserve heterogeneous elements through their inclusion in a construct that must exhibit a certain measure of formal unity. Such aesthetic salvaging of particulars that escape conceptual subsumption is, to be sure, always on the verge of becoming an *Aufhebung* in that Hegelian double sense of preservation and cancellation within an overarching framework. However, at least some works of art—the compositions of the second Viennese school, Hölderlin's late hymns, Beethoven's last quartets—have succeeded in outwitting this tendency; and as we are about to see, Adorno's redemptive critique of the *Odyssey* ends by uncovering in the ancient epic an anticipation of precisely this sort of paradoxical, and peculiarly modern, artistic feat.

In a concession to naive musical enjoyment that seems untypical for Adorno, he suggests that untrained music listeners who cherish "pretty passages" exempted from the ironclad logic of large-scale form unwittingly respond to a vestige of the nonidentical preserved in musical works.[9] Of course, in the absence of any analytical grasp of the dialectic of the one and the many, such naive responsiveness to sensuous particulars enjoyed in isolation is merely a kind of aesthetic regression. The musical hedonist fixated on pretty passages does not even notice the large-scale formal structures from whose totalizing claim the nonidentical aspects of the work of art must be rescued. If, then, the work of art is to serve as a refuge for the nonidentical, it cannot remain a self-sufficient object given for immediate apprehension. Buried beneath the unity of aesthetic form, which tends to present itself as a closed totality, vestiges of the nonidentical in the work of art call out for a mode of response on our part that might give them their due. It is the task of critique to rescue nonidentical elements from their reduction to mere constituents of an abstractly conceived whole—and to do so in anticipation of a reconciled state in which different things might exist alongside one another free of domination.[10]

Steadfastness Together in the Face of Death

This line of thought suggests a new approach to Adorno's marking of a caesura in the excursus on Odysseus in *Dialectic of Enlightenment*, as discussed in the previous chapter. By focusing on a seemingly perfunctory consoling phrase in book 22 of the *Odyssey*, Adorno—as we have seen in the previous chapter—salvages the perspective of subjugated female characters whose suffering the epic totality makes light of and indeed threatens to pass over. His critical act responds to that self-undoing tendency of the artwork which Adorno will associate with the figure of Penelope in *Aesthetic Theory*. That is to say, Adorno highlights a trace of the nonidentical that the work has managed to preserve thanks to the successive revisions through which its extant form gradually emerged. The redemptive critique that Adorno practices in approaching this juncture extends, as it were, the centuries-long process of textual revision and reimagines the *Odyssey* as a novel with a minimally compassionate narrator.

Beside suggesting a new perspective on Adorno's marking of a caesura in book 22 of the *Odyssey*, the allegory of Penelope in *Aesthetic Theory* draws attention to a passage in the excursus that explicitly associates the figure of Penelope with a caesura in the epic. For in addition to the caesura of book 22, Adorno also posits, albeit with a lighter emphasis, a second caesura in the *Odyssey*. Although this second caesura occurs at a later point in the Homeric narrative, in book 23, Adorno's comments on it precede his dense concluding remarks on the caesura of book 22. I will hazard a hypothesis about the reason for this inversion at the end of this chapter. Before this question can be addressed, however, we need to clarify the significance of the caesura in book 23 for Adorno's argument.

In the passage at issue now, Adorno remarks on the scene in which Odysseus's recollection of the marital bed that he had built finally allows Penelope to identify her husband:

> By this the ingenious Penelope recognizes him, flattering him with praise of his exceptional intelligence. But her flattery, which is not without a touch of mockery, is followed, in an abrupt caesura [*in jäher Zäsur*], by words which seek the reason for the suffering of all spouses in the gods' envy of the happiness guaranteed only by marriage, the "confirmation of the concept of permanence": "All our unhappiness is due to the gods, who couldn't bear to see us share the joys of youth and reach the threshold of old age together." Marriage represents not only the account-balancing order of the living but also steadfastness together, in solidarity, in the face of death. In it reconciliation grows up around subjugation, just as in history up to now true humanity has flourished only in conjunction with the barbaric element which is veiled by "humane values." Even if the contract between the spouses sets aside the old hostility only with difficulty, nevertheless the couple aging in peace vanishes in the image of Philemon and Baucis, as the smoke from the sacrificial altar is transmuted into that rising beneficently from the hearth. Undoubtedly, marriage forms part of the primal rock of myth at the base of civilization. But its mythic solidity and permanence jut from myth, as the small island realm rises from the endless sea. (*DE* 58–59, translation modified)

Adorno thus views marriage as the site of a transmutation of mythic sacrifice into contractually safeguarded fidelity. This idea lends substance to his earlier claim in the excursus, to the effect that marriage represents "society's middle way" between the paradigmatically masculine domination of the natural realm and reconciliation with that realm (*DE* 56). Crucially, however, the passage in book 23 that Adorno calls "an abrupt caesura" is one in which marriage briefly appears as more than a compromise, more than the flawed realization of an unattainable ideal.

By extension, mortality is envisioned here as something other than a source of dread. This point seems particularly significant, for it suggests that Adorno's claim a little further on in the excursus, to the effect that the motif of "abolishing death" is "the innermost cell of all antimythic thought" (*DE* 60), should not be taken in the literal sense. Indeed, when understood literally, the idea of abolishing death must sound positively horrifying to anyone who takes the trouble to imagine what it might entail.[11] In light of Penelope's remark, however, the hyperbolic talk of abolishing death may be deciphered as expressive of the desire for a fearless, because shared, anticipation of mortality.

Still, it might be tempting to make light of Penelope's claim about the gods' envy of mortals as a rapturous exaggeration. For one thing, the celebration of shared steadfastness in the face of death seems oblivious to the accidents of temporal order. In *Minima Moralia*, Adorno construes the inescapable role of such chronological contingencies in the genesis and dissolution of erotic relations as a mark of their tending toward possessiveness and reification: who was there first matters.[12] In a similar way, the fact that spouses are unlikely to die at the same time may be thought to preclude a genuinely shared being-toward-death. This problem already surfaced in the essay on *Elective Affinities*, in which Benjamin declared that "every love grown within itself must become master [*Herr*] of this world—in its natural exitus, the common (that is, *strictly simultaneous*) death, or in its supernatural duration, marriage" ("GEA" 345, my italics).

As should be clear from Benjamin's demand that love "must become master of this world," his version of utopia asserts the sublime transcendence of spirit vis-à-vis the mythic entanglements of empirical reality. Adorno's utopia of reconciliation, and his dialectical understanding of the relation between myth and enlightenment, lead him in a markedly different direction. In envisioning emancipation from the mythic forces that burden the marital bond with domination and fear of death, Adorno turns to the mythic fable of Philemon and Baucis, who grew old together and were granted their wish—

> . . . that the same hour take us both together,
> and that I should not live to see her tomb
> nor she survive to bury me in mine.[13]

It is telling that in Adorno's utopia "the couple aging in peace vanishes in the image of Philemon and Baucis," for of course that image created by Ovid finally shows Philemon and Baucis vanish together as they turn into a pair of entwined trees. Emancipation from myth is thus likened—in keeping with Adorno's dialectical framework—to mimetic assimilation to a myth of mimesis.

How to decipher this anti-mythic myth in the rational terms of an enlightenment that is enlightened about itself? One might say, in Freudian terms, that the Ovidian myth evoked by Adorno registers a wish that transcends the distinction between Eros and Thanatos. What would alleviate the terror associated with the prospect of one's reabsorption into nature is mimetic reconciliation with the nonidentical. Such is the utopia embodied by the poetic genius whom Adorno envisions near the end of his essay on Hölderlin: the willingness of the genius to relinquish domination of nature is inseparable from his espousal of mortality.[14] Along the same lines, in *Negative Dialectics* Adorno rejects the anthropological speculation that fear of death has an ineradicable basis in our animal nature; such fear of death is instead, as he insists, the product of a socioeconomic totality that conditions subjects to conform to a stunted rationality descended from the self-preservational drive that we have in common with nonhuman animals. Under the heading of "humanity" (*Humanität*) Adorno envisions a form of subjectivity that has been sufficiently strengthened for a free and fearless opening to otherness, a being-toward-death beyond the natural compulsion of the drive to self-preservation.[15] The strengthening of the subject is compatible with openness to experience because, for Adorno, the stance essential to being a subject is not spontaneous activity, as idealism would have it, but receptive openness to experience.[16] The strengthening of the subject that Adorno has in mind would presumably eliminate the possessiveness that tends to contaminate human relationships, such that the prospect of predeceasing one's spouse would no longer raise the specter of infidelity on the part of the survivor.

In all of these speculations that he hazarded at various points in his career, Adorno imagines a reconciled state in which an overcoming of the logic of self-preservation through domination would make possible novel forms of solidarity, fidelity, and happiness. And it is worth underlining that Adorno's utopia of experiential openness converges with the one anticipated by the self-undoing tendency of artworks, whose allegorical image he discerns in Penelope's subterfuge. Whether this utopia can serve as a source of moral and political orientation may well be doubted. It is difficult to see how the sting of mortality could be lessened to the point where dying is seen merely as an ultimate form of experiential openness to the nonidentical. Here, as elsewhere, Adorno seems vulnerable to the criticism that he conflates historically conditioned shortcomings of societal organization with the constitutive limitations of human life.

We can nevertheless see why Adorno views Penelope's effusive statement as a caesura. For, construed as an intimation of the utopian condition just outlined, Penelope's statement may be said to transfigure a necessity of nature—namely, the final rupturing of the continuum of experience—into the source of a possible happiness that would surpass not only the compromised satisfactions of a myth-bound humanity, but also the blithe contentment of the gods. This notion amounts to a radical break with the hierarchical worldview underlying the Homeric poems.[17] And yet this rupture discerned by Adorno, while "abrupt," nevertheless occurs on the diegetic level, within the world portrayed by Homer.

There is thus a doubling of the caesura in Adorno's excursus on Odysseus, a doubling that Adorno makes explicit by using the same technical term in reference to both passages. Whereas the caesura he marks in book 22 interrupts the very act of narration, the caesura in book 23 occurs on the level of the narrated events and receives a lighter emphasis in Adorno's reflections. To highlight this difference between a strongly marked extradiegetic caesura and a lightly marked diegetic one, I will refer to them as "hard" and "soft." Adorno does not comment on the relation between the two caesuras. However, a significant relation comes into view when we consider the centrality of death to both caesuras and the role of the female characters involved in the two episodes.

The alignment of the two caesuras juxtaposes Penelope with the maids who have "sunk back into harlotry" (*DE* 61). Commenting on her recent translation of the *Odyssey*, Emily Wilson has highlighted the connection between these two versions of female subjectivity. As already noted in the previous chapter, Wilson's translation corrects an entrenched bias that led generations of readers, including Adorno, to label the slave maids executed in book 22 as harlots. Conversely, Wilson points out that Penelope is neither an innocent victim nor a proto-feminist heroine but "a woman of privilege, who colludes in, indeed insists on, the silencing of more vulnerable women."[18] Wilson draws out the connection between Penelope's narrowly circumscribed autonomy and the lethal entrapment of the slave girls by noting a textual detail: "Birds in Homer are the ultimate image of speech and of freedom . . . The silenced slave girls are 'like doves or thrushes,' caught in a hunter's net. Penelope, meanwhile, is like a 'pale gray nightingale' who 'sits among the leaves / that crowd the trees.' She can't fly, but her warbling amounts to a 'symphony of sound.'" Tellingly, the passage quoted by Wilson is followed by Penelope's subsumption of her female slaves under the heading "my property," protection of which property she takes to be mandated by respect for her departed husband.[19]

These philological minutiae linking Penelope to the slave maids lend support to Adorno's comments apropos of the Circe episode. "Harlot and wife," writes Adorno, "are complementary forms of female self-alienation in the patriarchal world: the wife betrays pleasure to the fixed order of life and property, while the harlot, as her secret accomplice, brings within the property relationship that which the wife's property rights do not include—pleasure—by selling it" (*DE* 58). This comment offers a clue to the alignment between the caesura of Penelope's speech and the caesura that registers the mute agony of the maids. What Adorno calls the secret complicity between wife and harlot rests on the anthropological premises of his account of subjectivity. Whereas the institution of marriage supports the domination that constitutes the self-identical subject, that of prostitution brings even indulgence in the subject's repressed mimetic impulses within the purview of the exchange principle and hence of domination.

Yet the relation between the caesuras associated with the two figures of femininity also corresponds to the distance between utopian possibility and repressive reality. Although the institution of marriage originates, according to Adorno, in the logic of domination constitutive of the self-identical subject, the soft caesura of book 23 intimates a utopian possibility that lies dormant in this institution. For marriage participates in an unfinished civilizing process through which the brute domination of a nature coded as feminine might eventually be gradually transfigured into a site of domination-free solidarity. By contrast, the caesura of book 22 remembers the violence that has been inflicted upon a reified "feminine" nature so as to contain potentially disruptive erotic impulses arising from the vestigial mimetic tendencies of the subject's natural substrate. The deadly reification inflicted upon the maids is thus the price paid for the subjection of mimetic tendencies to that principle of identitarian domination which called the institution of marriage into existence in the first place. In sum, whereas in the caesura of book 23 marriage is shown to hold the promise of a utopian reconciliation, the caesura in 22 lodges a protest against the violence bound up with its unredeemed actuality.

Immanent and Transcendent Critique: The Double Caesura Model (I)

In Adorno's meditation on the *Odyssey*, the wife's rapturous speech and the maids' mute agony, the transfiguration of mortality and the ordeal of dying like an animal point toward the same utopian idea of reconciliation. Whereas the former intimation of utopia is the work of a diegetic caesura that occurs within the reality represented by the narrative, the latter is made possible by an extradiegetic caesura that interrupts the very act of narration. The alignment of the two caesuras in Adorno's excursus answers to a deeper theoretical necessity, which has to do with a fundamental question around which much of Adorno's thinking revolves. The question is easily stated: are utopian tendencies inherent in historical reality, or is the utopian standpoint of critique a construct of wishful thinking, a perspective that philosophy must establish by a forceful break with reality?

This dilemma can be traced back to an ambiguity in the works of Hegel and Marx that has been incisively analyzed by Seyla Benhabib in her account of the transformations of the idea of immanent critique.[20] As Benhabib argues, the young Hegel's putatively immanent critique of natural right theories actually depended on a retrospective ideal of "ethical life" that was extrinsic to the theories he was considering. Likewise, Marx wavered between two notions of utopia: on the one hand, an immanent utopia that defined emancipation as the "fulfillment" of needs already present in capitalist society; and on the other hand, a transcendent, "transfigurative" notion of utopia according to which emancipation would require a negation of the present through the accomplishment of a qualitatively new task.

It is also worth noting in this context that a cognate difficulty complicates Benjamin's reflections in the late *Arcades Project* on humankind's "awakening" from captivity to mythic "dreams." At times Benjamin states that every epoch dreams of awakening, that awakening is an actualization of tendencies latently at work already within the dream state. Other passages in Benjamin's work suggest, however, that the spell of mythic delusion is so pervasive that it needs to be be broken through a "Copernican turn" that enables us to reimagine the past with a view to projecting a better future. In this view, historical interpretation must by a forceful critical act redefine the present *as* a moment of lucid alertness and retroactively define the past *as* a period of mythic dreaming that in such retrospective light appears to have gestured all along toward awakening.[21]

Although Adorno often suggests that the contours of a good life are somehow implicit in the present state of things, his notion of utopia is closer to the transfigurative one found in Marx and to the interventionist strand in Benjamin's writings. The dominant orientation of Adorno's thinking emerges quite clearly from his critique of Hegel. Throughout Adorno's engagements with Hegel, the charge recurs that the argument of the *Phenomenology of Spirit* could not make good on its program of immanent critique because the dialectical transitions between successive figures of consciousness depended on a speculative premise that was unavailable to finite consciousness.[22] Although in pressing this line of criticism Adorno emphasizes Hegel's inconsistency, and he furthermore opposes the falsely affirmative content of Hegel's speculative presupposition, he nevertheless takes Hegel's covert reliance on such a presupposition to express a true insight about the limits of immanent critique. Already in his 1931 inaugural lecture, Adorno insists that a phenomenologically faithful description of reality in all its shortcomings and contradictions does not suffice for unleashing energies necessary for its critical transcendence.[23] There is, according to Adorno, a discontinuity between the "riddle" posed by a flawed, ideologically occluded reality and its "resolution," a gulf that only active construction can bridge. Rather than looking for the answer as an intention hidden in the riddle, critical thought must actively rearrange the elements of reality that pose a riddle in order for the answer to emerge.

And yet, the distinction drawn by Benhabib between utopia as the fulfillment of present desires and utopia as a transfiguration of those desires does not always take the form of a strict disjunction in Adorno's work. Not ready to resign himself to arbitrariness, Adorno insists that critical intervention becomes more than a purely intellectual exercise, it becomes actual and effective, only insofar as it harnesses a self-critical potential and transformative energy within the ideological formation at issue. "The ideology which affirms life," he writes, "is forced into opposition to life by the immanent drive of the ideal . . . As a result of the social dynamic, culture becomes cultural criticism."[24] In the excursus on Odysseus in *Dialectic of Enlightenment*, Adorno's overarching thesis that myth already gestures toward enlightenment commits him to the task of showing that his utopian projection does have a basis in the Homeric world. To be sure, the transcendence of utopia requires an act of radical projection that negates that which is historically given, a disruption of the very forms of representation through which historical reality articulates itself. Yet critical thought must also have a foothold in actually existing cultural formations if its normative idea of utopia is to have any positive content and ethical traction.

In some of his later writings, Adorno occasionally argues for the decidedly optimistic view that the immanent critique of culture and its transcendent critique from the external standpoint of social totality only appear disparate so long as the autonomy of culture is fetishized, such fetishization being just another symptom of the reifying tendencies that call for critique; and he accordingly claims that a properly dialectical understanding of the boundary between inside and outside, culture and social totality, can show immanent and transcendent critique to be reciprocally mediated by one another.[25] *Negative Dialectics* posits a cognate dialectic between the immanent self-critique of rigorously argued systematic thought and the critique of system in the name of concrete worldly experience (*ND* 28–31). Given his criticism of Hegel, however, it is not clear how Adorno can avail himself of the Hegelian dialectic of the boundary. In any event, Adorno's arguments for a dialectical synthesis between immanent and transcendent critique remain quite abstract and are therefore difficult to evaluate, much less endorse.

Failing such a dialectical resolution, systematic theorizing cannot resolve the antinomy generated by Adorno's insistence on both the immanence of utopia and its transcendence. According to Gordon Finlayson, this aporia surfaced in Adorno's work in the 1950s.[26] During the postwar years, Adorno's deepening sense of the "pervasively evil" character of social reality led him, according to Finlayson, to conclude that a reliable standard for social criticism could not be drawn from the existing state of things, and that immanent critique must therefore be combined with transcendent critique. How this could be done was a question to which Adorno never managed to work out a viable answer. The famous concluding section of *Minima Moralia* may be read as a candid admission of this, perhaps inevitable, failure:

> *Finale.*—The only philosophy which can be responsibly practised in face of despair is the attempt to contemplate all things as they would present themselves from the standpoint of redemption. Knowledge has no light but that shed on the world by redemption: all else is reconstruction, mere technique. Perspectives ought to be fashioned that displace and estrange the world, reveal it to be, with its rifts and crevices, as indigent and distorted as it will appear one day in the messianic light. To gain such perspectives without velleity or violence, entirely

> from felt contact with its objects—this alone is the task of thought. It is the simplest of all things, because the situation calls imperatively for such knowledge, indeed because consummate negativity, once squarely faced, delineates the mirror image of its opposite. But it is also the utterly impossible thing, because it presupposes a standpoint removed, even though by a hair's breadth, from the scope of existence, whereas we well know that any possible knowledge must not only be first wrested from what is, if it shall hold good, but is also marked, for this very reason, by the same distortion and indigence which it seeks to escape. ("153. Finale," *MM* 247, translation modified)

Although reality is riddled with "fissures" that reveal its imperfection and open onto a utopian horizon, such fissures only become visible in the retrospective light introduced by a critical act. Adorno's use of the unreal subjunctive mood ("*Perspektiven müßten hergestellt werden*") signals his admission of the difficulty of measuring reality against a condition defined by complete disjunction from it. Since critique cannot rely on either the self-transcending tendencies of historical reality or the sovereign assurance of a transcendent standpoint, the critical theorist cannot immunize himself against the charge of "velleity and violence."

The difficulty is brought to a head in another mini-essay from *Minima Moralia*, numbered 46, which is concerned with "the morality of thinking": "Nothing less is asked of the thinker today," writes Adorno, "than that he should be at every moment both within things and outside them" (*MM* 74). It is no accident that Adorno arrives at this aporetic formulation after invoking the Kantian stipulation that thought must be "neither blind nor empty." The impossible task of combining immanence with transcendence may be viewed as a late, meta-theoretical descendant of the basic Kantian dichotomy between the particular sensible contents and the conceptual form of knowledge. For Adorno, the persistence of both dualisms follows from the untenability of Hegel's claim to have dialectically sublated them.[27]

These passages from *Minima Moralia* bear out Finlayson's diagnosis of the aporia facing Adorno. However, I want to argue that the aporia surfaces at a somewhat earlier point in Adorno's career than Finlayson supposes. In particular, it already determines the excursus on Odysseus in *Dialectic of Enlightenment*, where it helps to motivate the turn to literary narration. If the two standpoints do not admit of systematic synthesis and hence their conjuction must remain a task for practical agency, at least their conflicting claims can be given their due and conjoined in the medium of philosophical reading. Adorno's formulation in the final mini-essay of *Minima Moralia* can thus be brought to bear upon the caesuras marked in the excursus. One might say, then, that the soft caesura of Penelope's speech in book 23 is "the simplest of all things," namely, a vision of human happiness that arises almost of its own accord from within the reality portrayed by Homer, through a character's recollection of ordeals endured. By contrast, the hard caesura that Adorno inserts after the narrator's consoling line in book 22 is "the utterly impossible thing," a break in the very act of narration that cannot be explained in terms of tendencies or aspirations immanent to the world portrayed by the Homeric narrative. This caesura is the product of a critical intervention that affords a fleeting glimpse of the "rifts and crevices," the "distortion and indigence" that the world would reveal if it were to be seen "in the messianic light" available from the standpoint of redemption. Aligning the intradiegetic caesura of Penelope's speech with the extradiegetic caesura of the execution episode is Adorno's way of construing the idea of reconciliation as both discontinuous and continuous with the mythic world portrayed by Homer—as its "transfiguration" and its "fulfillment" at the same time, to borrow Benhabib's terms. Dependent as it is on literary fiction and critical construction, the double caesura model does not so much resolve the aporia just outlined as it offers a perspicuous presentation of it.

Here is the place to note another feature of the critical model employed by Adorno—in addition to the previously noted stipulation that critical thought must be "neither blind nor empty" (*MM* 74)—which attests to the Kantian complexion of his thinking. By construing the beautiful as a "symbol of morality," Kant's *Critique of the Power of Judgment* identified a positive presentation of the moral law, a presentation characterized by sensuous plenitude.[28] According to this doctrine, the intelligible determination of our sensibility in the delight we take in the beautiful offers a positive actualization—if only in the anticipatory, subjective register of aesthetic experience—of the task of self-legislation that we face as moral agents. However, Kant complements this positive presentation with an equally important negative one, which is characterized by the higher-order pleasure we take in certain displeasurable experiences of satisfaction denied. Explicitly likened by Kant to the Jewish prohibition on graven images of God, the experience of the sublime represents the transcendent authority of reason's demand *ex negativo*, namely, by demonstrating the infinite power of this demand to override any empirically determined incentive.[29]

As we have seen in chapter 1, Benjamin revives the Kantian duality of the beautiful and sublime, although with the key difference that sublimity becomes in his conception a moment internal to beauty. We can now conclude that a reverse movement occurs in Adorno's excursus on Odysseus. That is to say, there is a sense in which Adorno reinscribes the duality of the beautiful and the sublime within the anti-mythic register of the sublime. For, if the negative presentation in the hard caesura of a transcendent utopia is a moment of unmitigated sublimity, then the positive presentation of utopia in the soft caesura may be viewed as a variant of the sublime that verges on the positivity of the beautiful. Whether this aspect of Adorno's double caesura has a precedent in Benjamin's original articulation of the model is a question that must be postponed until the following chapter.

In *Aesthetic Theory*, Adorno invokes the Kantian category of the sublime to refer to the paradoxical "spiritualization" (*Vergeistigung*) that the consummate order of artistic form undergoes when it is disrupted by traces of nature, which Adorno keeps invoking under such headings as "the elemental," "the non-identical," and "the intentionless" (*AT* 196). To be sure, what Kant described as a sublime awareness of spirit's sovereignty over nature is no longer possible once the concept of spirit is reinterpreted to mean the anticipation of reconciliation with the nonidentical. What then remains as "the legacy of the sublime" is "unassuaged negativity" (*AT* 198–99).

Adorno's negative dialectics does not permit a sublation of the difference between positive and negative presentation under the aegis of the former.[30] Their duality persists in Adorno's conception—and it persists with a marked primacy of the negative. For, by reversing the sequence of the two caesuras in the *Odyssey* and concluding his excursus with the negative presentation, Adorno refuses to grant the last word to the impulse to elaborate utopia in determinate terms borrowed from the existing order of things. Indeed, a curbing of that impulse is already evident in the cursory manner in which Adorno notes the "abrupt caesura" in Penelope's speech (*DE* 58). This lack of emphasis is in keeping with the fact that the image of happiness flashing up in Penelope's remark about the envy of the gods is invoked only as a measure of the sufferings endured by the separated spouses. That idea arises merely as a whimsical surmise, and it remains bound to Penelope's necessarily limited perspective. By contrast, we have seen in the previous chapter that the reflective pause that Adorno inserts after the consoling remark in book 22 occurs on the more authoritative plane belonging to the very act of narration. The extradiegetic status of this caesura, which evokes the idea of reconciliation in a strictly negative way, only serves to reinforce its primacy and rightful claim to the last word.

Chapter 4

✦

Benjamin's Soft Caesura

The Immanent Utopia of the Embedded Novella

The Double Caesura Model (II)

One way of summarizing the previous chapter is to say that the most important "saving line" of the *Odyssey* in Adorno's reading is not the line in book 22, so described by Gilbert Murray, but the virtual line connecting that caesura with its positive, intradiegetic counterpart in book 23. In establishing this structure defined by complementary caesuras, Adorno's excursus on Odysseus does not simply follow the Benjaminian critical model. Rather, between the lines of Adorno's novelistic reading of the *Odyssey* we find a probing interpretation of Benjamin's essay—and, by extension, of Goethe's *Elective Affinities*. By explicitly identifying two caesuras in a meditation on the *Odyssey* that conspicuously relies on the Benjaminian model, Adorno may be taken to suggest that the overarching conception of Benjamin's essay requires the marking of two caesuras in *Elective Affinities*.[1]

In this chapter, I will argue that there is indeed a sense in which Benjamin too posits not one but two caesuras in *Elective Affinities*, which complement one another as positive and negative presentations of a utopian dimension. In addition to the novelistic narrator's comment before the catastrophic turning point of the novel, Benjamin's interpretation comes close to attributing the status of a caesura to the novella "Strange Neighbors" embedded in the novel. Benjamin admittedly refrains from using the term "caesura" in this connection. To clarify the reasons for this avoidance will be one of the central aims of this chapter. In pursuing this matter I will also identify a blind spot in Benjamin's treatment of the novella and propose a corrective that remains in keeping with his critical orientation.

At first glance, it may seem far-fetched to suggest that Adorno's excursus implies a reading of Benjamin's essay along the lines just indicated. However, that hypothesis gains in plausibility in view of another piece of evidence that we have for Adorno's concern with the doubling of the caesura. As Bernadette Meyler has shown, Adorno's sustained preoccupation with Alban Berg's opera *Wozzeck* was marked not only by the influence of the Benjaminian caesura model but also by Adorno's vacillation as to where exactly the caesura of the opera falls. In outlining this issue, Meyler casually, yet perceptively, asserts the very point about Benjamin's essay that this chapter will develop in more detail: "Despite Benjamin's own identification of two caesurae in *Elective Affinities*," writes Meyler, "the concept of the caesura as the organizing force of the tragedy implies that there is only one. So which is the caesura of *Wozzeck*? The scene at the inn . . . or the space concluding and beginning the penultimate and last acts?"[2] Adorno's evident sense of a strict disjunction in this regard reflects his understanding that a tragic work such as *Oedipus* or *Wozzeck* can have only one caesura, at least if the term is used in the sense outlined by Hölderlin. By extension, then, the excursus on Odysseus may be taken to reflect Adorno's agreement with Benjamin as to the possibility of two caesuras in an epic work.

Meyler's observation helpfully highlights the genre-theoretical implications of the category introduced by Hölderlin and its adoption by Benjamin and Adorno. Whereas the metrical analysis of verse allows for multiple caesuras in a poem, and sometimes even in a single line, in Hölderlin's theory of tragedy the caesura figures as a singular juncture in a large-scale formal construct. In particular, Hölderlin's theory postulates a single point at which the succession of representations is arrested by a "pure word" that reveals representation itself. The tragic caesura is the point at which an unstable dynamic of diachronic succession is stabilized by a synchronic dynamic, thus affording the contemplative distance from which the tragic process can be grasped as a necessary, formally balanced whole.[3] As Paul Fleming has noted, the Hölderlinian conception of caesura as a "counter-rhythmic rupture" has close affinities with Émile Benveniste's recuperation of the ancient understanding of *ruthmos*: "*Ruthmos* in its original, etymological significance," writes Fleming, "is neither a fixed form nor an ordered movement under the dictate of a ruling measure (e.g., the body in dance), but rather the momentary interruption of such a movement, its petrifaction into a configuration. That is, *ruthmos* is not a temporal but a spatial category."[4]

The notion that a caesura has the effect of conferring a quasi-spatial, sychronically graspable order on an essentially diachronic artwork offers a clue for understanding the doubling of the caesura in Benjamin's and Adorno's critical texts. If the singularity of the caesura in Hölderlin's reflections is due to the transferral of the term from the metrical analysis of verse to the theory of tragedy, by extension the doubling of the caesura in Benjamin's and Adorno's reflections may be viewed as a consequence of its transposition from Hölderlin's tragic framework to a narratological one. In keeping with the quasi-spatial character of the formal order introduced through the caesura, a geometrical analogy can illuminate the need for this doubling. Tragic action, with its inexorable logic, may be likened to a straight line. Just as a single point on a straight line univocally defines a line perpendicular to it, a single caesura in the tragic process can open up a transcendent dimension. For epic narration, however, we need another spatial analogue. Although the Homeric narrative eventually vindicates a subject who persists in pursuing the telos of homecoming, that emergent subject must assert himself against the forces of dispersal at work in the mythic realm, rather than against a clearly defined opposing principle. The spatial analogue for his course is a meandering line, not unlike the geographical path of Odysseus's journey; and a single interruption of this meandering line would not yet suffice for defining a vector of transcendence. Much the same could be said, mutatis mutandis, about a modern work of narrative literature such as *Elective Affinities*. If tragic resolve is not yet possible in Homer's world, in the world portrayed by Goethe it is no longer an option. Goethe's novelistic narrative, as interpreted by Benjamin, bears witness to a form of consciousness on the part of the author as well as his heroes that has succumbed to a modern version of mythic self-opacity and irresolution.[5] A single point of interruption in the errant course of the novelistic plot would thus fail to define an arrow of transcendence.

Given the meandering course of both narratives, their opening unto a transcendent dimension requires more than one caesura. Yet why should it require precisely two caesuras and not more? Again, an elementary geometrical consideration can be of help here. Two points in space univocally define a geometrical line, whereas three or more points may or may not do so. Similarly, a pair of caesuras can best define a line that intersects a meandering narrative path, opening up a dimension transcendent to the immanence of the depicted reality. Originally used by Gilbert Murray in reference to the Homeric passage that Adorno subsequently terms a caesura, the phrase "saving line" thus acquires a more resonant meaning as a shorthand for that line of transcendence projected by the double caesura model.[6] As we have seen, Adorno's excursus aligns the two caesuras of the *Odyssey* with one another by explicitly identifying both *as* caesuras, and by means of his reflections on the wife and the "hetaera" as complementary feminine roles. In Benjamin's essay, a more subtle connection on the level of motifs has been noted by Thomas Zabka: in the quote from Stefan George near the end of the essay, the phrase "seize the body [*den leib ergreifen*]" ("GEA" 356, translation modified) refers back, on the one hand, to the boy's rescue of the girl in the embedded novella and, on the other, to the lovers' embracing for the first time in the scene interrupted by the apparition of hope.[7]

It is perhaps not entirely surprising that the saving line that emerged through Adorno's reading of the *Odyssey* has a precursor in the essay by Benjamin from which Adorno borrows that critical model. More remarkable is the fact that this structure, when made explicit, throws into relief a crucial textual detail in Goethe's novel that Benjamin's interpretation elides. For, its unparallelled illuminating power notwithstanding, Benjamin's essay does have a blind spot, which can be shown on closer examination to be indicative of an aporia at the heart of his critical conception. These shortcomings can help explain Benjamin's reluctance to identify in an explicit manner the second caesura implied by his argument. Besides making explicit the double caesura model at the heart of Benjamin's essay, Adorno's excursus on the *Odyssey* also contains valuable hints that allow us to remedy the blind spot in Benjamin's reading of *Elective Affinities*. Two themes that emerged in my analysis of Adorno's excursus will turn out to be especially suggestive in this regard: first, the reinscription of the dichotomy between the beautiful and the sublime within the register of the sublime, and second, the transformative effect of the process by which stories are transmitted.

Framing the Novella

These claims now need to be spelled out through a consideration of the novella "Strange Neighbors" embedded in Elective Affinities and its complicated role in Benjamin's interpretation of the novel. Even a reader who approaches Benjamin's essay for the first time cannot fail to appreciate the centrality of this embedded narrative to his argument. Benjamin's enumeration of the correspondences between the particulars of the novel and those of the novella is exhaustive and need not be recapitulated here. For our purposes, it should suffice to note that Benjamin construes the embedded novella as a redemptive antithesis to the mythic world of the novel. To make a less obvious but equally important point, we may understand Benjamin's elaboration of this antithesis as an attempt on his part to fulfill the desideratum, stated in "On the Program of the Coming Philosophy," of a "decisive transformation" of the correlative Kantian conceptions of experience and freedom. For whereas the protagonists of the novel are driven by a "chimerical striving for freedom" to make blind choices uninformed by their prehistory that expose them to mythic compulsion, in the redeemed world of the novella the children attain to a lasting bond through an authentic decision founded on the transfigured memory of their shared tempestuous past ("GEA" 332). As Benjamin puts it, the novella is "the day of decision shining into the dusk-filled Hades of the novel" ("GEA" 331). Benjamin sums up the relation between the novel and the novella in a memorable image of illumination:

> With regard to the freedom and necessity that it reveals vis-à-vis the novel, the novella is comparable to an image in the darkness of a cathedral—an image which portrays the cathedral itself and so in the midst of the interior communicates a view of the place that is not otherwise available. In this way it brings inside at the same time a reflection of the bright, indeed sober day. ("GEA" 352)

Although Benjamin's essay can hardly be faulted for a lack of subtlety, on this crucial point it is marred by a simplification. Neither is the relation between the novel and the novella reducible to an antithesis, nor is the novella as limpidly clear as Benjamin would have us believe.

To complement Benjamin's one-sided view of the relation between the novel and the novella, we must attend to a textual feature on which Benjamin remarks only in a cursory fashion. I mean the narrative framing of the novella, which establishes a significant linkage to the plot of the novel. Goethe sets the stage for the embedded narrative by introducing two new characters who represent the wider world for which Eduard has left the estate. An English Lord whom Eduard had gotten to know during his earlier travels visits the estate with his companion. These travelers introduce a vantage point of heightened perception into the narrow and occluded microcosm inhabited by the two women left behind by Eduard. Through the Lord's eyes, we are told, "the women first fully appreciated their surroundings," and "through his observations the park grew and was enriched."[8] We soon find out the reason for this sovereign power of vision from the Lord's own explanation:

> I have accustomed myself to being at home everywhere [*überall zu Hause zu sein*] and have come to feel it the best possible arrangement that others should build, plant, and exert themselves domestically on my behalf. I have no longing to return to my own estates, partly for political reasons but principally because my son, for whom, in the end, all the work I did was done, to whom I hoped to bequeath it all, with whom I hoped for a time still to enjoy it, takes no part in any of it but has gone to India like many another to lead a more useful life there or, for all I know, to waste himself completely. (*EA* 183)

Thanks to the centrifugal effects of post-Revolutionary politics and the rupturing of transgenerational continuity owing to the dynamics of colonialization, the English Lord claims to have attained to the cosmopolitan condition that Novalis saw as the true object of philosophy's yearning. His espousal of displacement is a matter of stoic acquiescence in the instability of worldly affairs, but also an aristocratic privilege that grants him the luxury of aesthetic detachment from the turmoil of the age:

> "It seems to me," he said, "that I do best to think of myself as a perpetual traveller, giving up a great deal in order to enjoy a great deal. I am used to change, indeed I find it necessary, just as at the opera we are always waiting for a scene-change precisely because there have already been so many . . . and if the place goes up in flames the servants will calmly pack my bags and load my carriage and I leave town." (*EA* 184–85)

Presenting a cynical counterpart to the pathos with which the first bridegroom of *Herrmann and Dorothea* espoused the uprooting forces of history in his farewell to Dorothea, the Lord's remarks convey an attitude of flippant complacency.[9] Yet the violence of the historical experiences evoked by the Lord reverberates in the impact of his statements upon Ottilie, whom they remind of the rootlessness from which Eduard must suffer in his self-imposed military vicissitudes:

> The Englishman had no idea how deeply the two friends were affected by his observations . . . Ottilie was thrown by these confidences into the cruellest state: the graceful veil [*anmutige Schleier*] before her eyes was violently torn asunder [*zerriß mit Gewalt*] and it seemed to her as if everything done till then for the house, the garden, the park, and the whole environment was in fact for nothing, because the man to whom it all belonged had no joy of it since he, like their present visitor, was wandering the world, and in the most dangerous fashion, having been driven to do so by those who were closest in his love. (*EA* 184, translation modified)

The violent tearing-asunder of a veil of beautiful semblance, a tearing that begins with these remarks by the Englishman and soon thereafter culminates in the novella told by the companion, agrees quite closely with the terms in which Benjamin describes the sublime irruption of "the expressionless" that arrests the play of semblance in the caesura ("GEA" 340–41).

Had Benjamin acknowledged the applicability of that term to the English visitors' discourse, he might also have noted that the tear is due, not to something foreign, but to the conjunction of the familiar and the foreign that characterizes the uncanny. Unlike Benjamin in his essay, the Lord's companion notices the disquiet caused by the similarity between the Lord's and Eduard's condition; an inquisitive observer of human affairs, he has "in advance, but then especially when arriving in the house, made himself acquainted with all that had happened and was still happening" (*EA* 185). In view of his knowledge of the predicament of Charlotte and Ottilie, it is all the more curious that, having presented "a series of strange, instructive, cheerful, moving, and terrible stories" for the diversion of the ladies, the companion ends with "an admittedly odd but none the less gentler happening, and did not guess how near it was to his listeners" (*EA* 186). That embarrassingly familiar story is of course the novella "Strange Neighbors."

What we must now examine with great care are the tantalizingly vague comments made by the novelistic narrator following the embedded novella. These comments concern the novella's relevance to the innermost concerns of the novelistic characters:

> The story-teller paused [*machte eine Pause*], or rather had already finished before he noticed that Charlotte was greatly agitated; indeed, she rose and with a gesture of apology left the room. She knew the

> story. Those things had happened in reality to the captain and the daughter of a neighbouring family, not entirely as the Englishman had described them, it is true, but in the chief features there was no distortion [*in den Hauptzügen nicht entstellt*], only in the details it had been developed and embellished, as is usually the case when stories of that kind pass from mouth to mouth and finally through the imagination of an intelligent and sensitive narrator [*die Phantasie eines geist- und geschmacksreichen Erzählers*]. In the end scarcely anything and almost everything remains as it was [*Es bleibt zuletzt meist alles und nichts, wie es war*]. (EA 194, translation modified)

Benjamin makes only passing references to the plot connection noted by the narrator between the novel and the embedded novella ("GEA" 331, 333). He summarily dismisses the linkage as a red herring, a banal exoteric explanation for Charlotte's distress that merely serves to conceal the deeper significance of the "saving correspondences" between the novel and the novella ("GEA" 361–62). That deeper significance resides, according to Benjamin, in the antithetical relation underscored by the correspondences. Accordingly, Benjamin locates the true reason for the two women's vehement turning-away from the novella in the offense caused by the heroine's "surrender of beauty" and "urgent, healing wildness," these being hallmarks of the genuine love that eludes them ("GEA" 344).

It would be easier to accept Benjamin's antithetical construction if the narrator's intriguing comments were the sole indication of a plot connection between the novel and the novella. However, that is not the case. The incident from the captain's past is also mentioned in chapter 4 of part 1, apropos of the precautions taken by the protagonists to forestall the threat of drowning posed by the ubiquitous lakes and waterways of the estate: "Eduard let slip the remark that a case of that sort had made a very strange and momentous intervention into his friend's life [*in dem Leben seines Freundes auf die seltsamste Weise Epoche gemacht*]. But when the captain said nothing in reply and seemed to be evading some unhappy memory, Eduard likewise went no further, and Charlotte too, being herself in a general way *au courant*, passed over the remark" (*EA* 27). Thus, the narrator's comments following the novella only render more precise an earlier allusion, carefully planted by Goethe, to the captain's prehistory. Given the obvious importance of this matter, Benjamin's failure to take it into account cannot be dismissed as a sign of oversight. Rather, we must assume a theoretical commitment on Benjamin's part that is sufficiently central to skew a reading that is otherwise finely attuned to textual details. In what follows, I attempt an interpretation of the occluded plot connection between the novel and the novella with a view to clarifying this commitment.

The first thing to note here is that both passages adverting to the captain's prehistory show us Goethe engaged in the same sort of artful obfuscation, which draws attention to the importance of the intimated connection but withholds the specifics. Thus, even if we consider the two passages together, they raise more questions than they answer. First, they fail to clarify whether the captain was the male protagonist or the spurned bridegroom of the novella—a question with obvious implications for the nature of the embarrassment that prompts Charlotte to leave the room. Second, the narrator's remarks are so provocatively coy that one cannot help wondering if his assurance regarding the faithful preservation of "the chief features" of the story ("as is usually the case when stories of that kind pass from mouth to mouth") is merely an ironic gloss on the notorious unreliability of oral transmission. The sense of mystery only deepens in the wake of the narrator's cryptic and deeply paradoxical claim that "scarcely anything and almost everything" is left unchanged in such a transmission.

Finally, a third perplexity is posed by the narrator's claim that the Englishman had "paused, or rather had already finished" when Charlotte got up and left. The narrator thus refuses to decide whether the story is now complete or perhaps there is still something else to be reported, in which case the "unheard-of event" that according to Goethe's famous definition defines the novella as such remains literally unheard because of Charlotte's inability to hear it. This equivocation about the act of storytelling corresponds to an ambiguity in the story told, and in particular in the comment concerning the children's demand for parental blessing: "and who could have refused it!" (*EA* 193, translation modified). It is of course tempting to read the question as a rhetorical one—which is precisely what Benjamin does ("GEA" 333). The storyteller's question would then echo the parents' rhetorical questions: "'Who am I seeing?' the mothers cried. 'What am I seeing?' cried the fathers" (*EA* 192, translation modified). On this reading, no one any longer has the power to refuse the children's demand, for, as Benjamin puts it, "the lovers step out maturely from the ties with their parental home, and . . . transform its inner power" ("GEA" 331). However, if the question mark customarily placed at the end of a rhetorical question serves to underscore the constative force of the sentence, conversely, the exclamation mark at the end of the last sentence of the companion's narration deviates from rhetorical convention and thus reintroduces the hint of a question. This hint is reinforced by the suggestion that perhaps the companion only meant to pause for a moment, and the real conclusion has been preempted by Charlotte's departure.

The Lacuna of Prehistory

We have thus arrived at another curious pause in narration. Similar to the "pause for breath" that Kraus inserts into Luxemburg's letter and the pause that Adorno postulates after the Homeric "saving line" identified by Murray, this pause too is not "in" the text of the novella but is the effect of a constructive citation. In particular, it is Goethe's narrator who leaves open the possibility that perhaps the companion merely paused when Charlotte stood up and left. What might this possibility entail? Pausing for a moment could be the companion's way of registering through his own performance what arguably constitutes the true "unheard-of event" of the novella, namely, the fact that "everyone/the whole world fell silent in astonishment [*da alle Welt staunend verstummte*]" in response to the children's demand, possibly indicating that nobody any longer had the authority to refuse it.[10] Yet we cannot exclude the opposite possibility either. That is to say, the pause might also register the stunned disappointment that overwhelms the storyteller as he prepares to report the parents' response.

What the novelistic narrator thus leaves open is the question of whether the lovers' demand for the blessing of the parents is backed by a transcendent warrant so powerful that assent cannot be denied, or it is simply a heartfelt plea that might still be met with refusal. Because the narrator equivocates between conclusion and interruption of the narrative, the ensuing chapter break marks something that remains unsaid, indeed expressionless: namely, an all-important truth that the narrator of the novel either withholds, in complicity with the protagonists' false tact, or more likely cannot bring himself to decide. What I am suggesting, then, is that the second caesura in *Elective Affinities* is not the novella itself—as Benjamin's interpretation implies—but the break that follows upon its equivocal ending.

The lacuna that becomes visible at this point has to do with the backstory to the novelistic plot, which in many ways constitutes the hidden center of the novel. Benjamin's comments on this matter have a direct bearing on his attempted "decisive transformation" of Kantian philosophy. In particular, these comments should be read against the backdrop of Benjamin's thesis that the criterion of a genuine decision lies "in the character of the experience [*Erfahrung*] preceding the decision," where experience is to be understood as an integral dimension in contradistinction to lived experience ("GEA" 347). Although Benjamin's interpretation strongly suggests that the bond between Eduard and Charlotte does not rest on such an unshakable foundation, arguably his more important suggestion on this point is that Goethe failed to answer this question in an unequivocal fashion. Presumably because Goethe could not resolve his struggle against the mythic right that tends to usurp the hollowed-out institution of marriage, in writing *Elective Affinities* he tried to have it both ways. That is to say, he could neither assert that Eduard's and Charlotte's marriage was based on a genuine decision, nor condone their adulterous passion on the grounds that it was not. Benjamin suggests that the backstory of the novelistic plot is an artful device that allows Goethe to leave this question open:

> If this necessary condition of conjugal fidelity is given [namely, the criterion of integral experience], then fulfillment of duty amounts to its sufficient condition. Only when one of the two can remain free

> of doubt as to whether it was there can the cause of the rupture in the marriage be stated. Only then is it clear whether the rupture is necessary from the outset [*von Hause aus*]: whether, through reversal, salvation is still to be hoped for. And with this, that prehistory which Goethe devised for the novel comes forth as evidence of the most unerring feeling. Earlier, Eduard and Charlotte already loved one another, yet despite this they entered into an empty marriage bond before uniting with each other. Only in this one way, perhaps, could the question remain in the balance: the question of where, in the life of both spouses, the blunder lies—whether in their earlier irresoluteness or in their present infidelity. For Goethe had to sustain the hope that a bonding which had already once been victorious was destined to last now, too. . . . Yet since union is no longer granted to the couple, at the end the question prevails, which, doing the work of exculpation, accompanies everything: Wasn't that merely liberation from an undertaking which was misguided from the start? ("GEA" 347–48, translation modified)

If the flashbacks given in the opening chapters have the function of keeping this question in suspense as regards Eduard and Charlotte, the riddles posed by the framing of the novella inject into the narrative a corresponding uncertainty concerning the captain's past. The caesura that separates the novella from the novel signals a failure on the novelistic narrator's part, and indeed on Goethe's part, to clarify the captain's prehistory and thereby to adopt an unequivocal stance regarding the dilemma facing him, and by extension, the other characters. One might go even further and say that the caesura marks a failure to complete the work as a self-contained construct that projects a determinate fictional universe. The puzzlement that lingers in the wake of this caesura acknowledges the fact that the significance of a given act is often a function of antecedent events that are themselves shrouded in obscurity and hence require further retrogressive inquiry, and so on ad infinitum.[11] To the extent that it opens up this vertiginous perspective, the novella introduces the register of the sublime not only through its plot elements—the fierceness of the heroine, the violent current of the river—and through its vexing impact on the companion's audience, but also and more importantly by pointing to something that eludes representation in the text. The obscurity of the prehistory undermines the epistemic and moral authority of the narrator as well as of the author. Here, to quote Benjamin's formulation, "something beyond the poet interrupts the language of the poetry" ("GEA" 341). The unresolved struggle between myth and liberation that Goethe was unable to decide surfaces in the novelistic narrator's indecision, which in turn prevents an unambiguous resolution of the English companion's narration.

Since the narrator does not decide the question regarding the backstory but the text keeps artfully teasing this question, the reader is left to weigh hints in favor of each alternative. Let us briefly review, then, the alternative possibilities of filling the lacunae left in the novel. To begin with the most straightforward alternative, the captain may be identical with the spurned bridegroom of the novella (1). This would imply that the repeated retelling and transmission of the original story altered only such relatively insignificant matters as the captain's social status. In terms of Benjamin's ethical reflection, this version of the backstory would suggest that whatever attraction had once existed between the captain and the girl of the novella was not strong enough to become "master of the world" ("GEA" 345), presumably, because its basis was not a decision born of integral experience. The memory of this bond, while embarrassing for the captain and Charlotte, would hardly explain Charlotte's vexation, and it would not stand in the way of the decision that they would have to make in order to enter a new and lasting union.

However, the novelistic narrator suggests that the events related in the novella happened to the captain and "the daughter of a neighbouring family [*Nachbarin*]," and this echo of the title of the novella suggests that the captain may actually be the male protagonist of the novella (2). The question that arises, then, is why the captain is unattached in the novel. In filling this lacuna, we must choose either of three suppositions. According to the first, favored by Wolf Kittler, Friedrich Kittler, and Alexander Honold, the incident recounted in the novella must have ended with the drowning of the girl, and it is only the process of oral transmission that transfigured this disaster into a story of deliverance (2/A).[12] Since, according to Benjamin's stipulation, "every love grown within itself must become master of this world—in its natural exitus, the common (that is, strictly simultaneous) death, or in its supernatural duration, marriage" ("GEA" 345), the lethal outcome of the girl's act, together with the captain's survival and subsequent love for Charlotte, show that the fraught love between the children did not rest on a transcendent warrant. Still, the traumatic memory of the girl's death might preclude the decision that the captain would have to make together with Charlotte in favor of a new marital bond. On this hypothesis, the captain is unattached not by accident but by a psychological necessity rooted in his past. The second possibility is that the precondition of a lasting bond was fulfilled, the children got married, but the girl subsequently died (2/B). This loss would likely stand in the way of a later decision, in the emphatic Benjaminian sense, in favor of a new bond with Charlotte.

The third possibility that we must consider is that the children's love was in fact not founded on a transcendent sanction rooted in integral experience, and hence their marriage did not even come about due to the parents' denial of the authorization demanded by the children—or was destined to fail (2/C). Here, to complicate matters, a further bifurcation is called for. If the final sentence of the companion's narration is read as a rhetorical question, then our supposition would mean that this concluding suggestion of a union founded on an incontestable, transcendent sanction is just a fictional element that accrued to the story as it was passed on by successive storytellers (2/C/a). Alternatively, the clause "and who could have refused it!" could be a prequel to the disappointing revelation—preempted only by Charlotte's departure—that the parents did in fact refuse to confer their blessing on the children (2/C/b).[13] These two cognate versions of the prehistory, similarly to alternative (1), would leave the door open for a decision in favor of a lasting bond between the captain and Charlotte.

André François-Poncet, whose 1910 book earned the epithets "shallow" and "bloated" from Benjamin ("GEA" 337), takes for granted that the captain is the hero of the novella. Benjamin, for his part, voices doubt regarding this view in his unpublished notes. "Is the captain really the saving hero in the novella and not the rejected one?" he asks.[14] Whether Benjamin rejected the latter hypothesis as unilluminating or he could neither solve the puzzle nor explain why it had to persist, in the essay he cuts through the Gordian knot by declaring the whole conundrum to be a red herring. Instead, his argument is single-mindedly focused on the antithetical relation between the novel and the embedded novella. Why Benjamin sidelines the plot connection between the two is a question to which we are not quite ready yet to hazard an answer. For we must first identify that conjecture about the captain's past which is most in line with Benjamin's interpretation of the novel as a whole. It seems reasonable to assume that the implications of this conjecture might shed some light on the motive behind Benjamin's avoidance of the whole issue. In other words, we have to assess each of the hypotheses just outlined in view of Benjamin's critical orientation.

Let us begin, then, with hypothesis (1), according to which the captain is the spurned bridgegroom of the novella. We can dismiss this possibility because it presumes a coincidence that seems too striking in view of its ultimate irrelevance to the plot of the novel. Moreover, the prominence and the teasing suggestiveness of the narrator's comments on the transformative power of oral transmission make it appear unlikely that this power affected only such minor details as those pertaining to the captain's social standing. We must see, then, if there is any basis in the text for choosing between (2/A), (2/B), and (2/C). If (2/A) or (2/B) held true and the incident had ended with the girl's drowning, then the upshot of the nexus between the novella and the novel would be that the death of a beloved inflicts an irremediable trauma upon the survivor. Although plausible enough, this lesson seems unilluminating in the broader context of the novel and irrelevant to the broader concerns evident in Benjamin's essay.

If, however, (2/C) held true, then the union between the captain and the girl never came about, or eventually foundered, in the absence of a transcendent warrant based on integral experience. This hypothesis can draw textual support from the narrator's remarks in chapter 4 of part 1. The suggestion that an incident involving the danger of drowning "had made a very strange and momentous intervention [*auf die seltsamste Weise Epoche gemacht*]" in the captain's life and left him with "an unhappy memory [*eine traurige Erinnerung*]" (*EA* 27) is too equivocal and lacking in gravity to suggest a deadly outcome. It is, however, consistent with a happy rescue from the river followed by an anticlimactic foundering of the union. What matters above all, however, is the implication of this hypothesis about the backstory for the current plight of the lovers. For this version of the past would pose no insurmountable obstacle to a new union between the captain and Charlotte; which is to say that this backstory cannot justify the lovers' indecision. Their failure to fight for a happy resolution would thus have to be chalked up to that bourgeois decorum which complacently adheres to abstract scruples devoid of experiential substance, and which Benjamin's essay shows to be the hallmark of an incomplete enlightenment. This is clearly the hypothesis about the backstory that is most consistent with Benjamin's critical agenda.

Moreover, this version of the backstory also explains the fact that Charlotte feels compelled to leave the room at the very point in the novella when the narration hovers irresolutely between resolution and irresolution. To recall a point made earlier, we cannot be certain if Charlotte's exit is a reaction to the rhetorical question concluding the novella (2/C/a) or it cuts short the novella just before the narration reaches a disappointing conclusion (2/C/b). When Goethe's narrator explains Charlotte's departure with the words "she knew the story," the implication cannot be that she knows the novella itself as a verbal artifact; what she knows, presumably, is the factual truth that has been embellished and, to a degree unknown to us, transformed in the novella. That is to say, following the hypothesis we have just adopted, Charlotte knows full well that the captain's love for the girl eventually proved transient and hence does not justify her and the captain's indecision. Crucially, however, what seems to disconcert Charlotte is not the familiarity of the incident on which the novella is based. If *that* was what vexed this woman portrayed as a paragon of self-possession, then she would not wait until the end of the English companion's narration to get up and leave. The fact that she leaves when she does suggests that what unsettles her is not the real incident of which she is reminded but the story being narrated, irrespective of its factual accuracy. More specifically, she cannot bear to find out whether or not the story has come to an end with the phrase: "and who could have refused it!" (*EA* 193, translation modified).

What thus remains in suspense is the bundle of questions we have just reviewed: whether the storyteller has ended his story or only paused, whether his question is rhetorical or not—and most importantly, whether or not the novella has a happy ending that shows the children's love to be confirmed by a genuine decision founded on integral experience. Since, according to our hypothesis, the children of the real incident did not as a matter of fact attain to such a decision, this last question can be rephrased as asking whether the novella is an accurate account of a failed love, or the product of a transmission that has turned the story of that failure into a utopian tale of fulfillment.

It is as if Charlotte could not bear to find out the answer to this question—as if she had to arrest the narrative in a state of suspense between a disappointing truth and its fictional utopian transfiguration. Each of these possible resolutions of the ambiguity would confront her with something unbearable. A factually accurate conclusion to the story would disappoint whatever utopian wish she may secretly harbor; whereas a fictionalized happy outcome would imply a severe indictment of her decorum. Since Charlotte is a fictional figure, the fact that her unease in the face of a piece of fiction here becomes formally significant—determining as it does the discontinuous transition from the embedded novella to the novel—ultimately attests to Goethe's ambivalence, his inability to either wholeheartedly affirm or dismiss the ethical ideal that would find vindication in an unequivocally happy resolution of the novella. Hence the caesura introduced by Charlotte's departure, which suspends the narrative progression of the novella on the brink of the decision between disappointment and redemption, anecdote and fairy tale, factual truth and fictional transfiguration.[15]

Storytelling

The argument of the previous section directs our attention to the process of oral transmission that resulted in the novella, and to its power to transmute the factual truth. Benjamin's failure to give serious consideration to the framing of the novella prevents him from addressing this matter, even though it touches on one of his central concerns. On this point, in fact, we need not resort to new or borrowed theoretical constructs. For we can consult the reflections on storytelling that Benjamin himself would develop more than a decade later in his great essay on Nikolai Leskov.[16]

To draw on these reflections in the present context might appear like a conflation between distinct stages of Benjamin's intellectual trajectory. However, such a procedure is justified by an underappreciated continuity in Benjamin's preoccupations. As we have seen, the overarching concern with integral as opposed to lived experience (*Erfahrung* versus *Erlebnis*), which will feature prominently in Benjamin's late writings, already determines the terms in which the essay on *Elective Affinities* approaches the problem of novelistic narration and its bearing on ethical quandaries. We have also seen that the narrator's stance in the caesura of *Elective Affinities* owes its authority, according to Benjamin, to an expressionless truth that transcends every authorial intention and only becomes accessible in light of a chance biographical episode recalled by an observer. This view of Goethe's narrator anticipates Benjamin's later characterization of the challenge to which Proust had to rise: namely, that of an isolated individual for whom it has become "a matter of chance . . . whether he can take hold of his experience" because his "inner concerns" are no longer connected by integral experience to his external situation and his place in a shared lifeworld (*SW* 4:315). Given this continuity, it seems legitimate to consider the narrator's remarks on the genesis of the embedded novella in light of the physiognomy of the storyteller that Benjamin would outline in the late 1930s.

It will suffice here to recall only the most directly relevant features of that physiognomy. "Experience [*Erfahrung*] which is passed on from mouth to mouth is," as Benjamin declares in 1936, "the source from which all storytellers have drawn" (*SW* 3:144). As it emerges quite clearly already in Benjamin's early neo-Kantian reflections, experience in this sense is not a transaction between subject and object that yields mathematizable knowledge. Rather, it is a "systematic specification of knowledge," where knowledge is "a sphere of total neutrality in regard to the concepts of both subject and object" that possesses the authority of a "doctrine," or *Lehre* (*SW* 1:104, 108). Stories are vehicles of experience in this sense inasmuch as the process of their handing-down transcends the opposition between the individual's subjective consciousness and the objectivity of her social world. A story that participates in such a living tradition "does not aim to convey the pure 'in itself' or gist of a thing, like information or a report. It submerges the thing into the life of the storyteller, in order to bring it out of him again. Thus, traces of the storyteller cling to a story the way the handprints of the potter cling to a clay vessel" (*SW* 3:149). What the storyteller remembers and passes on is not factual information but "counsel," practical "wisdom," which is "less an answer to a question than a proposal concerning the continuation of a story which is in the process of unfolding" (*SW* 3:144–45). The bearing of this ethical conception of storytelling on *Elective Affinities* may be inferred from Benjamin's claim that, whereas the plot of the novel ends with a catastrophe that remains a merely "phenomenal" event, the potentially lethal catastrophe of the embedded novella—the girl's leap into the river—occupies the "center" of the story, where it functions as an "animating principle" that brings about the resolution ("GEA" 331). In other words, the "unheard-of event" of the novella is not just a disastrous incident, but the didactic vehicle of a practical wisdom regarding the need for a daring wager, guided by remembrance, to resolve an impasse.

A further theme in the essay on Leskov that must be mentioned here concerns the role of iterated retelling in endowing stories with normative authority under the premodern regime of epic wisdom. Following Valéry, Benjamin writes of "the perfect things in nature—flawless pearls, full-bodied mature wines, truly developed creatures" that have been produced by "a long chain of causes that are all similar to one another," and which people in the premodern era used to imitate by fabricating "miniatures, ivory carvings elaborated to the point of greatest perfection, stones that are perfect in polish and engraving, lacquerwork or paintings in which a series of thin, transparent layers are placed one on top of the other." Stories that survive in oral traditions develop by a similar "slow piling up, one on top of the other, of thin, transparent layers which constitute the most appropriate image of the way in which the perfect narrative is revealed through the layers of various retellings" (*SW* 3:150).

In his essay on Leskov, Benjamin invokes as a model case of epic storytelling Johann Peter Hebel's celebrated calendar story "Unexpected Reunion" (*SW* 3:151–52). Based on a real incident, this story recounts how the corpse of a young miner killed in an accident was found decades later deep in the mine—preserved by the chemical effect of minerals in such perfect condition that the aged bride's reunion with the dead miner prefigured their future reunion beyond the grave. Against the backdrop of Benjamin's argument, we may understand this story as an allegory for that slow process of transmutation by transmission which according to Benjamin imitates a slow natural process. In a celebrated passage cited by Benjamin, Hebel identifies the year 1809 as the time of this promise of reunion beyond the grave. It cannot have escaped Benjamin's attention that the same year also saw the publication of the novel by Goethe that ends with the narrator's gesture toward "some future day" when the lovers resting in their grave will finally "wake together" (EA 247).

If we are to believe Goethe's narrator, the story of deliverance presented in the novella emerged precisely through the type of transformative process just described.[17] In order to understand why this process might have effected a transfiguration of disaster into deliverance, we can turn to a passage from the essay "On Some Motifs in Baudelaire" that takes up Benjamin's lifelong preoccupation with Goethe:

> "What one wishes for in one's youth, one has in abundance in old age," said Goethe. The earlier in life one makes a wish, the greater one's chances that it will be fulfilled. The further a wish reaches out in time, the greater the hopes for its fulfillment. But it is experience [*Erfahrung*] that accompanies one to the far reaches of time, that fills and articulates time. Thus, a wish fulfilled is the crowning of experience. (*SW* 4:331)

Because integral experience owes its coherence and intelligibility to a tacitly shared idea of happiness, the stories that serve as vehicles for such experience tend in the process of their transmission to give increasingly clear expressions to that vision. As the desires and fantasies of subsequent storytellers are deposited in it, the story is gradually reconfigured to represent not the factual truth about what actually happened but what might have happened and indeed what ought to have happened—a truth that is shared and binding precisely because it is counterfactual. Thus anecdotes become fairy tales.

The fairy tale is the paradigm of the story because it offers counsel in the face of the very source of all exigencies afflicting humans, namely, myth. Benjamin's comments on this point anticipate with striking precision the dialectic of myth and enlightenment that Horkheimer and Adorno will outline a few years later:

> "And they lived happily ever after," says the fairy tale. The fairy tale, which to this day is the first tutor of children because it was once the first tutor of mankind, secretly lives on in the story. The first true storyteller is, and will continue to be, the teller of fairy tales. Whenever good counsel was at a premium, the fairy tale had it, and where the need [*Not*] was greatest, its aid was nearest. This need was the need created by myth. The fairy tale tells us of the earliest arrangements that mankind made to shake off the nightmare which myth had placed upon its chest . . . The wisest thing—so the fairy tale taught mankind in olden times, and teaches children to this day—is to meet the forces of the mythical world with cunning and with high spirits. (This is how the fairy tale polarizes *Mut* [courage], dividing it dialectically into *Untermut*—that is, cunning—and *Übermut* [high spirits]) The liberating magic which the fairy tale has at its disposal does not bring nature into play in a mythical way, but points to its complicity with liberated man. (*SW* 3:157)

It is not hard to see how this characterization of the fairy tale applies to the novella in *Elective Affinities*. The "strange neighbors" achieve deliverance by entrusting themselves to a natural force that turns out to be, in Benjamin's words, complicitous with liberated man, or in Goethe's words, "a friendly element for whoever knows it well and is able to manage it" (*EA* 191). The children's death-defying leap into the river may be viewed as a "high-spirited" counterpart to the "low-spirited" cunning that guides Odysseus's mimetic adaptations to the forces of myth. The juxtaposition is all the less far-fetched because Benjamin's identification of the seafarer as one of the two archetypes of the storyteller all but invites an extension of his line of thought to Odysseus.

It is also the archetype of the seafarer that at first appears to find embodiment in the English Lord and his companion. Through the detour leading to the companion's narration, the familiar story about the captain is transmuted into a fable of redemption. This fairy tale possesses an aura not unlike that of the stories told by seafarers: "intelligence [*Kunde*] that came from afar—whether over spatial distance (from foreign countries) or temporal (from tradition)—possessed an authority which gave it validity, even when it was not subject to verification" (*SW* 3:147). We can now appreciate the complementarity between Eduard's military adventures abroad, whose failure to make any experiential difference all but guarantees a disastrous homecoming, and the long detour mediated by the English travelers which allows the story about the captain to return to its source with a redemptive difference precisely while Eduard is away. Through this complementarity, Goethe's novel opposes the productivity of integral experience to that sterile regime of lived experience which begins to be consolidated in this very period.[18]

Yet we should not simply conflate the English Lord's companion with the seafarers who brought fables of faraway lands in the premodern era. Because the story in which the novella originated passed "from mouth to mouth and finally through the imagination of an intelligent and sensitive narrator," the chain of transmission that led from Germany to England and back is not a homogenous one. The story first traversed an anonymous crowd by mouth-to-mouth transmission (*den Mund der Menge*) in order finally to be returned to its source by an ironically reflective, cosmopolitan citizen of the nation at the vanguard of modernity around 1800. The novella thus came about by a process that crossed the threshold separating the premodern realm of epic wisdom from the "birthplace of the novel," namely, "the individual in his isolation . . . who can no longer speak of his concerns in exemplary fashion, who himself lacks counsel and can give none" (*SW* 3:146). This is why the novelistic narrator's term "*Erzähler*" for the English companion should be translated as "narrator" rather than as "storyteller." Instead of counsel, this visitor has only diversion, natural-scientific knowledge, and medical expertise to offer to his audience (*EA* 194–96).

And yet, if the novella recited by this narrator nevertheless succeeds in salvaging something of the power of integral experience under modern conditions, it is precisely because the archaic wisdom that accrued to the story during its passage through a traditional lifeworld subsequently received the imprint of reflective subjectivity. It is by conjoining these two perspectives that the novella can portray that near-miraculous reconciliation of freedom with embeddedness which defines the utopia envisioned in Benjamin's reading:

> For it is certain that the lovers step out maturely from the ties with their parental home, and no less certain that they transform its inner power. . . . For both of them not only the abyss of sex but even that of family has closed . . . Even the greatest extremity does not expel the two young lovers [of the novella] from the circle of their own people . . . ("GEA" 331–32)

The novella thus transfigures the captain's obscure past through the interposition of a dual optic that combines the archaic with the modern. To that extent, the genesis of the novella exemplifies what Ernst Bloch called the synchronicity of the nonsynchronous: namely, the potentially revolutionary co-presence of progressive aspirations with the utopian energies latent in vestiges of premodern, earthbound life.[19] Construed in Blochian terms, the novella presents a revolutionary conjunction between the cosmopolitan, reflective modernity embodied by the two Englishmen and the archaic anonymity of the multitude who handed down the story about the captain to them. The intrusion of the two Englishmen into the seemingly self-sufficient life of the estate thus reflects the same necessity which finds expression in the epigrammatic last sentence of Adorno's excursus on Odysseus: "Only as novel is the epic transmuted into fairy tale" (*DE* 62). Only a novelistic, modern sensibility can transform the epic wisdom preserved in the story about the captain into a fairy tale concluding with a utopian vision.

The key role of spatiotemporal distance in charging the sad story about the captain with utopian anticipation points ahead to a motif in Benjamin's later reflection on storytelling as a medium of integral experience. In his late essay on Baudelaire, Benjamin associates this anticipation with a symbol evocative of cosmic space: "a wish fulfilled is the crowning of experience. In folk symbolism, distance in space can take the place of distance in time; that is why the shooting star, which plunges into infinite space, has become the symbol of a fulfilled wish."[20] In a way, however, this shooting star now begins to resemble a comet that periodically returns in the stellar constellation of Benjamin's oeuvre. The essay on *Elective Affinities*, we may recall, located the hard caesura of the novel in Goethe's comparison of hope to a falling star, evoked in terms that equivocate between shooting star and comet. As we can see now, in one of the last texts written by Benjamin, the shooting star returns to symbolize the utopian fulfillment whose positive image Benjamin earlier discerned in "Strange Neighbors"—the other, soft, caesura of *Elective Affinities*. The line in which the shooting star speeds along over Eduard's and Ottilie's heads thus terminates in that infinitely distant state of reconciliation which lies on the far side of the equivocal chapter break ending the novella.

Benjamin's Aporia

We are now in a position to hazard a conjecture as to why Benjamin sidelines the framing of the embedded novella and its connection to the novelistic plot. The central role of the novella for Benjamin's interpretation emerges clearly from the scheme that he outlined in preparing to write his essay. According to this scheme, the inventorying of the mythic material content in the first part was to play the role of a "thesis"; the demonstration of the redemptive content of the novella in the second part constituted the "antithesis"; and the third part devoted to hope yielded the "synthesis" (*GS* 1/3:835–37). Although scholars writing about the essay often assume that it follows this outline, there is presumably a good reason why Benjamin abstained from using the pseudo-Hegelian triad of concepts in the essay. Consider Benjamin's formulation for the relation between redemption and hope: "to the certainty of blessing that, in the novella, the lovers take home with them responds [*erwidert*] the hope of redemption that we nourish for all the dead" ("GEA" 355, translation modified). In chapter 1 I argued that the hope registering in the narrator's sentence may be understood in terms of the negatively understood principle of saving phenomena. It follows that hope's response to the certainty transpiring from the novella does not have the character of a reassuring conclusion at all. Instead, we are dealing here with an uncertainty responding to a certainty. Such a response cannot be construed as a synthesis between the actuality of myth and the utopia of reconciliation. As in the relation between experience and freedom, in this connection, too, the key to understanding Benjamin's conception lies in his previously quoted remark in "On the Program of the Coming Philosophy." "Besides the concept of synthesis," to recall Benjamin's remark, "another concept, that of a certain nonsynthesis of two concepts in another, will become very important systematically, since another relation between thesis and antithesis is possible besides synthesis" (*SW* 1:106). Hope is precisely a determinate relation of nonsynthesis between the actuality of mythic entrapment and the utopia of redemption.

Nevertheless—and herein lies the difficulty facing Benjamin—that nonsynthesis presupposes the positively conceived antithesis of redemption. This idea of redemption had better not be a construct of pure thought. Rather, in order to have some determinate content, it must have a foothold within that which is historically given—in the case of Benjamin's essay, it must have a foothold in the text of *Elective Affinities*. This key desideratum of Benjamin's critical agenda is fulfilled through his interpretation of the novella as a positive presentation of redemption. Without such a construal of the novella, Benjamin's highly formal and necessarily indeterminate theory of the ideal of the problem would be the sole content envisioned in the transient opening of hope in the novel's hard caesura. This would render his interpretation speculative in the pejorative sense as well, in addition to the technical one. As we have seen in chapter 1, the marking of the hard caesura, which shatters the semblance of closed totality that attaches to the novel, does in fact require the critic to overstep the limits of immanent interpretation. However, Benjamin also claims that this act of critical violence responds to a moment of the expressionless latent within the novel, a self-critical moment internal to the novel viewed as a beautiful object. Accordingly, Benjamin's critical project requires him to construe the truth content that manifests itself in the expressionless as more than just a formal, negatively defined ideal of systematic totality to which critique might refer every artwork: that truth content must appear in the novel in a positive form, enlivening the novel's presentation of a historically specific material content displaying a particular philosophical problem. Otherwise put, the hope that flashes up in the narrator's sentence cannot just be a generalized hope for a rational totality that has attained to the status of doctrine, capable of resolving all philosophical questions; the hope at issue must be legible as hope for the settlement of a particular problem, peculiar to a historical lifeworld, that such a future doctrine would lay to rest. Without the luminous backdrop provided by the positive presentation of the novella, the narrator's fleeting invocation of hope in chapter 13 of book 2 would be but an empty gesture.

Yet the problem is that Benjamin's most deeply held commitments likely preclude a positive presentation of utopian transcendence. The framing of the novella presents an embarrassment for Benjamin's reading because it reveals this antinomy entailed by his uncompromising conception of utopian transcendence. The novella owes the determinate, positive content of its utopian projection to its origins within the stagnant social world of the novel—which is to say, to its immanence. Acknowledging the continuity between the oppressive reality portrayed in the novel and the fairy tale of redemption in the novella would therefore have undercut Benjamin's construal of the latter as a moment of radical transcendence. I hope to have shown that Benjamin's later theory of storytelling offers a framework that might allow for something like immanent transcendence, that is to say, for the emergence through storytelling of utopian projections from within the immanence of historical reality. However, although the seeds of the later conception—such as the distinction between integral and lived experience—are already discernible in the essay on *Elective Affinities*, Benjamin is evidently not yet in the position to make use of it.

The antinomial demands of positivity and utopian transcendence can also explain why Benjamin refrains from explicitly referring to the novella as the second caesura of *Elective Affinities*. In thinking about this question, it is instructive to note a seemingly marginal detail in Benjamin's interpretation of the novella. Before commenting on the children's attainment to a redemption that others have yet to reach, Benjamin evokes the "great image [*Bild*] of the boat landing at the place of their union" ("GEA" 332). This emphasis on the iconic character of the representation of redemption in the novella recurs later in the essay when Benjamin compares the novella to "an image [*Bild*] in the darkness of a cathedral—an image which portrays the cathedral itself and so in the midst of the interior communicates a view of the place that is not otherwise available" ("GEA" 352). If not quite "Nazarene"—to recall Benjamin's pejoratively used epithet for the final transfiguration of Ottilie ("GEA" 355)—this literary image, centering as it does on the image of a cathedral (*Münster*), nevertheless belongs to a distinctly Christian, and more specifically Catholic, order of representation. What I am suggesting is that, by highlighting the image-character of the novella, Benjamin tacitly acknowledges the fact that it falls under the Judaic prohibition of images. To the extent that the novella paints a positive image of reconciliation, it cannot be taken to represent a utopian transcendence of reality. To confer upon it the status of a caesura would be to compromise the negative theology to which Benjamin is so rigorously committed, and which forbids recognizing "the sublime violence of the true" in any form other than "the expressionless."[21]

The problematic status of the novella in Benjamin's essay thus shows the strain placed upon his reading by the Judaic ban on images. Benjamin is compelled by the logic of his conception to construe the novella as a moment of transcendence, and hence as a second caesura—without which the hard caesura of the narrator's comment would be an isolated, empty gesture—and at the same time he is barred from doing so. Similarly, the novella can serve as a necessary complement to the hard caesura by virtue of its positive content; but the origins of that content within the immanence of the portrayed reality must be elided, for a projection of utopian transcendence cannot draw on the mythic nexus that holds the novelistic characters captive. Thus, in what may be the most drastic instance of critical violence in the entire essay, Benjamin severs the connection between the novel and the novella so as to insist on their antithetical relation. In the words of the poem by Stefan George quoted near the end of the essay, the novella is transformed into a fragment from "higher stars" ("GEA" 355), a meteorite lodged in the fabric of novelistic narration.

It may be tempting to conclude that Benjamin's distinctly Jewish conception of transcendence makes the moment of violence in his reading of Goethe all but inevitable. This would be a premature conclusion, however. Close attention to the framing of the novella suggests a corrective to Benjamin's reading that respects the spirit of his critical project and avoids the violence just described. At the end of the previous chapter, I argued that Adorno reinscribes the Kantian duality of the beautiful and the sublime within the latter register, with the soft caesura of Penelope's speech construed as a variant of the sublime that verges on the positivity of the beautiful; and I indicated that perhaps a similar strategy would turn out to be at work in Benjamin's essay as well. Since—as discussed in chapter 1—Benjamin's conception of the expressionless makes sublimity a moment internal to the beautiful, the reinscription of the distinction between the two within this sublime moment would result in an intricate, recursive structure of aesthetic representation. It is now possible to take up this hypothesis in more precise terms.

While Benjamin's essay does not quite reinscribe the duality of the beautiful and the sublime in the sublime pole, my corrective to his interpretation yields precisely such a structure. Benjamin, as we have just seen, does not succeed in reconciling the antinomial theoretical pressures that surface in his reading of the novella. Although his conception requires him to view the novella as a positive presentation of utopian transcendence, the epistemic authority of the novella can be upheld only if it is construed as a purely negative presentation, a caesura of the expressionless. However, if we attend to the framing of the novella it becomes possible to mark here a soft caesura—that is to say, a negative presentation that may nevertheless be called positive in a qualified sense, *relative* to the unmitigated negativity of the hard caesura in the narrator's comment on hope. For my argument about the framing of the embedded novella could be summarized in the claim that the soft caesura of *Elective Affinities* is not the novella itself but the expressionless pause, marked by a chapter break, that ends the English companion's narration. This moment of arrest suspends the all-important decision between pausing and ending, factual reporting and fictional transfiguration, disappointment and fulfillment. However vivid and luminous the fable of decision presented in the novella, the finally decisive moment of reconciliation is not included in the chain of narrated events. Rather, reconciliation remains a mere possibility that the narrative evokes through its cessation, and through its refusal to dispel the shadow of doubt even as it propels our hopeful imagination beyond the point of arrest.

Chapter 5

✦

Adaptations, Conclusions, Limits

The Song of the Cicada

When Hölderlin defined the caesura as a "counter-rhythmic rupture," he thereby highlighted a moment in tragedy at which the flow of language is disrupted by a musical principle of organization through disarticulation. In the caesura, the proximity between literature and music that everywhere informs Hölderlin's poetological writings reaches a point of utmost and tense intimacy. It is thus not surprising that Adorno found the concept of caesura congenial to his thinking about music and repeatedly made use of it in his musicological writings. Nor does it seem accidental that Adorno's borrowing of the term from Benjamin can be traced back to the conversations prompted by their joint encounter with a musical work, namely, Alban Berg's opera *Wozzeck*.

Apart from this encounter, however, Benjamin would appear to belong to a distinguished group of writers whose attunement to language required a displacement, or even a drastic sidelining, of musical sensibility.[1] In Benjamin's case, to be sure, one cannot speak of an outright suppression. Intriguing observations regarding sound, acoustics, and even music do occasionally rise to the surface of his writings.[2] The scarcity of Benjamin's comments on music is nevertheless striking when compared to the sheer volume of his reflections on other art forms. The essay on *Elective Affinities* is a notable exception to this rule. Towards the end of the essay, the topic of music assumes a prominence in light of which one cannot but wonder what Adorno might have made of these reflections. Let me hazard a speculation regarding this connection, for it is important enough in its own right, and by addressing it I can set the stage for a broader assessment of the lessons that have emerged from my argument.

Benjamin's comments on the role of music in Goethe's novel are suggestive and cryptic in equal measure. In attempting to make sense of them, it helps to identify the two premises that guide these reflections: first, that music is the art form least implicated in semblance ("GEA" 350), and second, that "semblance once again dawns sweetest before its vanishing" ("GEA" 348). The tension between these two premises charges Benjamin's reflections on music with a refractory ambivalence. In keeping with the early Nietzsche's Schopenhauerian conception, Benjamin claims that music does not depend on semblance for its medium. Touching on a deep temperamental basis for his elective affinity with Goethe, Benjamin suggests that those "from the beginning moved in their innermost being by music" are to that extent "proof against the power of living beauty"—in a way in which Goethe was not, and neither was, we may infer, Benjamin himself ("GEA" 349). However, Benjamin complicates the Schopenhauerian-Nietzschean metaphysics of music by suggesting that music can engender a type of second-order semblance that is less apparent, but for that reason more insidious than the first-order semblance endemic to the art forms that traffic in visual or verbal representation. This second-order semblance is prone to arise whenever musical harmony holds out the false promise that reconciliation might be attained without an antecedent interpersonal or political conflict, and without the transcendent warrant which must, according to Benjamin, be secured through the solitary individual's reconciliation with God.

Such is the case with the music-making of the protagonists of Goethe's novel. The musical expression of their merely apparent reconciliation is, as music, not dependent on semblance. Since, however, what the music expresses is a specious idea of reconciliation, music's very freedom from semblance will in this case delude the characters who draw consolation from their joint music-making into thinking that real reconciliation has been achieved. A semblance-free expression of reconciliation is thus mistaken for an expression of real reconciliation. The aesthetic response proper to this delusion is a sentimental "emotion" (*Rührung*) that stops short of deepening to the shattering effect (*Erschütterung*) of Dionysian sublimity ("GEA" 349).

Benjamin associates this shallow musical sentimentality with the cicada, which according to Greek mythology sings without food or drink until it dies; and he draws a suggestive parallel between the mythological transformation of this lowly insect into a stellar constellation and Goethe's transfiguration of Ottilie, whose gently extinguishing beauty suffuses the novel with a lyrical mood. If we now recall that Plato's *Phaedrus* figures cicadas as victims-turned-agents of musical enchantment, indeed as "sirens" whose sleep-inducing noontime song the philosopher must "sail past" and counter with dialectical reasoning, then we may begin to suspect that Adorno's silent dialogue with Benjamin extends into his meditation on the story of Odysseus and the sirens.[3] According to this allegory of the birth of aesthetic subjectivity, song becomes a medium of reconciliation with the nonidentical from which the subject originally had to distinguish itself—but only because the discipline constitutive of the aesthetic stance banishes this reconciliation to the autonomous and hence practically inconsequential domain of pleasing semblance, "beauty deprived of power" (*DE* 26). The figure of the cicada thus establishes a connection between Benjamin's critique of Goethe's lyrical enchantment and the Adornian primordial history of aesthetic subjectivity.

To be sure, Benjamin's suggestion that musical emotion can deepen beyond sentimentality to a Dionysian shattering still leaves open the possibility of a liberating sort of musical experience. It is presumably music of the emancipatory type that Benjamin has in mind when he writes that the world inhabited by the music-making protagonists is in truth "wholly deserted by music," "a mute world" ("GEA" 348, 355). Yet the closing of Benjamin's essay suggests that the distinction between musical sentimentality and the musical sublime is not to be understood as one between "good" and "bad" musical works. Rather, the very same music can be an object of both types of response. This, at least, is one way of understanding Benjamin's closing comments apropos of Stefan George's lines about Beethoven, whose "singing" is said to portend heroic action:

> Before you wage the battle of your star,
> I sing of strife and gains on higher stars.
> Before you seize the body on this star,
> I shape you dreams among eternal stars. ("GEA" 355, translation modified)

These lines appear "destined for a sublime irony," as Benjamin puts it, because even though music can be a spur to emancipatory action, it can also be a substitute for it; and in fact the aestheticism of the George circle strongly tends toward the latter, escapist alternative. Benjamin's reflections on music thus adumbrate the dialectic of emancipatory potential and ideological semblance that will stand in the forefront of Adorno's decades-long meditation on Beethoven.

Wolkenriss, Nebelstreif: Keller

In developing this musical theme, uncovering one last thread in the tacit dialogue between Benjamin's and Adorno's texts was not my only aim. Rather, I also wanted to bring into view a motif in Benjamin's essay, namely, the spurious musical sentimentality symbolized by the transfiguration of the cicada into a celestial constellation. This motif directs our attention to a literary work that involves at a key juncture a similar musical transfiguration, and which can serve as a suitable basis for demonstrating that the double caesura model has considerable heuristic value beyond its application to Homer's and Goethe's narratives. The work I have in mind is "A Village Romeo and Juliet" by Gottfried Keller.

A celebrated exemplar of so-called poetic realism, Keller's novella about "strange neighbors"—to recall the title of Goethe's embedded narrative—recounts the love and death of a boy and a girl whose fathers are caught in a destructive feud over a contested plot of land. My choice of this work is anything but arbitrary. Benjamin praised this novella as "imperishable" in an essay on Keller that was published in 1927, and which notes Keller's affinities with both Homer and Goethe. The Homeric aspect of Keller's work is foregrounded in Benjamin's characterization of Keller's Switzerland as a diminutive version of the universe of the *Odyssey*. As for Goethe, Benjamin links "A Village Romeo and Juliet" to *Elective Affinities* when he claims that Keller's demonstration of the mythic powers unleashed through the hollowing-out of property right parallels the problematic of Goethe's novel.[4] Whether redemptive energies can still surface in the face of this inexorable logic is the question at stake in the passages that I am about to examine. In an attempt to extend the line of critical succession that connects Benjamin's and Adorno's interpretations, I will now consider Keller's novella in terms of the double caesura model in order to illustrate the adaptability and the disclosive potential of that model.

We can begin to address the question regarding the possibility of redemptive moments by turning to a passage in which Keller foregrounds the equivocal character of musical enchantment. Having found a fleeting happiness in the Dionysian musical revelry of a village fair, and just before they resolve to drown themselves in a river, the lovers pause to listen:

> The stillness of the world sang and made music in their souls; they could hear nothing but the soft, pleasant gurgling of the river below, as it slowly flowed by. "How beautiful it is around us! Don't you seem to hear something resounding [*tönen*] like a beautiful song or a ringing of bells?" "It's the swish of the water in the river. Everything else is still." "No, there's something else—here, out there, it resounds everywhere [*überall tönt's*]!" "I believe we hear our own blood swooshing in our ears." ("VRJ" 115, translation modified)

The repeated occurrences of the untranslatable verb *tönen* echo the narrator's earlier comments, which construe the musical enchantment experienced by the lovers as an echo effect amplifying the peal of church bells: "Every sound or distant call that died away in the Sunday stillness sent a shock through their souls [*klang ihnen erschütternd durch die Seele*]; for love is a bell which echoes back anything [*widertönen lässt*], however remote or insignificant, converting it into a peculiar music" ("VRJ" 99, translation modified). Both passages hearken back to the opening scene of the novella, in which the children's innocent-sadistic game takes an ominous turn as they imprison a buzzing fly inside the severed head of a puppet: "As it still had on the red poppy hood, the resonant object [*der Tönende*] now resembled a prophet's head, and the children with their arms around each other listened in profound silence to its oracles and tales" ("VRJ" 57). As Justus Fetscher notes, the children's play with the puppet is a miniaturized enactment of the founding of a new family, which intimates a possibility that would remain unrealized in the novella.[5] To that extent, the episode resembles, in a further miniaturization, the embedded novella that represents the resolution that eludes the protagonists of *Elective Affinities*. To be sure, the idyllic fantasy is rehearsed in a sinister register. Keller's characterization of the buzzing puppet head as a "prophet" led Benjamin to write in this connection of an "orphic head"—a keen deciphering of the oblique way in which this scene unfolding by a river evokes the myth according to which Orpheus's severed head kept singing as it floated down the river.[6] In the compositional logic of Keller's novella, the prophetic buzzing emitted by the severed head of the puppet foreshadows not only the fateful head injury that will reduce Vrenchen's father to nonsensical babbling, but also the intracranial noise that the girl will mistake for the music of the spheres.

For the reader who can look back upon these scenes and notice the proleptic logic linking them, the effect of their linkage is a deflation of the spurious experience of musical sublimity undergone by Vrenchen near the end of the novella. In terms of Benjamin's comments on the cicada as a symbol of a spurious musical transfiguration, one might say that the mythic stellar constellation is brought down to the earth and revealed to be an insect. This effect epitomizes the disenchantment that Keller's narrative furthers even as it incessantly deploys diverse effects of poetic enchantment. Again and again, Keller tentatively suggests transfigurative, astral interpretations of the human lives narrated in the novella. Thus, the two fathers plowing their respective fields are likened in the opening of the novella to "two setting stars" (*wie zwei untergehende Gestirne*, "VRJ" 53, translation modified); and when, years later, their children walk hand in hand on the contested plot of land, the narrator comments that "this happy pair also resemble[s] a constellation [*Sternbild*]," whose harmony is soon disrupted by a "dark star," namely, the "black fiddler" whose unrighteous dispossession gave rise to the feud that now vitiates the children's happiness ("VRJ" 79). To put the matter in the terms of the George poem that Benjamin cites at the end of his essay on *Elective Affinities*, Keller's novella repeatedly asks whether a glimpse of "higher stars" might be caught from "this star," from the earthly realm in which a contested plot of land can divide lovers. The narrator persists in toying with the idea of such a transcendent dimension even as the fateful progression of the plot again and again gives the lie to these intimations.

The interplay between disenchantment and enchantment in Keller's novella has received a nuanced treatment in an essay by Gerhard Kaiser that focuses on Keller's religious imagery.[7] According to Kaiser, the religious vocabulary employed in the narrative marks the children's imaginary transposition of marriage from the sphere of bourgeois convention into an inwardness that demands an ideal unity of spontaneity and norm. Kaiser convincingly argues that the unconditionality of this ideal is born of the characters' inability to face the task of living together under the flawed conditions inherited from their fathers; the ideal marriage they invent together is thus a "a beyond within this world, a transcendence of the world through a falling short of it," a transcendence that can be actualized only through a dreamlike game of make-believe ending in death.[8] It is this dialectic between failure and transcendence, conditioned reality and unconditional ideal, that registers in the narrative stance devised by Keller, which blends absolutization with relativization. The characters are transfigured in recognition of the ideal of perfection enacted in their playful fantasy, but they are treated with humor insofar as this ideal remains a mere figment of "inconsequential inwardness." As Kaiser puts it, the lovers "achieve the heavenly Jerusalem by being, remaining, and becoming children"—a formulation intended to mark both the limited, regressive character of this utopia and its parallels to the pagan Christology that Kaiser identifies in the anticipation of a "heroic child" in Keller's poem "Stille der Nacht."[9]

If Keller recurs to images resonant with Christian soteriology, however, he does so in order to recognize an older divinity. According to Kaiser, Christianity functions in Keller's novella merely as a vocabulary for imagining a perfection that humans cannot realize in the world yet must demand of it, "a god radiant with worldliness" who is revealed only amid human conflicts in the silent splendor of nature. The peculiar *Weltfrömmigkeit*, or "piety towards the world," that Kaiser discerns in Keller's novella is thus tinged with a negative theology. Accordingly, he detects in Keller's tentative projections of a theological dimension something of that "infallible metaphysical tact" which Adorno praised in commenting on Eichendorff's famous counterfactual analogy: "And my soul spread / her wings wide, / flew through the silent countryside / as though she were flying home."[10]

Kaiser briefly extends his argument to passages from other works by Keller that evoke scenes of apotheosis. In these scenes, characters on the verge of death appear in the transfigurative light of celestial apparitions: rays of sun piercing through clouds, ghostly cloud formations lit by the setting sun. Oddly, however, Kaiser neglects to discuss two passages in "A Village Romeo and Juliet" that involve similar effects. These passages introduce narrative caesuras that are aligned with one another in a manner that both recalls and contrasts with the saving line identified by Benjamin and Adorno. Whereas in the sentence highlighted by Benjamin the narrator of *Elective Affinities* invokes the shooting star as a simile, the two caesuras in "A Village Romeo and Juliet" are marked by the actual occurrence of celestial phenomena that complement one another. These are the erratic phenomena that I will now attempt to "save" in the sense elucidated at the end of chapter 1.

The concept of caesura seems especially apt in connection with the first of these junctures, since it marks a moment of arrest even on the level of the plot. The moment in question occurs in the scene in which the two children first encounter each other as young adults in the company of their enraged fathers. The four characters meet on a bridge during a gathering storm, and as the two fathers begin to wrestle with each other, the children make a desperate bid to separate them:

> So for a moment the fight stopped, or rather the entire group strained restlessly back and forth without separating. Meanwhile the young people, pushing further in between their fathers, had come into close contact with each other. At that moment a break in the clouds [*Wolkenriss*] let the bright evening sunshine through, illuminating the girl's face, and Sali looked into this face, so familiar to him, yet now so different, so much more beautiful. ("VRJ" 74)

By chance the momentary standstill, which arrests the group to an emblem, coincides with a sudden illumination. This illumination afforded by a break in the clouds is nothing short of an epiphany, at least if the narrator's characterization of its aftermath is to be trusted. Remembering the encounter the following day, it seems to Sali

> as if he had learned something worthwhile and knew infinitely many good and beautiful things, since he was now so definitely and distinctly aware of what he had seen the day before. This science [*Wissenschaft*] seemed to him as if it had fallen from heaven, and his mind was in a state of endless and happy amazement over it. Yet it seemed as if he had in truth always known and realized that which now filled him with such wonderful sweetness. For there is nothing like the wealth and the unfathomable depth of that happiness which comes to a man in such a clear and distinct form, baptized by a parson and fully provided with a name of its own, one which does not sound like other names. ("VRJ" 75)

Yet this revelation is not an experience of positive plenitude. In fact, Keller emphasizes the negativity and dispossession that this experience involves—its sublimity, however ironically refracted. The sublimity at issue here must be attributed to the imagination, for Sali imagines (*er bildete sich ein*) that he cannot recall the particular features of the "image" (*Bild*) that haunts him. His yearning anamnesis impels him to look for Vrenchen in the village of their shared childhood, and so, as the narrator puts it, "Sali strolled out of the gate toward his old home, which now seemed to him [*zu sein schien*] like a heavenly Jerusalem with twelve shining gates."

It is worth dwelling on this passage for a moment. The locution "seemed to him" might be taken to suggest that the analogy to heavenly Jerusalem is drawn by Sali himself. There are reasons to doubt this, however, not the least of which is the fact that not a single passage can be found in which either Sali or Vrenchen invoke a transcendent authority in their muddled deliberations about love, guilt, and death. Throughout their conversations, the children's thinking is shown to be thoroughly wedded to the immanence of the world. Much the same applies to the story's broader social context. In this society, baptism is merely a bureacratic matter that underpins the legal order, and the journalistic reference to the children's "God-forsaken marriage" that the narrator ironically quotes at the end of the novella is merely an instance of bourgeois hypocrisy—although, importantly, the description happens to be true. The hyperbolic characterizations of Sali's experience as a kind of epiphany are thus clearly instances of what one might describe—playing a variation on Adorno's expression—as lapses into metaphysical tactlessness on the narrator's part, whose perspective here intrudes upon Sali's. Otherwise put, these characterizations express the narrator's construal of how things appear to Sali.

Bearing this in mind, we should ask what might be meant by the analogy between the village and "heavenly Jerusalem," which seems both fitting and wildly out of proportion for a clueless lad who goes by the diminutive form of "Salomon." The analogy has an obvious enough basis in the plot, since Sali's family was forced to sell their land in the village and move to the city, where they now live in poverty and disrepute. However, for readers who are willing to pursue intertextual references—as indeed the very title of the novella invites us to do—the hyperbolic invocation of heavenly Jerusalem gains in weight against the backdrop of Keller's antecedent quotation from Heine's "Jehuda ben Halevy" ("VRJ" 59). For that poem from the cycle "Hebrew Melodies" opens by invoking the injunction to remember Jerusalem from Psalm 137 and goes on to commemorate Judah Halevi, the great twelfth-century Jewish poet and philosopher who died on a pilgrimage to Jerusalem. Whereas Heine portrayed Halevi as a minnesinger whose love for the "dame" Jerusalem was inflamed by reports of the city's decline, its ruins overgrown with weeds, Keller now inverts Heine's allegory by having his protagonist elevate the "old home" he formerly shared with his sweetheart to "a heavenly Jerusalem"—which, to be sure, Sali will soon find in a state of dereliction not unlike the one lamented by Heine's Jerusalem pilgrims.[11] With this inversion, which follows the key operation of the left Hegelian critique of religion that Keller knew so well from Feuerbach's lectures, Keller makes explicit Heine's tacit acknowledgment of the basic anthropomorphism of religion.[12]

To the negative revelation afforded by the sunlight shining through the break in the clouds, there comes in answer a fleeting occlusion of lunar light near the end of the novella. Following the scene of deceptive music discussed earlier, the children betoken their love by exchanging rings:

> "And so we're really and truly engaged now—you're my husband and I'm your wife. Let's think we are, just for a minute—only until that streak of fog [*Nebelstreif*] over the moon has passed, or until we've counted twelve! Kiss me twelve times!" Sali's love was certainly just as strong as Vrenchen's, but for him the question of marriage [*Heiratsfrage*] was not as passionately alive—not so much a definite either-or, and immediate to-be-or-not-to-be—as it was for Vrenchen, who was capable of feeling only the one thing, and saw in it with

> passionate decisiveness a simple issue of life or death. But now at last he saw a light [*jetzt ging ihm endlich ein Licht auf*], and what was womanly feeling in the young girl immediately became in him a wild and hot desire, and his senses were alight with a burning clarity. Vehemently as he had embraced and caressed Vrenchen before, he now did it in a different and more tempestuous way, overwhelming her with kisses. In spite of her own intense feeling Verena noticed this change at once, and a violent trembling coursed through her entire being; but before that streak of fog [*Nebelstreif*] had crossed the moon she too was seized by passion. ("VRJ" 116, translation modified)

In a chiaroscuro effect, the transient occlusion of the moon coincides with a metaphorical "light" seen by Sali. The bid to suspend the fateful course of things for the brief duration of this celestial phenomenon prompts an access of uninhibited passion, the first and last such moment in the novella. This suspension of time is followed by the protagonists' resolve to "go out of this world together" in a bid to transcend time: "We shall have been together—whether for a long time or a short time doesn't matter."

The compound words *Wolkenriss* ("a break in the clouds") and *Nebelstreif* ("a streak of fog") stand for inverse and complementary celestial phenomena which the novella aligns with a subtle poetic logic. The first is a solar phenomenon that affords a sudden illumination, while the second is lunar and causes a temporary darkening. Although both phenomena involve enduring heavenly bodies, their proximate cause is in each case an atmospheric episode of the vaguest, most fleeting and contingent type. These atmospheric phenomena created by celestial light instantiate in a literal manner the concept that the narrator invokes for analogical purposes in relating the lovers' reunion: "They stared at each other for a moment, as if observing an aerial apparition [*Lufterscheinung*]" ("VRJ" 78, translation modified). Actually occurring aerial apparitions charged with allegorical meaning dictate the two decisive turning points in this story of doomed love. As the light emitted by a heavenly body traditionally coded as masculine suddenly shines through the break in the clouds, it reveals to Sali a grand but empty "science" that will prompt him to look for Vrenchen. Correspondingly, the fleeting occlusion of the heavenly body associated with femininity brings to a head "the question of marriage" that occupies Vrenchen's mind. Although the allegorical patterning deployed by Keller is not legible to his characters, nevertheless the two atmospheric apparitions have the power to prompt decisive action because in them the constricting social world is briefly breached by intimations of a wider dimension. The sun shining through the break in the clouds as well as the streak of fog passing before the moon are manifestations of a natural world whose beauty Keller does not tire of celebrating, but whose promise of this-worldly happiness the protagonists eventually decline when they turn down the Black Fiddler's invitation to exit society.

As we have seen, the sequence of the caesuras is crucial to the double caesura model used by Benjamin and Adorno. In Keller's novella, the first caesura must be viewed as an extradiegetic one. Whereas Sali sees only Vrenchen's illuminated face, the narrator also notes the celestial source of illumination. Likewise, it is the narrator's perspective that subsequently intrudes upon Sali's in the analogy to heavenly Jerusalem. Although the fleeting break in the clouds allows a glimpse of a reconciled state to flash up—the lovers exchange smiles and surreptitiously hold hands—this presentation remains negative insofar as it occurs in the midst of the embittered scuffle between the fathers; and accordingly it is followed by Sali's inability to recollect Vrenchen's features. The second caesura, by contrast, occurs within the diegetic frame, in the form of Vrenchen's proposal regarding the passing streak of fog. What we have in this make-believe wedding is a positive presentation, however fleeting and illusory, of reconciliation.

The sequence of the two caesuras reverses that of the caesuras in *Elective Affinities*—and thus conforms to the sequence we find in the *Odyssey*, which Adorno had to reverse in his novelistic reimagining of the epic. Such a sequence might appear to conform to the eschatological pattern of prefiguration and fulfillment. Indeed, the invocation of "heavenly Jerusalem," anticipated by the Heine quote as well as by recurrent allusions to the Song of Songs, participates in a series of textual vignettes that evoke theological motifs. It is telling, however, that these vignettes combine theological resonance with the suggestion of vagrancy and instability. Suffice to note two examples: the droll description of Vrenchen's old bedstead, carried by a farm-boy whom the narrator likens to Samson, as a "moving temple";[13] and the passage in which Vrenchen carries a gingerbread house bought at a church fair and is said to resemble "one of those old paintings of a saintly patron of the church holding in her hand the model of a cathedral or cloister which she has established; but," the narrator adds, alluding to Vrenchen's fantasies of a respectable bourgeois marriage, "the pious founding [*fromme Stiftung*] that Vrenchen had in mind could come to nothing" ("VRJ" 108, translation modified). Kaiser is certainly right to note the thread of Christian allusions that runs through Keller's novella. However, the preponderance of motifs from the Old Testament and the quote from Heine's "Jehuda ben Halevi" make the narrative resonate with another, older variety of religious experience. Again and again, the fateful necessity that condemns the lovers to a lot that mirrors the initial dispossession and forcible vagrancy of the Black Fiddler is allegorically linked to a pervasive loss of metaphysical anchoring, a "transcendental homelessness" (to recall Lukács's famous coinage) whose archetype is the Jewish experience of diaspora.

It is, then, in keeping with these echoes of a theology of nonfulfillment and absence that the eschatological pattern evoked by the alignment of the two caesuras—promise and fulfillment—is subtly undercut by the sequence of the corresponding celestial phenomena, with a sudden illumination followed by an undramatic darkening. This incongruity highlights the contingency of the two apparitions at these plot junctures, as well as the arbitrariness of their investment with transcendent meaning. As for the theological language employed in the rendering of Sali's memory of the illumination, Sali's new "science" has no more to do with the wisdom of King Solomon than does the ringing heard by Vrenchen with the music of the spheres. The supposed singularity of the promise of happiness that Sali has come to associate with Vrenchen's name is ironically undermined when that name is said, in free indirect discourse, to be "one which does not sound like other names"—a claim contradicted by the typologizing use of names in the very title of the novella. The groundlessness of these lofty interpretations of Sali's encounter with Vrenchen is confirmed by the second caesura that answers to the first. For Vrenchen's proposal to treat the streak of fog occluding the moon as a higher sanction for their union is nothing but a whim, no less contingent than that fleeting phenomenon.

Most importantly, the high-minded theological construal that the narrator imposes on Sali's amorous recollection is belied by the fact that the children's passion is, to borrow Benjamin's formulation apropos of *Elective Affinities*, "a vacillating love" over which "the norm of law makes itself master" ("GEA" 345). Since, as the narrator remarks, the children's mutual attraction is fueled by nostalgia for the squandered respectability of their families, they are unable to envision a lasting bond without the sanction of the very social order whose corruption has entrapped them in mythic guilt in the first place. The commentary given by Keller's narrator is unambiguous on this point. We are told that "the question of marriage [*Heiratsfrage*]" was for Vrenchen—in a surprising echo of Kierkegaard—"a definite either-or [*ein bestimmtes Entweder-Oder*]," the "one thing" alone that she was capable of feeling, and that "the idea of being a bride raged in her blood [*das Brautwesen tobte ihm im Blute*]" ("VRJ" 116, 113, translation modified). These passages suggest a thoroughgoing captivity to the mythic delusion of which Stanley Corngold, writing about Benjamin's essay on *Elective Affinities*, offers the following epigrammatic diagnosis: "what one marries par excellence is marriage, the marriage par excellence of the banal and the obscure."[14] It is the lovers' inability to exit this narrowly circumscribed mythic realm that warrants the narrator's explanation of their failure in terms of their "inexperienced passion" (*unerfahrene Leidenschaft*), a phrase that seems particularly apt in view of Benjamin's ethical reflections on Goethe's novel. In the novella embedded in *Elective Affinities*, the remembered experience of an attraction originating in childhood becomes the foundation for a redemptive decision that takes the form of a death-defying plunge from a boat into the river. By contrast, the shared past recollected by Keller's children leads them to consummate their union by passively merging with the deadly element: as their drifting boat approached the city in the morning twilight, the narrator tells us, "two pale forms, locked in close embrace, glided down in the frost of the autumn from the dark mass into the cold water" ("VRJ" 118).

We must therefore reconsider Gerhard Kaiser's conclusion regarding Keller's pagan religiosity. "The eschatological metaphor of the coming child [in the poem 'Stille der Nacht'] stands," writes Kaiser, "not for the appearance of the eternal God as a futural one, but for the transitory lighting up [*Aufleuchten*] of the heavenly Jerusalem within time, of the ancient God in the primordial bedrock of the ancient Earth."[15] Indeed, Kaiser goes so far as to claim that the children are shown in the novella to have attained to "the heavenly Jerusalem" through their deadly serious yet inconsequential game. If, however, the caesuras in "A Village Romeo and Juliet" are recognized as such and considered in connection with the elaborate web of theological motifs, then this positive thesis no longer appears tenable. For the "ancient God" glimpsed again and again in Keller's narrative is not a pantheistic divinity older than Christianity but an absent one, or one to whom humans have lost access. By celebrating the beauty of a natural world that the protagonists simply take for granted or merely use as a setting for their make-believe marital idyll, Keller's narrative may indeed be thought of as offering the reader something like the Benjaminian hope for the sake of the hopeless. Yet even though the chance apparitions of this natural dimension in the two caesuras have the power to prompt action, they are also shown to be insufficient to guide resolute, purposive agency. They cannot free the protagonists from their captivity to myth. The two moments of sublime intimation in "A Village Romeo and Juliet" turn out on closer examination to be hyperbolic simulacra of transcendence that only serve to highlight its absence. That dimension is absent from the consciousness of the protagonists as well as from their social world, and it appears on the horizon of narration only as an ironic counterpoint.

An attempt at redemptive critique in relation to Keller's novella would therefore have to depart from the "metaphysical tact" that Adorno praised apropos of Eichendorff. To assert utopian hope, a redemptive critique of Keller's novella would have to resort to forceful critical construction. This would probably require an abandonment of literary criticism—the dominant register, if not the only one, of Benjamin's essay—in favor of the type of philosophical reflection that we find in Adorno's excursus, which can take greater constructive liberty in dealing with the literary work. Such a hypothetical philosophical essay about Keller's novella might, for instance, follow the model of Adorno's excursus and reverse the sequence of caesuras in order to leave the last word to Sali's epiphany on the bridge.

These observations about Keller's novella were meant to show that the double caesura model that Benjamin and Adorno developed in reference to *Elective Affinities* and the *Odyssey*, respectively, is sufficiently flexible to be adapted to other works as well. If such adaptations of the model are possible, the explanation for this is twofold. First, since literary works can call forth successor works that respond to them, a critical model developed in reference to the earlier work may also shed light on its successor. Thus, as I noted at the beginning of chapter 2, a Homeric subtext is discernible in *Elective Affinities*; and a much closer relation of literary succession obtains between *Elective*

Affinities and "A Village Romeo and Juliet," since the latter may be viewed as a disenchanted counterpart to Goethe's embedded novella "Strange Neighbors."[16] This literary filiation all but invites the sort of critical succession that I have tentatively undertaken here.

A second, more general, point to be made here is that a critic does not encounter a given work in hermetic isolation. Prior readings of other literary works are among the factors that determine which aspects of the work under consideration stand out. It is thus reasonable to assume that the critical perceptions crystallized in Benjamin's and Adorno's articulations of the double caesura model are not limited in their scope to the literary works that stand in the thematic focus of their texts. Although Benjamin does not anywhere comment on the particular passages from Keller's novella that I examined here, his praise for "A Village Romeo and Juliet" as "imperishable," the novella's thematic affinities with Goethe's novel, and the relevance of the double caesura model, all suggest that the critical sensibility at work in the essay on *Elective Affinities* may well have been subliminally informed by Keller's novella, among countless other sources.[17]

Mann's Temple and Kafka's Cathedral

It is only reasonable to wonder whether the double caesura model is limited in its relevance to successor works to the *Odyssey* and *Elective Affinities* and literary texts that might have informed the works of critical theory examined in this book. Let me therefore suggest exemplary applications of our model to two literary works written in the same period as Benjamin's essay that belong to neither category. In both cases, the possibility of the application that I propose was, knowingly or unknowingly, hinted at by Benjamin himself.

The first hint that I want to follow can be found in a letter to Gershom Scholem dated April 6, 1926. In it Benjamin makes a curious confession:

> Thomas Mann published a short essay on Goethe's *Elective Affinities* in the last issue of *Neue Rundschau*. I have not read it yet. But it caught my attention because recently I have repeatedly come upon this author's work. I hardly know how to begin telling you that this man, whom I hated like few public intellectuals [*Publizisten*], has gotten positively close to me because of the last great book of his, which I happened to read, *The Magic Mountain*. In this book something that unmistakably belongs to my ownmost being [*untrüglich Eigenstes*], something that moves me and has always moved me, has spoken to me in a way that I can accurately evaluate [*die ich streng kontrollieren kann*] and which I must acknowledge and indeed in many respects greatly admire. However charmless such constructions are, I can only imagine, indeed I am absolutely certain, that an

> internal change must have taken place in the author while he was writing. I still do not know whether he knows my essay on *Elective Affinities*. In any case, I can no longer see anything purely arbitrary in the fact of his recent statement regarding the book. Beyond that, I must [let] the subject drop: it is not suitable for a letter.[18]

Benjamin must have known that there could be little question of his essay's influence on *The Magic Mountain*. After all, when Mann's novel was published in November 1924 the second part of Benjamin's essay still awaited publication (until January 1925). Moreover, although Benjamin could not have known this, Mann had already written six of the seven chapters of *The Magic Mountain* by the time the first part of Benjamin's essay appeared in April 1924 in the journal *Neue deutsche Beiträge*.[19]

Yet these philological facts do not diminish the interest of the question provoked by Benjamin's mystery-mongering: wherein lay the affinities that Benjamin saw between his essay on *Elective Affinities* and *The Magic Mountain*? In trying to answer this question, we must complement Benjamin's speculation with our own. We can quickly identify a parallel between, on the one hand, Benjamin's argument that a deficient form of Enlightenment reason tends to revert to myth and, on the other hand, the vertiginous dialectic of the disputes staged by Mann, in which the rather sterile "freethinking" position of the humanist Settembrini and the pious obscurantism of the conservative revolutionary Naptha prove increasingly difficult to keep apart from one another.[20] One may surmise, furthermore, that Hans Castorp's infatuation with the languid and consumptive Clawdia Chauchat might have struck Benjamin as a decadent counterpart to Goethe's portrayal of Ottilie's extinguishing beauty. Benjamin would have also been intimately familiar with the dialectic between the present and the past in the hallucinatory erotic anamnesis that allows Castorp to connect his infatuation with Madame Chauchaut to his teenage fascination with a schoolmate.[21] However, for the purposes of my argument, the most intriguing gloss on Benjamin's assertion of an affinity between his essay and Mann's novel concerns the relevance of the Benjaminian double caesura model.

If we look for an intradiegetic caesura in Mann's novel, the most plausible candidate is surely the chapter "Snow," in which Hans Castorp goes on a solitary outing on skis and, overcome by exhaustion in a snowstorm, experiences a revelation in the form of a dream. The dream first shows an Arcadian landscape populated by people of beguiling grace and friendliness. One of them, "a pretty lad," is looking at Hans Castorp, "watching the watcher"; but as this boy suddenly looks past and behind Castorp, his face becomes "earnest, quite as if it had been made of stone, expressionless [*ausdruckslos*], inscrutable," displaying a "deathlike reserve."[22] Following the boy's gaze, Castorp turns around and discovers a very different space: a vast, dark, elaborate temple, in the sanctuary of which witches are tearing apart and devouring a baby. After a brief, frightened awakening, the dream resumes with an interpretation of this vision. Castorp now understands that the genial life of the "sunny folk" was based on "a silent regard for" the horror in the temple, that Settembrini and Naphta each only cling dogmatically to one side of this contradictory truth, and that our dignity as humans rests on our ironic sovereignty in the face of both the rational imperatives of this-worldly life and the metaphysical piety dictated by death.[23] This ethical vision culminates in a distinction between "lust" and "love." In this context, the former term stands for pleasure taken in a potentially deadly loosening of the forms that must be strenuously maintained for the sake of biological and political life. By contrast, according to Mann's daring synthesis of German Romanticism and Whitmanian democracy, love is an ethically and politically constructive orientation based on a sympathetic awareness of our shared mortality, which nevertheless upholds the dignity of perishable form. Although the relation between lust and love will later turn out to be considerably more complicated, the binary opposition reached at this stage in the novel entails a repudiation of lust and an espousal of love.

Much as the embedded novella of *Elective Affinities* instantiates the genre that was Goethe's original template for the novel, the chapter "Snow" has a novella-like compactness, fulfilling the requirements of the genre that Mann initially had in mind when he set out in 1913 to write a story about a sanatorium in Davos.[24] As should be clear from the above summary, the dream at the heart of the chapter offers a humanistic recasting of Nietzsche's decidedly anti-humanistic conception in *The Birth of Tragedy*. In fact, Mann borrowed the very title of his novel from the young Nietzsche's re-imagining of Greek antiquity.[25] Nietzsche's book was also, as we have seen, a key source of inspiration for the Benjaminian theory of the expressionless; and it so happens that the word "expressionless" ("ausdruckslos") marks the literal turning point of Castorp's dream. Thanks to Castorp's turning around, the dream gives rise to an insight that momentarily transcends his bewilderment, only to become unintelligible to him by the end of the day.

If Castorp's dream constitutes a diegetic caesura, one that takes place on the plane of a fictional consciousness, where in the novel might we locate its extradiegetic counterpart? One would have to say, I think, that the hard caesura occurs in the narrator's closing remarks in the chapter "Fullness of Harmony." In this chapter near the end of the novel, the sanatorium's acquisition of a gramophone prompts Castorp to develop a passion for music. Having described some of Castorp's favorite musical pieces, all of which resonate in one way or another with his remembered adventures, the narrator finally zeroes in on the recording that is closest to the protagonist's heart, namely, that of Schubert's well-known song "Der Lindenbaum" (The Linden Tree). Since this song belongs to the cycle *Winterreise* (Winter Journey), its evocation here recalls Castorp's near-lethal, visionary journey in the chapter "Snow." As I will show now, this motific linkage signals a more consequential correspondence between the two passages which is best understood in terms of the double caesura model.

In commenting on Castorp's attachment to "Der Lindenbaum," the narrator's sympathy for the protagonist reaches a degree that is unusual in *The Magic Mountain*. This sympathy is self-involved, however. The narrator's prefatory remarks on his own task suggest that his exposition calls for the same artistic skill that the challenging genre of the art song demands of singers: after appealing to his readers as "our listeners," the narrator notes that explaining what the song meant to Castorp requires "the utmost delicacy of intonation."[26] Such delicacy is called for because, much like the song of the sirens in Adorno's analysis, Schubert's song is said to epitomize a beauty whose enchanting spell is due to the lure of death. Without a deep affinity for this "emotional sphere," we are told, Castorp would have never become stranded for seven years in the decadent microcosm of an Alpine sanatorium. Yet the perilous intellectual experiences undergone by Castorp during his entrapment have led him to understand that such devotion to morbid beauty can only lead to Naphta's terroristic misanthropy. Strikingly, this critical insight is said to heighten, rather than weaken, Castorp's love of the song, for such ethical doubts "are what add the prick of passion to love, so that one could define passion as doubting love."[27] For Castorp as well as for the narrator, Schubert's song becomes a symbol of this paradoxical passion, in which enchantment with the beauty of death is both enhanced and tempered by the pain of critical "self-overcoming" for the sake of an affirmation of life. We might add that the song can epitomize this contradictory attitude because—in yet another modern version of Odysseus's encounter with the sirens—it evokes both the deadly-seductive promise of rest emanating from the linden tree and the resistance mustered by a distressed wanderer who closes his eyes while passing by the tree and refuses to return to it.

As the narrator ponders Castorp's conflicted love of this song, his reflections detach themselves from the protagonist's consciousness and blend disarmingly forthright self-reflection with oracular pronouncement:

> Oh, it was mighty, this enchantment of the soul. We were all its sons, and we could all do mighty things on earth by serving it. One need not be a genius, all one needed was a great deal more talent than the author of this little song about a linden tree to become an enchanter of souls, who would then give the song such vast dimensions that it would subjugate the world. One might even found whole empires upon it, earthly, all-too-earthly empires, very coarse, very progressive, and not in the least nostalgic—in which the song would wither to electric gramophone music. But the song's best son may yet have been the one who consumed his life in triumphing over himself and died, the *new* word of love on his lips, which he did not yet know how to speak. It was truly worth dying for, this song of enchantment. But he

> who died for it was no longer really dying for this song and was a hero only because ultimately he died for something new, for the new word of love and for the future in his heart— —
>
> Those, then, were Hans Castorp's favorite recordings.[28]

In this remarkable passage, the royal "we" routinely used by Mann's narrator gives way to a "we" that embraces a national community, albeit one whose sovereignty is fraught with doubts about the future. For this community might turn the quintessentially German Romanticism epitomized by Schubert's song into the basis of a Wagnerian dark magic of aesthetic manipulation or, alternatively, it could reduce musical Romanticism to a mere ornament instrumentalized by a militaristic empire. However, most faithful to the spirit of Schubert's song is a third possibility, which the narrator associates, in a proleptic passage that will become legible in light of the novel's conclusion, with Hans Castorp himself.[29] For in the final pages of the novel we will catch one last, cinematic glimpse of Castorp as a soldier in the First World War, singing Schubert's song as shells explode around him in the inferno of Flanders. This concluding passage merely hints at the long odds of Castorp's survival. In the earlier, proleptic reflection on "Der Lindenbaum," however, the narrator indicates in no uncertain terms that Castorp will be killed.

Crucially, however, the key sentence does not mention Castorp by name. It is as if, through Mann's barely veiled proleptic remarks, Castorp had become the anonymous unknown soldier whose remembrance is enshrined in the national pantheon. The passage suggests that anonymized Castorp lives on in Mann's novel because his narration is animated by hope for "a *new* word of love." This phrase points us back to the ethical conception reached at the end of "Snow," that of a loving community of humans who uphold civilized form with a lucid awareness of mortality. The fragile hope invested in this humanistic vision gives the final, questioning note on which Mann ends the novel as the narrator addresses his hero one last time: "There were moments when, as you 'played king,' you saw the intimation of a dream of love rising up out of death and lascivious excess. And out of this worldwide festival of death, this ugly rutting fever that inflames the rainy evening sky all round—will love someday rise up out of this, too?"[30]

The oracular quality that this question has in common with the narrator's remarks on "Der Lindenbaum" reflects the nebulousness of the hard-won democratic republicanism that Mann espoused in response to the crises of the early 1920s. It is quite unclear why Castorp's final homecoming to the "flatland" and his apparently vigorous participation in the carnage unleashed by chauvinism should qualify as a sacrifice made for the sake of a new word of love—rather than, much more plausibly, as a definitive succumbing to deadly lust. To accept Mann's favorable interpretation would be to surrender to the enchantment wrought by his seductive song. That song is not underwritten by a coherent vision of the hoped-for future. Nor can it be, for the future in question must remain uncertain so long as the cataclysmic upheavals that began with the First World War "have not yet ceased to begin," as Mann puts it in his metanarrative foreword to the novel.[31] Accordingly, the two dashes (omitted in both English translations) at the end of the narrator's remarks on "Der Lindenbaum" suggest an anxious trailing off, a concession to the formless, an admission on Mann's part of the limits of his artistic sovereignty in the face of a future pregnant with both hope and foreboding. This momentary surrender of narrative authority is only accentuated by the abruptness of the subsequent return to a soberly factual register in the final sentence of the chapter: "Those, then, were Hans Castorp's favorite recordings."

What we have here, then, is indeed something akin to the hard caesura that Benjamin marks in the narrator's remark in *Elective Affinities*. The sovereign posture of narration suddenly becomes unsettled by a hope harbored by the author that transcends the limited concerns of the protagonist. Benjamin stipulates, as we may recall, that the hope of redemption that we harbor for all the dead "must never be kindled from one's own existence," for such hope can persist only in a narrator's stance towards his hero ("GEA" 355). Accordingly, Mann's narrator suggests in the final paragraph of *The Magic Mountain* that Castorp may yet "survive in spirit what [he] probably will not survive in the flesh." The spirit by virtue of which Castorp survives is that of hope for the sake of the hopeless, kindled by sympathy for a doomed hero and nourished by narrative's power to transmit the lessons of his demise to future readers. This hope manifests itself as a lapse into vagueness and silence that attests to the uncertainty of the hoped-for future. Yet, although the hope that surfaces at this key juncture takes the form of what Benjamin calls the expressionless, it is not for that reason entirely indeterminate. For this hard caesura in the narrator's reflection on a song from *Winterreise* corresponds to the soft caesura of the dream vision that was previously reached on Castorp's winter journey. Thus the double caesura model can help us discern a deep structure that defines both the literary form and the philosophical substance of Mann's novel.

If there is no line of influence linking *The Magic Mountain* with Benjamin's essay, similarly any relation of influence can safely be ruled out in connection with the second exemplary application that I now want to propose. Franz Kafka's novel *The Trial* was published posthumously in April 1925, three months after "Goethe's Elective Affinities," and Benjamin would not read the novel until more than two years later.[32] And yet his essay contains an uncanny anticipation of *The Trial*. I am thinking of Benjamin's comparison of the novella embedded in *Elective Affinities* "to an image in the darkness of a cathedral—an image which portrays the cathedral itself and so in the midst of the interior communicates a view of the place that is not otherwise available" ("GEA" 352). This passage calls to mind the penultimate chapter of *The Trial*, titled "In the Cathedral," which contains the embedded story in which countless critics have sought a key to the novel. In the darkness of the cathedral, the prison chaplain confronts Josef K. with an enigmatic revelation in the form of the parable "Before the Law." Famously, this parable ends, in the manner of a cruel metaphysical joke, with the doorkeeper telling the dying man from the country that he is now going to close the door to the Law that was meant for the man alone.

If we consider this embedded story ending with the closing of a door as the intradiegetic soft caesura of the novel, we may locate the corresponding hard caesura in the sudden opening of a window near the very end of the text:

> Like a flash of light [*Wie ein Licht aufzuckt*], the two casements of a window parted and a human figure, faint and thin from the distance and height, leant far out in one swift movement then stretched its arms out even farther. Who was it? A friend? A kind person? Someone who felt for him? Someone who wanted to help? Was it just one? Or all of them? Was help still possible? Were there still objections he'd forgotten? Of course there were. Logic may be unshakeable, but it cannot hold out against a human being who wants to live. Where was the judge he had never seen? Where was the high court he had never reached? He raised his hands and splayed his fingers.[33]

Although the opening of the window answers to the closing of the door at the end of the parable, that answer immediately prompts a series of questions, questions that the man from the country neglected to ask during the years of his waiting before the open door to the Law. At first glance, it may not be obvious that this proliferation of questions represents an extradiegetic caesura, one that occurs on the level of the act of narration. However, this idea becomes plausible if we consider that the narrator's free indirect discourse here becomes resonant with a questioning that cannot possibly be the protagonist's own, since he has by this point become entirely acquiescent. Rather, in this passage, to quote Benjamin's formulation, "something beyond the poet interrupts the language of poetry" ("GEA" 341): namely, a "small, nonsensical hope"—Benjamin's phrase apropos of Kafka in a letter to Scholem—that outlives the protagonist only because it is registered by the narrator.[34]

The correspondence between the opening of the window that prompts these questions and the closing of the door at the end of the parable is suggestive. For that embedded narrative, which has all the trappings of a privileged albeit enigmatic moment of truth, offers the very opposite of utopian hope. Thus, the hope that unexpectedly breaks through to interrupt the act of narration has no foothold within the fictional world. Therefore, it can only be understood as issuing from a standpoint external to the fictional world, and as contradicting—by the mere act of asking—the bleak revelation of the parable. A more fully developed interpretation of these passages would also have to consider the theological implications of Kafka's parable about waiting, told by a Christian priest; its embedding within the novel via the ensuing aporetic exegetical exchange; and the fact that the two caesuras are placed even closer together, and nearer to the end of the novel, than are the caesuras of the *Odyssey* and *Elective Affinities*. For the limited purpose of demonstrating the relevance of the double caesura model to Kafka's text, however, the pointers just given may suffice.

The double caesura model drawn from Benjamin's essay thus allows us to discern a non-obvious formal analogy between two novels that otherwise belong to very different regions of interwar-era modernism. In both novels, an embedded story affords an insight whose privileged status is signaled by its being staged in a space traditionally reserved for the sacred. This diegetic caesura has an extradiegetic counterpart in an unsettlement of the narrative perspective by a hope that must appear tenuous at best in *The Magic Mountain* and downright "nonsensical" in *The Trial*.

Antiquity, Modernity, and Critical Violence

The fact that versions of the double caesura model can be discerned in Benjamin's essay as well as in Mann's and Kafka's novels tells us something about the paradoxical conjunction of anguish and hope in the post-1914 decade that gave rise to these three works. Since, however, the model in question was originally developed in reference to a novel by Goethe and has now been shown to be relevant to narratives by Homer and Keller as well, its object domain is clearly not limited to interwar-era modernism. Whether there are further works that exhibit some version of the structure aligning two caesuras is, however, a question that must be left open here. To try to define in advance the range of literary works to which the double caesura model might be applied would be to turn a flexibly adaptable model into a genre concept. There is nothing to be gained from such a move. The heuristic reach of the model can be established only through its adaptation to particular works. Each adaptation must be justifed by its critical yield and the unique specification of the model that it makes possible.

The preceding consideration of narratives by Homer, Goethe, Keller, Mann, and Kafka suggests that the formal effects attainable through the alignment of two caesuras admit of variations that in each case reflect the ontological horizon of the work. By marking caesuras in a work of fiction, critical reading takes a stance vis-à-vis that horizon. It is one thing for a critic to notice junctures in a narrative at which a constricting fictional world is breached by intimations of a wider metaphysical horizon; and it is an altogether different thing to put maximal hermeneutic pressure on select passages in a bid to break through the ontological horizon of the work toward another horizon. This basic distinction suggests an angle of approach for a final assessment and comparison of Benjamin's and Adorno's critical texts.

The insight at the heart of both texts is that close attention paid to the act of literary narration can make the otherwise elusive topic of hope accessible to philosophical thought. For Benjamin as well as Adorno, what distinguishes hope from both optimistic expectation and purposive striving is that it can persist even in the face of irremediable failures and damages. Philosophical critique can grasp such hope for the sake of the hopeless by zeroing in on a narrator's stance toward literary characters at the moment of their succumbing to the insidious and pervasive unreason that Benjamin and Adorno theorize under the heading of myth. What underwrites the hope that surfaces in such moments is not the possibility that the impending disaster might perhaps still be averted, but the insight that the very act of narration can precipitate an emancipatory truth content out of irremediably failed lives and pass this truth on to future readers. Benjamin and Adorno concur in suggesting that this type of hope enters narration in the form of abrupt shifts to a perspective that transcends the characters' and the narrator's standpoint as well as the author's intentions.

Both of the critical texts examined in this book align the negative presentation of utopia, which exceeds the perspective of the characters and unsettles the very act of narration, with a positive presentation within the diegetic frame. An important difference has emerged, however, from the joint reading developed in the preceding chapters. Not unlike the Englishman who brings back to the heroines of *Elective Affinities* a version of the story about the captain that has been transfigured through repeated retelling, Gilbert Murray's philological scholarship draws Adorno's attention to the rudimentary form of enlightened self-reflection that was at work in the genesis of the Homeric text. Yet, whereas philology can show transformative transmission to be a factor in the textual genesis of the *Odyssey*, in *Elective Affinities* the transmutation of a story through iterated retelling is a motif internal to the reality portrayed within the diegetic frame. To this contrast we can add a second one. The transformative transmission that gave rise to the *Odyssey* underwrites a historicized conception of the work that enables Adorno to mark a negative presentation of utopia in the form of a hard caesura. By contrast, the process of storytelling thematized in *Elective Affinities* allows for a positive presentation of reconciliation.

Both differences may be understood in terms of the more fundamental one between the ancient epic and the modern novel. As the characteristic genre of a modernity marked by heightened historical consciousness, the novel can incorporate a memory of the premodern world in which storytelling was still at home. In particular, a novel can bring archaic wishes within the purview of the reflective disposition that modern subjects can no longer disown. Thus, in *Elective Affinities*, the genesis of the embedded story refracts the epic wisdom and the utopian desires of an anonymous multitude through the cultivated perspective of the English companion. Such an embedded story can serve as a positive counterpoint to the unhappy self-consciousness of the novelistic narrator, from whose vantage point the idea of reconciliation only appears *ex negativo*. By contrast, much of the appeal of the ancient epic in the eyes of modern readers is due to its supposedly naive depiction of scenes of fulfillment. However, the historically hardened appearance of naïveté that attaches to the ancient epic also implicates it in barbaric inhumanity. If, therefore, the modern discontent with historical actuality is to find resonance in the ancient epic, the appearance of its naïveté must be dispelled as a false semblance—which is to say that the posture of epic narrator must be viewed from that historical perspective whose "baselines," to recall Benjamin's formulation, "converge in our own historical experience."[35]

The presentism of this construction informs, moreover, not only the "baselines" of Adorno's interpretive perspective, but also the saving line that runs from a positive intimation of the idea of reconciliation, less clearly identified as a caesura, to its more emphatically marked negative counterpart. In keeping with the progression of Goethe's narrative, Benjamin's exposition gives the negative presentation the last word. In order to establish the same order in his excursus, Adorno must reverse the sequence of the two caesuras in the *Odyssey*: his remarks on the recognition scene in book 23 precede his concluding meditation on the execution of the slave women in book 22. By departing from his literary object in this manner, Adorno can give the last word to a narrator whose perspective bears witness to the expressionless. This reversal must be seen as a forceful act of critical construction, a key move in Adorno's reimagining of the *Odyssey* in accordance with the novelistic paradigm elaborated in Benjamin's essay on *Elective Affinities*.

For Adorno's reliance on the Benjaminian caesura model should not obscure the fact that that model fulfills a different function in Adorno's argument than in its original articulation by Benjamin. The model cannot have the same function in the two contexts for the simple reason that it is brought to bear on works that belong to different historical periods. Benjamin is writing at a relatively small remove from the literary work he is considering, which is an eminently modern novel that incorporates moments of critical self-reflection. Hence, a redemptive critique undertaken from the vantage point of Benjamin's crisis-fraught present does not necessitate as radical a reconstitution of the work as is required by Adorno's disenchantment of antiquity. In the latter case, the philosophical construction of the truth content of the literary work calls for a more selective use of, as well as a bolder departure from, the minutiae of philological commentary. As a consequence, Benjamin's anti-Platonic saving of the semblance of reconciliation gives way in Adorno's excursus to a critical fiction, a retroactive construction underwritten by a radically transcendent idea of utopia. This may not be the only reason why most readers will likely find Benjamin's essay more finely responsive than Adorno's to its respective literary object, but it is certainly an important reason for that difference.

In considering the degree of critical violence employed by Benjamin and Adorno, however, we must also take into account their divergent views on the relation between myth and Enlightenment reason. For the young Benjamin, full actualization of Enlightenment rationality would require a completed integration of Kant's architectonic system to a "doctrine." According to the dichotomous conception that underlies Benjamin's essay on *Elective Affinities*, the fully achieved Enlightenment rationality envisioned in such philosophical terms would constitute a genuine alternative to myth. Intimations of such an alternative, though necessarily evanescent, are possible even in the world of an incomplete enlightenment that tends to revert to myth. Benjamin can thus posit a hard caesura in *Elective Affinities* by construing the fleeting hope registered by the narrator as the unintentional marking of an enduring hope. Moreover, this moment of hope is aligned in Benjamin's essay with the embedded novella, whose fable of redemptive decisiveness originates in the reality portrayed in the novel and hence lends a measure of determinate ethical content to the hope that Benjamin means to salvage.

Whereas the young Benjamin sees the project of correcting and completing the Enlightenment as coextensive with the consummation of the philosophical system—a task which in the interim requires philosophy to take an indirect route through art criticism—Adorno holds that completion of the Enlightenment requires a self-critique of philosophical reason. In his view, reason as we know it is merely a continuation of myth by other means, a late outgrowth of the fearful drive to self-preservation that permeates the immanence of nature, and its totalizing character precludes any determinate intimation of a genuine alternative. According to this more pessimistic view, the sole path to a genuine enlightenment leads through the reflective recognition—through remembrance of the nature within the subject—that the Enlightenment is itself a late descendant of myth. Accordingly, Adorno marks a hard caesura, not at a juncture in the text where fleeting hope registers, but at a point where remembrance of nature faintly stirs—in the narrator's comment on the maids' agony—but is immediately made light of. The critical leap from fleeting phenomenon to philosophically significant experience is thus occasioned by a recognition of suffering, rather than by a moment of hope. It is only through the modern reader's recoil that the death throes trivialized by the phrase "but not for long" call forth a remembrance of "unspeakably endless torment" (*DE* 62) and thus elicit, though merely *ex negativo*, an idea of reconciliation. Adorno's assertion that "homeland is a state of having escaped [*Entronnensein*]" (*DE* 61) registers his conviction that we can form no concept of reconciliation except as the opposite of the suffering that domination inflicts upon human nature. That a mere recognition of somatic suffering provides a determinate orientation towards a reconciled condition is a claim made by Adorno that I have disputed, objecting in particular to his reliance in this connection on an unworkable Hegelian construal of the Judaic ban on images. Benjamin's resolutely un-Hegelian conception of hope as a determinate relation of "nonsynthesis" between myth and redemption testifies to a more consistent theoretical posture.

Given this difference regarding the relation between myth and enlightenment, it is not surprising that Adorno's utopian construction remains significantly less determinate than Benjamin's. Notwithstanding the commitment to aniconism and negative theology that the two authors share, by hewing close to Goethe's text Benjamin can flesh out a truth content in the concrete terms of the ethical dilemmas that drive the novelistic plot. The ethical determinacy of Benjamin's argument most clearly comes into view in his forthright repudiation of hollow bourgeois decorum and in his plea for a decisiveness whose criterion lies in integral experience. This is the positive ethical conception that emerges from Goethe's embedded novella, according to Benjamin. To be sure, the status of this positive conception within the overall framework of Benjamin's interpretation remains unresolved. In order to avoid violating the prohibition on presenting images of redemption and to uphold his antithetical scheme, Benjamin feels compelled to suppress the origins of the novella in the backstory of the novelistic plot. As a consequence, he overstates the degree of critical violence needed for rescuing the truth content of *Elective Affinities*. I have argued in some detail that this excess of critical violence is unnecessary; it could have been avoided if Benjamin had appreciated the caesura marked by the ambiguous ending (or interruption) of the novella.

The critical violence involved in Adorno's postulation of a caesura answers to a more fundamental aporia at the heart of his project. Such critical violence is required, first of all, by the nature of the very text that Adorno is considering, which contains only rudiments of self-reflection traceable to later phases of its genesis. Of course, Adorno's choice of that ancient text as an exemplary object of disenchantment is itself indicative of a feature of his conception that makes critical violence imperative. For the reason why a reflection on the *Odyssey* can shed light on the deficiencies of modern reason, according to Adorno, is that his totalizing understanding of the dialectic between myth and enlightenment makes Homer's world essentially continuous with ours.

This questionable view entails that the idea of an enlightenment freed of myth can only be conceived from the standpoint of a philosophical critic who intervenes from without in a bid to arrest the dialectic by which enlightenment again and again reverts to myth. Since the unreason underlying reason permeates the full range of historical reality, the domination-free alternative postulated by Adorno falls under the purview of the prohibition of images. No idea of that alternative can be conceived, other than as the opposite of the mute suffering that registers through remembrance of nature. While insisting that only uncompromising negativity can unlock this utopian dimension, however, Adorno also relies on the Hegelian logic of determinate negation to suggest that this negative concept of utopia is nevertheless a determinate one. Yet it is hard to see how he can have it both ways. If the myth endemic to enlightenment has its roots in the drive to self-preservation and hence distorts our forms of sociality and language on the most elementary level, then the alternative of reconciliation must remain so indeterminate, so radically foreign to every known lifeworld, that in attempting to conceive of it we cannot avoid running together historically specific forms of domination and delusion with the constitutive limitations of human life. Albrecht Wellmer is therefore right to conclude that Adorno's exaggerated sense of the obstacles that block human self-realization "leaves no conceptual space for an unperverted reason and selfhood except in the sense of an almost un-articulable utopian horizon of real history."[36]

In a counterpart to Wellmer's objection that leads to the same conclusion from the other side of a dialectic, Raymond Geuss takes Adorno to task for his failure to curb the impulse "fantastically to project . . . an exaggerated idealized conception of a perfect life."[37] Perhaps to absolve a thinker whose work evidently holds a deep appeal to Geuss in spite of its perceived irritating aspects, Geuss chalks up the "tired, diffuse religiosity" evident in Adorno's utopian projections to the influence of Benjamin's orientation towards a yet-to-be-formulated "doctrine" (*Lehre*). In a first, superficial approach this last charge may seem especially apt in view of the essay on *Elective Affinities*, in which Benjamin does not shrink from such unabashedly theological statements as the assertion that "true reconciliation exists only with God" ("GEA" 342). Closer examination shows, however, that these apodictic pronouncements are precisely what they appear to be, namely, articles of theological doctrine that are extraneously juxtaposed to Benjamin's interpretation of the novel.[38] One might be tempted to argue that the novel's portrayal of an unredeemed reality implies these claims *ex negativo*. Yet the very terms of Benjamin's reading preclude such a move when it comes to the novella embedded in *Elective Affinities*, whose turning point one would labor in vain to construe, by either philological commentary or philosophical critique, as a "moment of shared readiness for death through God's will" ("GEA" 345). Since the core of Benjamin's interpretation of *Elective Affinities* is unencumbered by such doctrinal elements, the cogency and the ethical determinacy of his utopian construction give the lie to Geuss's attempt to shift the blame for Adorno's failure on this score to Benjamin.

A more general lesson may, finally, be drawn from my joint reading of the two critical texts. For the tacit dialogue between Benjamin's exemplary criticism and Adorno's reimagining of the *Odyssey* suggests that the undertaking to save narrative fiction from myth is less prone to reverting to a specious reenchantment if it is undertaken in reference to a modern than to an ancient work. This, if little else, lends some support to the vanishingly faint hope for progress that emerges from *Dialectic of Enlightenment*.

Hans Jonas on Logos, Myth, and the Long Pause of Metaphysics

The preceding conclusion delimits, albeit quite broadly, the range of literary works to which the double caesura model can be applied without too much interpretive violence. Something also needs to be said, however, about the historical situations that might warrant, and indeed necessitate, a recourse to some version or other of this interpretive model—as opposed to situations that call for a different type of theoretical response. The preceding chapters have borne out a basic fact already noted in the "Introduction," namely, that Benjamin and Adorno are not engaged in scholarly exegesis. Through a critical reimagining of literary classics, they attempt to change the shape of the culture in whose canon these works are enshrined. The demands posed by a very specific historical emergency authorize their projects of redemptive critique. Responding to an atavistic and seductive obscurantism that became complicit in the rise of fascism, Benjamin and Adorno use the double caesura model to interrupt, in the name of a transcendent logos, narratives mired in mythic unreason. A different type of historical emergency may, however, call for a different stance toward discontinuity and a different strategy with respect to the ancient duality of mythic narration and philosophical logos.

To illustrate this point, I now turn to a later work by a third German-Jewish thinker, a book in which philosophical argumentation gives way at a key juncture to mythic narration. The book I have in mind is *The Phenomenon of Life: Towards a Philosophical Biology* by Hans Jonas. Against the foil of this work, it will be easier to appreciate the historical specificity of the critical model examined in the preceding chapters, as well as the limits of its applicability. Although the central insight of Jonas's book was conceived around the time Horkheimer and Adorno wrote *Dialectic of Enlightenment*, the book's publication in 1966 postdates *Dialectic of Enlightenment* by roughly the length of time that separated the latter from Benjamin's essay on *Elective Affinities*. Originating in a series of philosophical letters that Jonas wrote to his wife while serving in the British forces liberating Italy from German occupation, the argument of the book was first developed in a number of systematically interconnected essays written in English over the 1950s and the early 1960s. Jonas regarded this book as his central achievement: the ontological framework outlined in it serves as a bridge between his early work on Gnosticism and his later systematic work on ethics for a technological age.

Although this fact is rarely commented on, important points of convergence exist between Jonas's diagnosis of modernity and that of Horkheimer and Adorno.[39] Indeed, in certain respects the two arguments complement one another. If Horkheimer and Adorno claim that reason stems from a "mimesis of death," that is, from a fear that strives to master the destructive forces of nature through "deliberate adaptation" to the "rigidity" of "spiritless nature" (*DE* 44–45), similarly Jonas argues that the materialist monism of scientific modernity signaled the "total triumph of the death experience over the life experience."[40] Following Jonas's account, the stage was set for the scientific revolution when the inert materiality of the corpse came to be viewed as the default state of material nature and the constitutive principle of the universe. As a result, life became an accidental and transient anomaly that the fragile human being had to struggle to preserve in the teeth of a permanent emergency.[41] According to a maxim formulated by Francis Bacon, gaining control of nature to meet this challenge requires obedience to the laws of nature.[42] The dialectic of domination that Horkheimer and Adorno analyze in terms inspired by the Hegelian dialectic of lordship and bondage (*DE* 27) thus also informs Jonas's account of modern technology. We master nature at the cost of becoming dependent on the man-made second nature that grants us such mastery, leaving us shackled to the treadmill of blindly self-perpetuating technological progress.[43]

Essentially geared toward the objective of fending off misery and death through technological mastery, the project of the natural sciences inaugurated by Bacon, Galileo, and Descartes was never one of pure theory. "If we equate the realm of necessity with Plato's 'cave,' then scientific theory is," concludes Jonas, "entirely of the cave and therefore not 'theory' in the Platonic sense."[44] It is, moreover, precisely because technological invention is pursued as a means of gaining power over an otherwise overpowering world that the natural-scientific worldview must reduce nature to mathematizable forces.[45] For this reduction to quantity to succeed, all qualities, values, and purposes had to be extruded from the material world and attributed to the subject. This was indeed the founding act of Cartesian dualism. Perceptual qualities were thus chalked up to the constitution of our sensory organs. Similarly, post-Cartesian thinkers from Kant to the existentialists have tended to assume that values and purposes do not inhere in things but are projected onto the world by human subjects, and that consequently no moral "ought" can be deduced from what there is.

Once Cartesian dualism disintegrated under the weight of the aporias it engendered, the "fission products" left in its wake, according to Jonas's trenchant analysis, were two rival versions of monism: on the one hand, the one-sided idealist privileging of subjectivity, with the existentialist "stare at isolated selfhood" as its late descendant; and on the other hand, materialist monism, which reduces the subject to a plaything of exceptionless physical laws.[46] The unquestioned predominance of the latter position in the modern age conceals an insoluble paradox of self-refutation at its heart. For if our mental life is reduced to meaningless causal processes discoverable through natural-scientific explanation, then that very scientific pursuit, as a naturalized mental phenomenon, can no longer be understood as a normatively oriented, truth-seeking practice.[47] In the end, the monistic overreach of scientific naturalism subverts the humanistic premises that underwrite the very project of scientific modernity. As Jonas puts it: "So radically has anthropomorphism been banned from the concept of nature that even man must cease to be conceived anthropomorphically if he is just an accident of that nature. As the product of the indifferent, his being, too, must be indifferent."[48]

Significantly, this conclusion echoes Horkheimer and Adorno's claim that in scientific modernity "even the human being becomes an anthropomorphism for human beings" (*DE* 45). Peculiar to the way in which Jonas develops this claim, however, is the emphasis he places on its ethical implications. To be sure, the ethical dimension is hardly absent from Frankfurt School reflections. As I hope to have shown, already Benjamin was centrally concerned with the loss of ethical orientation that results when experience is flattened by a reductive rationality and rendered immaterial for free agency. Similarly, as we have seen, Adorno's meditation on the execution of the slave maids in the *Odyssey* epitomizes the diagnosis, incisively elucidated by J. M. Bernstein, that chalks up the ethical blind spot of modernity to its repudiation of moral realism: the disenchanted, abstractly self-legislating reason of the Enlightenment robs objects as well as persons of their "axiological colors, their intrinsic worth," destroying the "auratic" individuality that constitutes "the primary instance of anthropomorphism."[49] Moreover, Horkheimer and Adorno comment presciently on the dialectic by which the scientific-technological mastery of nature, born of the fear of individual death, ends up conjuring up the apocalyptic specter of collective self-destruction:

> The fatalism by which incomprehensible death was sanctioned in primeval times has now passed over into utterly comprehensible life. The noonday panic fear in which nature suddenly appeared to humans as an all-encompassing power has found its counterpart in the panic which is ready to break out at any moment today: human beings expect the world, which is without issue, to be set ablaze by a universal power which they themselves are and over which they are powerless. (*DE* 22)

In passages such as these, it is not difficult to discern an anticipation of Jonas's critique of scientific-technological modernity. Conversely, an important strand in Jonas's later reflections on technological modernity runs parallel to Frankfurt School analyses of the displacement of substantive reason by instrumental rationality.

Unlike Horkheimer and Adorno, however, Jonas develops this thought under a diagnostic heading that he adopts (via his former teacher Heidegger) from Nietzsche, namely, nihilism. One of the most instructive expositions of this problematic can be found in the 1973 essay "Technology and Responsibility: Reflections on the New Tasks of Ethics," which would later become the opening chapter of Jonas's final systematic work, *The Imperative of Responsibility* (1979). This line of thought warrants a somewhat longer quote:

> The very same movement which put us in possession of the powers that have now to be regulated by norms—the movement of modern knowledge called science—has by a necessary complementarity eroded the foundations from which norms could be derived . . . First, Nature had been "neutralized" with respect to value, then man

> himself. Now we shiver in the nakedness of a nihilism in which near-omnipotence is paired with near-emptiness, greatest capacity with knowing least what for.
>
> It is a question whether without restoring the category of the sacred, the category most thoroughly destroyed by the scientific enlightenment, we can have an ethics able to cope with the extreme powers which we possess today and constantly increase and are almost compelled to wield. Regarding those consequences that are imminent enough still to hit ourselves, fear can do the job—fear which is so often the best substitute for genuine virtue or wisdom. But this means fails us toward the more distant prospects, which here matter the most, especially as the beginnings seem mostly innocent in their smallness. Only awe of the sacred with its unqualified veto is independent of the computations of mundane fear and the solace of uncertainty about distant consequences. But religion as a soul-determining force is no longer there to be summoned to the aid of ethics. The latter must stand on its worldly feet—that is, on reason and its fitness for philosophy. And while of faith it can be said that it either is there or is not, of ethics it is true to say that it must be there.[50]

This passage can help us specify the difference in historical perspective that separates Jonas from Benjamin and Adorno. The distance between their positions can be assessed in terms of a historical framework established by Günther Anders, the unduly neglected, visionary theorist of technology who was a close friend of Jonas—and, as it happens, was Walter Benjamin's cousin. In 1956, Anders proposed that "all history can be divided into three chapters, with the following captions: (1) All men are mortal, (2) All men are exterminable, and (3) Mankind as a whole is exterminable."[51] With this scheme in mind, we might say that the young Benjamin was writing on the threshold of the age of mass extermination, and Adorno's work was written in view of the reality of genocide, whereas Anders and Jonas are struggling to muster an adequate intellectual response to the third era, that of potential human extinction. The hallmark of this era, according to Anders, is an "*apocalyptic* kind of temporality," marked by the ever-present possibility that not only the future of humankind but also memories of its past might be completely erased, such that it will be the case that "time was an episode."[52] We may recall that Benjamin and Adorno arrest fleeting narrative episodes in order to salvage a hope underwritten by the power of narration to transmit the lessons of failed lives to future readers. No foothold for such hope remains, however, in the face of a looming catastrophe that threatens to leave no survivor, reducing human history itself to an inconsequential episode.

In order to capture the distinctiveness of Jonas's vantage point, we need to introduce a further division within the third era identified by Anders. As Anders points out, even if all nuclear weapons were destroyed, the genie of humankind's nuclear know-how could no longer be put back in the bottle. To avert a nuclear armageddon and regain freedom in the face of a baleful invention of ours whose power we cannot fully comprehend, much less control, we must, according to Anders, "saturate" our souls with fear of our own destructiveness.[53] Significantly, however, Jonas in 1973 rejects the heuristics of fear that Anders propounded in the 1950s. His reason for doing so emerges quite clearly from the passage quoted above. Although fear is an effective deterrent when it comes to imminent threats, it fails in the face of "more distant prospects, which here matter the most, especially as the beginnings seem mostly innocent in their smallness." Here we must recall that Anders's reflections were still written in view of the most acutely perilous period of the Cold War. In the 1960s and 1970s, however, a relatively stable regime of mutual deterrence was achieved, bolstered by a series of arms control agreements, allowing the hitherto underappreciated dangers of environmental devastation to move to the forefront of philosophical attention. Jonas's reflection from 1973 already shows a clear awareness of a feature of this threat that distinguishes it from the threat of nuclear extinction. The ecological crisis deepens in an undramatic, gradual way, with a highly indirect causal connection and a large temporal lag, potentially spanning multiple generations, between decisions taken today and their impacts. Faced with such a slowly gathering, nebulous threat, whose full effects we may not even live to see, we are ill equipped to muster a sufficiently intense fear to motivate necessary changes in our form of life. It is Jonas's recognition of this impasse that prompts his remarks on the concept of the sacred as the sole source of authority that might underwrite a categorical imperative to safeguard the survival of humankind.

To be sure, these remarks remain highly tentative. Indeed, Jonas goes on to acknowledge that a turn to the sacred is not an option in a secular age. At least in the passage now under discussion, Jonas's commitment to secular reason would appear to be unshakable. In fact, his ambition to justify the imperative to secure the survival of humanity in purely secular terms is already evident in the later essays gathered in *The Phenomenon of Life*. However, as I will now demonstrate in some detail, the argument presented in that book also shows Jonas running up against the limits of secular reason; and it is when he reaches these limits that he feels compelled to switch to mythic narration.

In *The Phenomenon of Life*, Jonas undertakes to complement the natural-scientific picture of the world with a non-reductive philosophy of nature that overcomes the entrenched dichotomy between fact and value, ontology and ethics, thus reconstructing a long-buried understanding of nature as a realm of values towards which we have obligations. Having unmasked the seemingly self-evident Cartesian bifurcation of Being into extended matter and thinking mind as a piece of dogmatic metaphysics, Jonas exploits the ontological implications of evolutionary theory to combine the characteristically modern conviction in the natural origins of mind with an ancient intuition about the latency of mind in nature.[54] These ontological premises undergird a critique of the Cartesian view that mind is unique to humans and that all nonhuman organisms are just complex aggregates of inanimate matter governed by relations of mechanical causality. In place of this dogmatic view, Jonas develops an account of organic life that treats the interiority of self-concern, in varying degrees, as a constitutive feature of all living organisms. This self-concern is a function of the dialectic of freedom and needful dependence that defines the organism's essentially mediate relations to the world.[55]

This dialectic intensifies with life's ascent on the evolutionary ladder. Compared to plants, animal life brings a heightening of the mediate character of the organism's relations to the world. The exercise of higher powers that originally evolved as mere means to vegetative survival—motility, perception, and emotion—tends to be elevated to an end pursued for its own sake, such that the animal's purpose is not just survival but also continued enjoyment of these powers.[56] Finally, in humans the animal tendency to elevate means to ends becomes the basis for a genuine freedom to set oneself purposes according to a freely conceived normative image of oneself in relation to the totality of Being.[57] This normative self-conception grounds the obligation to assume responsibility for beings in the world that we must recognize as inherently valuable, including especially other living things with their intrinsic purposiveness.[58] Rejecting the strong anthropocentric thesis that humans are the sole sources of value in the world, Jonas acknowledges "a silent plea for sparing its integrity" that issues "from the threatened plenitude of the living world."[59] However, he also subscribes to the weaker anthropocentric tenet that only humans can assume responsibility for the preservation of valuable things. Since this uniquely human power to assume responsibility for value qualitatively heightens "the valuableness of *Being as a whole*," the existence of humans is itself a value for whose preservation we are responsible.[60] This, in a nutshell, is Jonas's attempt at a purely secular justification of the imperative to safeguard human survival.

However, the argument falls short of its stated goal. Even if we grant that the extinction of humankind would reduce the valuableness of Being as a whole, it is not clear why such a diminution in value would matter—and to whom. Since a hypothetical extinction of humans would abolish the very ability to care for values, it would appear immaterial whether there is more or less value left in a world without humans. It is, I want to suggest, precisely when we take this objection seriously that the rationale for Jonas's tentative appeal to the sacred comes into view. In short, he finds himself unable to justify the imperative of responsibility in purely secular terms. This is shown especially clearly by two texts, written at distinct stages of Jonas's career, which rehearse the same mythic creation story in order to address different philosophical puzzles. The first of these texts was presented in 1961 as the annual Ingersoll Lecture on Immortality at Harvard and eventually became the final essay included in *The Phenomenon of Life*, titled "Immortality and the Modern Temper."[61] Twenty-three years later, in a lecture titled "The Concept of God after Auschwitz: A Jewish Voice" that he delivered at the University of Tübingen, Jonas offered a verbatim repetition, explicitly identified as such, of this creation myth.[62]

It is neither possible nor necessary to cite this embedded narrative, which takes up roughly three pages, in its entirety. It will suffice here to rehearse only its turning points.[63] The narrative commences with a deliberate echo of Genesis: "In the beginning" the divine being abandoned all of his contents, holding back nothing, "to the chance and risk and endless variety of becoming." He "renounced his being, divesting himself of his deity—to receive it back from the odyssey of time weighted with the chance harvest of unforeseeable temporal experience: transfigured or possibly disfigured by it." Following aeons filled with the "gyrations of matter," governed by blind chance, "the first stirring of life" introduced "a new language of the world: and with it a tremendous quickening of concern in the eternal realm and a sudden leap in its growth toward recovery of its plenitude." Through "the briefly snatched self-feeling, doing, and suffering of finite individuals, with the pitch of awareness heightened by the very press of finitude . . . the deity comes to experience itself," with "every new dimension of world-response" actualizing "another modality for God's trying out his hidden essence." Finally, with the advent of the human capacity for freedom and knowledge, "the innocence of the mere subject of self-fulfilling life has given way to the charge of responsibility under the disjunction of good and evil." Thus, Jonas concludes, the "image of God . . . passes into man's precarious trust, to be completed, saved, or spoiled by what he will do to himself and the world."

This creation myth occupies a systematically central place in Jonas's thinking. It fills a crucial theoretical gap that Jonas admitted in the opening pages of *The Phenomenon of Life*, where the mystery surrounding the origins of life was met with the frankly subjective and hypothetical speculation "that even the transition from inanimate to animate substance, the first feat of matter's organizing itself for life, was actuated by a tendency in the depth of being toward the very modes of freedom to which this transition opened the gate."[64] Explicitly acknowledged by Jonas, even the anthropomorphism of the creation myth is not as arbitrary as it might appear at first glance. It is legitimized by Jonas's audacious bid to lift the modern ban on anthropomorphism—his assertion, that is, that the human being represents "the maximum of concrete ontological completeness known to us . . . from which, reductively, the species of being may have to be determined by way of progressive ontological subtraction."[65] The centrality of the myth is evident from the fact that Jonas rehearses it in two representative texts written almost a quarter century apart, to address markedly different concerns. In the Harvard lecture given in 1961 that would become the final essay included in *The Phenomenon of Life*, Jonas offered up this mythic story in order to help make plausible the vague surmise that we are "an experiment of eternity" and hence our "deeds inscribe themselves in an eternal memoir of time."[66] In the later Tübingen lecture, the same myth is recalled as part of Jonas's response to that radical modern version of the theodicy problem which is epitomized by the place name "Auschwitz." Here the myth allows Jonas to uphold the absolute goodness and intelligibility of God at the cost of rejecting the third traditional attribute, that of omnipotence.

Since the problem of theodicy already presupposes a religious framework, the later iteration of the creation narrative is less revealing of the reasons for Jonas's turn to myth than is its initial deployment. In the earlier lecture, however, Jonas resorts to the creation story in order to address a question that can be posed in purely secular terms: what explains our sense that the decision we make in a critical moment has a lasting significance above and beyond its worldly consequences? It is Jonas's justification for the turn to myth in the context of this inquiry that will prove most instructive in connection with the readings of Benjamin and Adorno presented in the preceding chapters. This justification follows immediately upon the mythic narration and needs to be quoted in full:

> Such is the tentative myth which I would like to believe "true"—in the senses in which myth may happen to adumbrate a truth which of necessity is unknowable and even, in direct concepts, ineffable, yet which, by intimations to our deepest experience, lays claim upon our powers of giving indirect account of it in revocable, anthropomorphic images. In the great pause of metaphysics in which we are, and before it has found its own speech again, we must entrust ourselves to this, admittedly treacherous, medium at our risk. The myth, if only it is conscious of its experimental and provisional nature and does not pose as doctrine, can from the necessity of that pause bridge the vacuum with its fleeting span. I at any rate felt driven to it for once under the constraint of a task which philosophy even in its helplessness must not deny.[67]

The myth is thus defended as a necessary postulate, not unlike Kant's postulations of God and immortality. A more specific justification for the mythic register chosen by Jonas can be gleaned from his later remarks on the project of demythologization propounded by his former teacher Rudolf Bultmann, which mandated the translation of religious myths into existential-philosophical terms. Countering this enterprise with a thought inspired by his friend Hannah Arendt, Jonas raises the possibility that "the road leads always only from metaphor to metaphor, from outworn and no longer viable to fresh and newly appealing metaphor, since the 'real' *can* perhaps be 'said' only indirectly or not at all."[68] Accordingly, Jonas claims that, although his attempt at cosmogony is no less fictional than the dualism and the reductive monisms that he rejects, nevertheless as a piece of speculative fiction it does more justice than its competitors to the evidence of a universe that has given rise to life and mind.[69]

In view of Jonas's later reflections on the metaphorical character of philosophical discourse, a striking feature of his apologia for myth is its metaphorical resonance with the narrative that it purports to justify. Much as the divine being allegedly surrendered the self-sufficiency of eternity and exposed itself to the perils of becoming, Jonas admits to having surrendered the sovereignty of philosophical reason and (to quote his formulations) "entrusted" himself to the "treacherous" medium of mythic narration. By weaving what he calls a mythic "tale," he opens up his discourse to a wealth of traditions drawn from Jonas's inheritance as a German-Jewish thinker, traditions whose often discordant echoes reverberate throughout the resultant narrative. Jonas himself identifies only two of these sources, namely, the Jewish teaching of the Book of Life and the Manichean doctrine of "the last image." In the lecture given in 1984, Jonas also acknowledges his debt to the doctrine of *tzimtzum* in Lurianic Kabbalah, according to which God restricted himself in order to make room for finite created things.[70] As for Jonas's characterization of creation as the "odyssey of time," it hearkens back to Schelling's claim that we might learn to decipher in the riddle of nature the "odyssey of spirit."[71] Similarly, Jonas's references to the "ground of being" and the "gyrations of matter" echo Schelling's "Ages of the World" project, itself influenced by Christian theosophical appropriations of the doctrine of *tzimtzum*.[72] Finally, it is not hard to discern echoes of Hölderlin and Hegel in the claim that the divine absolute experiences itself through the mediation of finitude.

This blend of Jewish theology and German philosophy becomes especially poignant in the context of the Tübingen lecture "The Concept of God after Auschwitz." A philosopher's self-surrender to the treacherous medium of myth does not get more audacious than here, in a post-Holocaust theodicy that allows Jewish theology to be filtered through figures of thought borrowed from the German idealists who set out from the Protestant theological seminary of Tübingen. Indeed, Jonas's reference in the Tübingen lecture to the "odyssey of time" undergone by the divine being hints, by oblique analogy, at the profound ambivalence of his own return to Germany—first in 1945, when he fulfilled his vow to return in the uniform of a conquering army and learned that his mother had been murdered in Auschwitz, and then repeatedly in subsequent decades as an invited speaker held in great esteem.[73]

One of the objective correlatives of these later returns to Germany was the publication in 1973 of the German-language version of *The Phenomenon of Life*.[74] Jonas himself translated most of the book, and in doing so, as he explains in the preface, he "permitted himself the author's freedom in relation to the original in substantive matters as well," significantly emending several passages.[75] For the present argument, two emendations in particular deserve attention.

The first one concerns the historical experiences that Jonas considers in light of his hypothetical creation myth. Near the end of the Harvard lecture that became the final essay of *The Phenomenon of Life*, Jonas hazarded a speculation about the theological implications of the Holocaust that anticipated the lecture on this topic that he would give twenty-three years later in Tübingen.[76] In the German version of *The Phenomenon of Life*, published in 1973, this retrospective reflection is replaced with a forward-looking line of thought concerned with "the endangerment of our entire lifeworld by technology, of which the specter of the atomic bomb is only the most dramatic (and possibly the most easily tractable) aspect."[77] In the face of this unprecedented threat, as Jonas goes on to argue, only a theological framework can establish an ontological foundation for the unconditional duty to safeguard the survival of humankind, for such a duty "cannot be derived from the mere immanence of worldly facts." Jonas is very clear on this point: "No unconditional duty stipulating that humans must exist can be justified on the basis of the cosmic accident of becoming that brought them into existence."

What prompted Jonas to replace his theological speculation about the Holocaust with a reflection on the threat of human extinction? We can only speculate as to the answer. Jonas may have felt that it was too early in 1973 to address, in a text intended for German-language readers, the Nazi violation of unconditional moral norms in connection with a merely hypothetical and hence noncommittal theological framing; if so, he must have changed his mind by the time he set out to write his 1984 Tübingen lecture. More to the point, however, a positive reason for Jonas's turn to a more immediately topical issue can be inferred from his parenthesized remark to the effect that the threat of nuclear annihilation is only the "most dramatic (and possibly the most easily tractable)" form of technological endangerment. In view of this remark, the emendation in the German-language text appears to reflect Jonas's insight, explicitly stated in the essay on "Technology and Responsibility" published in the same year, that the undramatic character of the ecological crisis defies the heuristics of fear and might necessitate a turn to the sacred. The emendation of 1973 thus reflects the change in historical perspective that had occurred since 1966, as the ecological threat to human survival began to loom larger than the more "easily tractable" danger of nuclear annihilation.

The second emendation in the German version concerns a seemingly minor lexical detail in Jonas's previously quoted apologia for mythic narration. In rendering the English passage in his native German, Jonas ended up translating a single word into a third language. The word in question occurs in the following crucial sentence: "In the great pause of metaphysics in which we are, and before it has found its own speech again, we must entrust ourselves to this, admittedly treacherous, medium at our risk." In the German version the word "speech" is rendered as "*Logos*."[78] By opting for this highly resonant Greek term, Jonas frames his procedure in terms of the ancient duality of *mythos* and *logos* that already informed Plato's dialogues. Indeed, in the 1984 lecture given in Tübingen, Jonas justifies the medium of myth as a "vehicle of imaginative but credible conjecture that Plato allowed for the sphere beyond the knowable."[79]

These two emendations in the German version of Jonas's book—the turn to the ecological crisis and the accentuation of the duality between logos and myth—help us highlight, by way of contrast, the sense in which Benjamin's and Adorno's critical strategies are conditioned by their historical vantage point. The contrast is prima facie evident from the divergent meanings attached to the concept of myth by Benjamin and Adorno on the one hand and Jonas on the other. Whereas eternal sameness defined the myth that encumbered Goethe's and Homer's narratives according to the Frankfurt School theorists, the type of narration to which Jonas tentatively resorts is the medium in which a deity reveals itself in irreversible historical time.

The opposition between the two concepts of myth is due to the difference between the underlying diagnoses of the historical present. For the emergency perceived by Jonas, as well as his response to it, represent the inverse of what we found in the works of the two Frankfurt School theorists. The hard caesuras postulated by Benjamin and Adorno interrupt, in the name of a transcendent logos, literary narratives mired in a pernicious mythic immanence of the sort that eventually triumphed in fascism. To complement the negative thrust of this interruption with a positive vision of utopia, the soft caesuras marked by Benjamin and Adorno identify mythic rudiments of freedom, namely, the novella embedded in *Elective Affinities* and Penelope's fantasy about the gods' envy of humans. In both of these critical interpretations, however, the negative, interruptive effect of the transcendent logos is given the last word. The threat that it counters stems from the persistence of myth in the Enlightenment. For Jonas, by contrast, the danger arises from the cessation of that metaphysical logos, paradigmatically expressed in Aristotle's philosophy, which formerly secured the connection between ontology and ethics. What disrupted this logos was an emergent scientific-technological rationality whose compulsive expansion is now destroying the natural conditions of human life.

Yet it must be stressed that Jonas writes of a "pause of metaphysics," not its definitive end, and that he presents the creation myth as a temporary, "revocable" device for the purposes of bridging the hiatus resulting from this pause. Moreover, this myth is not simply a wishful substitute for rational metaphysics, not a just-so story patched together from bits and pieces of defunct theology. Insofar as the mythic narrative recapitulates in another register the rationally grounded philosophy of nature developed in the preceding chapters of *The Phenomenon of Life*, it has a certain plausibility. At any rate, it is less fantastical than such sober-sounding, but ultimately incoherent or self-refuting, positions as Cartesian dualism and reductionist materialism. Jonas's philosophy of nature may thus be viewed as a first step toward a future, hinted at in his apologia for myth, in which metaphysics might once again find its logos. Whereas Benjamin's and Adorno's interventions in the name of a genuinely rational enlightenment are underwritten by a problematic negative theology, the tentative positive theology of Jonas's myth anticipates a rational logos. Deployed in order to bridge the hiatus of metaphysics "with its fleeting span," Jonas's provisional myth is a bold and uncertain, but far from arbitrary, reach for transcendence in an emergency whose contours were already visible in 1973. This emergency has become all too evident in the intervening decades, and it appears increasingly clear that neither the heuristics of fear nor fleeting moments of hope for the sake of the hopeless are any longer adequate to it.

ACKNOWLEDGMENTS

The puzzlement that prompted my work on this book first surfaced in the context of a graduate seminar I taught in autumn 2017 at Johns Hopkins University. If the project was quick to take off, this was partly due to the catalytic effect of the discussions with the wonderful group of students attending this seminar. The completion of the book was also aided by the congenial intellectual atmosphere that I found at Johns Hopkins, my institutional home during the relevant period. I am especially grateful to my colleagues in the German program: Rochelle Tobias and Katrin Pahl, both of whom welcomed me to Hopkins and encouraged me to explore new interests; Jennifer Gosetti-Ferencei, who was generous with advice; Deborah Mifflin, who helped me shoulder advising duties; and Sam Spinner. I also thank department chair Derek Schilling for his support, Kathy Loehmer and Teri Caughman for administrative help, and the Eisenhower Library staff for research assistance.

From the moment my proposal landed in his mailbox, Trevor Perri has been an unfailingly supportive and judicious editor. As the coronavirus pandemic brought normal life to a halt, project editor Maia Rigas remained unfazed and shepherded the book through the production process with wisdom, tact, and lightning-like efficiency. I am grateful to Paul Mendelson for his eagle-eyed copy editing. The reports submitted by the two readers assigned by Northwestern University Press were extremely insightful and constructive. The detailed suggestions made by Henry W. Pickford, who allowed himself to be identified as one of the readers, were particularly helpful in revising the manuscript.

Stanley Corngold gave me perceptive feedback on an early version of the the text, and I am much indebted to his work on some of the material discussed here. Hans Ulrich Gumbrecht's encouragement of the project was bracing. I have fond memories of a Princeton seminar, co-taught by Michael W. Jennings and Thomas Y. Levin, that first sparked my interest in Benjamin and Adorno.

Rereading the *Odyssey* a few years ago, Zsófia Zachár spoke to me memorably about the passage in book 22 that had also prompted Adorno's remarks on a pause in narration. Had it not been for her words in the back of my mind, I am not sure I would have paused for so long to think about those cryptic remarks and their ramifications.

NOTES

Introduction

1. Walter Benjamin, "107. To Gerhard Scholem [8 November 1921]," in *The Correspondence of Walter Benjamin, 1910–1940*, ed. Gershom Scholem and Theodor W. Adorno, trans. Manfred R. Jacobson and Evelyn M. Jackson (Chicago: University of Chicago Press, 1995), 194.

2. Albrecht Wellmer, *The Persistence of Modernity: Essays on Aesthetics, Ethics, and Postmodernity*, trans. David Midgley (Cambridge: Polity, 2007), 35–36.

3. See aphorism no. 1 in Friedrich Nietzsche, *Beyond Good and Evil*, ed. Rolf-Peter Horstmann and Judith Norman, trans. Judith Norman (Cambridge: Cambridge University Press, 2015), 5; Martin Heidegger, *The Fundamental Concepts of Metaphysics: World, Finitude, Solitude*, trans. William McNeill and Nicholas Walker (Bloomington: Indiana University Press, 1995), 185; sections no. 133 and no. 255 in Ludwig Wittgenstein, *Philosophical Investigations* (Oxford: Blackwell, 1999), 51, 91; and "GEA" 333–34.

4. Hans Robert Jauss, *Ästhetische Erfahrung und literarische Hermeneutik* (Frankfurt: Suhrkamp, 1991), 398.

5. See Odo Marquard, "Frage nach der Frage, auf die die Hermeneutik die Antwort ist," in *Abschied vom Prinzipiellen: Philosophische Studien* (Stuttgart: Reclam, 1981), 130.

6. Friedrich Schlegel, "Über Goethes Meister," in *Kritische Schriften und Fragmente*, vol. 2 (Paderborn: Ferdinand Schöningh, 1988), 165–66.

7. Immanuel Kant, *Critique of Pure Reason*, trans. and ed. Paul Guyer and Allen Wood (Cambridge: Cambridge University Press, 2000), 677 (A805).

8. Kant, *Critique of Pure Reason*, 680 (A811).

9. Kant, *Critique of Pure Reason*, 677 (A805).

10. Immanuel Kant, *Critique of the Power of Judgment*, ed. Paul Guyer, trans. Paul Guyer and Eric Matthews (Cambridge: Cambridge University Press, 2000), 67–74 (*AA* 5:180–88).

11. For Kant's tripartite model of the mind, see Immanuel Kant, "First Introduction," in *Critique of the Power of Judgment*, 11 (*AA* 20:205–6).

12. Rachel Zuckert, "Is Kantian Hope a Feeling?" in *Kant and the Faculty of Feeling*, ed. Kelly Sorensen and Diane Williamson (Cambridge: Cambridge University Press, 2018), 242–59.

13. Kant, *Critique of the Power of Judgment*, 89 (*AA* 5:204–5).

14. Zuckert, "Is Kantian Hope a Feeling?" 255.

15. Zuckert, "Is Kantian Hope a Feeling?" 258.

16. Zuckert, "Is Kantian Hope a Feeling?" 253–54.

17. Immanuel Kant, "Critique of Practical Reason," in *Practical Philosophy*, trans. and ed. Mary J. Gregor (Cambridge: Cambridge University Press, 1999), 241 (*AA* 5:125–26). See Eckart Förster, "'Was darf ich hoffen?': Zum Problem

der Vereinbarkeit von theoretischer und praktischer Vernunft bei Immanuel Kant," *Zeitschrift für philosophische Forschung* 46, no. 2 (1992): 176–77.

18. Förster, "'Was darf ich hoffen?'" 184–85.

19. *ND* 382. See also Theodor W. Adorno, "On Subject and Object," in *Critical Models: Interventions and Catchwords*, trans. Henry W. Pickford (New York: Columbia University Press, 2005), 246.

20. In this and the following paragraph I draw on Roland Reuss, "*Wo aber Gefahr ist, wächst das Rettende auch [. . .]*": *Philologie als Rettung* (Frankfurt: Stroemfeld, 2016), 30–37.

21. James McFarland, *Constellation: Friedrich Nietzsche and Walter Benjamin in the Now-Time of History* (New York: Fordham University Press, 2013), 72.

22. As Thomas Zabka puts it, "reflection *occasioned* by an object would be completely pointless if it did not lay claim to being an at least partially adequate discourse *about* the object" (Thomas Zabka, *Pragmatik der Literaturinterpretation: Theoretische Grundlagen–kritische Analysen* [Tübingen: Max Niemeyer Verlag, 2005], 177).

23. Theodor W. Adorno, "On the Final Scene of *Faust*," in *Notes to Literature, Volume One*, trans. Shierry Weber Nicholsen (New York: Columbia University Press, 1991), 111.

24. Adorno, "On the Final Scene of *Faust*," translation modified.

25. Theodor W. Adorno, "A Portrait of Walter Benjamin," in *Prisms*, trans. Samuel Weber and Shierry Weber (Cambridge, Mass.: MIT Press, 1983), 234.

26. Ulrich Plass, *Language and History in Adorno's Notes to Literature* (London: Routledge, 2007), xix.

Chapter One

1. "GEA" 333. Benjamin's consistent use of the plural form *Geschwister* suggests that each significant work of art has a plurality of philosophical siblings: "In just this way critique seeks to discover siblings of the work of art" ("GEA" 333). Paul North makes a convincing case for a sibling relationship between *Elective Affinities* and Plato's *Symposium*. See North, "Apparent Critique: Inferences from a Benjaminian Sketch," *Diacritics* 40, no. 1 (2012): 83. As it will emerge from my argument, I agree that the essay's central reflections on aesthetics refer *Elective Affinities* to a Platonic problematic. However, the related strand of ethical reflection that plays an equally central role in the essay is, in my view, best understood in light of a sibling relationship to Kant's critical project. Thus, the correspondence between the age of Goethe and Greek antiquity that surfaces in the relation of critical succession between Benjamin's reading of Goethe and Adorno's reading of Homer already determines the Platonic-Kantian problematic at the heart of Benjamin's essay.

2. J. M. Bernstein, *Adorno: Disenchantment and Ethics* (Cambridge: Cambridge University Press, 2001), 34.

3. Bernstein, *Disenchantment and Ethics*, 163.

4. Bernstein, *Disenchantment and Ethics*, 110.

5. Bernstein, *Disenchantment and Ethics*, 115–16.

6. Bernstein, *Disenchantment and Ethics*, 119.

7. Bernstein, *Disenchantment and Ethics*, 179.

8. I thus agree with Peter Fenves's claim that Benjamin's essay is concerned in equal measure with Goethe's and Kant's legacy. However, my interpretation of Benjamin's engagement with Kant follows a different route from the one taken by Fenves, since I claim that the central issue at stake for Benjamin is the problem of the connection between experience and freedom, first formulated in "On the Program of the Coming Philosophy." See Peter Fenves, "Kant in Benjamins Wahlverwandtschaften-Essay," in *Benjamins Wahlverwandtschaften: Zur Kritik einer programmatischen Interpretation*, ed. Helmut Hühn, Jan Urbich, and Uwe Steiner (Frankfurt: Suhrkamp, 2015), 221–37.

9. On the tension in Benjamin's writings between affirmative and melancholic responses to the decay of integral experience, see John McCole, *Walter Benjamin and the Antinomies of Tradition* (Ithaca, N.Y.: Cornell University Press, 1993).

10. See Sigrid Weigel, "Fidelity, Love, Eros: Benjamin's Bireferential Concept of Life as Developed in 'Goethe's Elective Affinities,'" in *Walter Benjamin and Theology*, ed. Colby Dickinson and Stéphane Symons (New York: Fordham University Press, 2016), 76.

11. This marks a point of great proximity to, as well as sharp difference from, Heidegger's claim that Dasein "has its weight in having-been [*Gewesenheit*]"; Martin Heidegger, *Being and Time: A Translation of Sein und Zeit*, trans. Joan Stambaugh (Albany: State University of New York Press, 1996), 353. Although both Benjamin's essay and *Being and Time* show clear signs of the two authors' reading of Kierkegaard, a few quotes from Heidegger's magnum opus should suffice to highlight how his reworking of the Kierkegaardian concept of repetition differs from Benjamin's: "We call authentic having-been *retrieve* [*Wiederholung*]" (*Being and Time*, 311). "And thus it *also* reveals the possibility of an authentic potentiality-of-being that must, as something futural in retrieving, come back to the thrown There" (*Being and Time*, 315–16). Heidegger's pronouncements on "fate" (*Geschick*) are particularly telling: "The resoluteness in which Da-sein comes back to itself discloses the actual factical possibilities of authentic existing *in terms of the heritage* which that resoluteness *takes over* as thrown. Resolute coming back to thrownness involves *handing oneself over* to traditional possibilities, although not necessarily *as* traditional ones" (351). "We characterize retrieve as the mode of resolution handing itself down, by which Da-sein exists explicitly as fate" (353). Benjamin's notion of remembrance as a faculty animated by utopian energies sharply contrasts with Heidegger's insistence that the freedom of "repetition" consists in the resolve to appropriate the fateful facticity of existence (to "take[s] over the *powerlessness* of being abandoned to itself," 351).

12. See Hegel's critique of "Reason as Law-Testing" in G. W. F. Hegel, *The Phenomenology of Spirit*, trans., intro., and comm. Michael Inwood (Oxford: Oxford University Press, 2018), 171, paragraph 431.

13. This too is a point made by Hegel, in his discussion of "Virtue and the Course of the World" (*Phenomenology of Spirit*, 153, paragraph 386).

14. As Michael W. Jennings points out, in the "esoteric afterword" on Goethe that Benjamin appended to his doctoral dissertation, he attributed the mythic character of Goethe's experience of nature to his failure to appreciate the linguistic character of *Urphänomene* and to his resultant tendency to seek such archetypal forms of nature in nature itself. Jennings, *Dialectical Images: Walter*

Benjamin's Theory of Literary Criticism (Ithaca, N.Y.: Cornell University Press, 1987), 135.

15. As Peter Fenves points out, Benjamin's reasoning here is inspired by the argument, originally devised by Georg Cantor, that inaugurated transfinite mathematics. Benjamin knew Cantor's work through his uncle, the mathematician Arthur Schoenflies, with whom Benjamin was staying in Frankfurt while he worked on the *Elective Affinities* essay. See Fenves, "Kant in Benjamins Wahlverwandtschaften-Essay," 231–32.

16. North, "Apparent Critique," esp. 79–81.

17. North adds, however: "Whether once this is revealed philosophy can go on believing in this phantasm and in turn repressing its *apparence*—that is another question" ("Apparent Critique," 81). The program of "apparent criticism" proposed by North suggests that an answer in the negative *might* be more desirable: "The madman—philosophy—conceals from himself the illusory nature of the ideal that governs his practice. The magician—an artwork—makes a similar illusion manifest as illusion, so that the madman, although he cannot have it on his terms, can at least name what is driving him mad. The impresario—critique—orchestrates the show and invites the philosopher to watch it" ("Apparent Critique," 86). As I will argue in chapter 2, Adorno's reworking of the Benjaminian theory of the expressionless implies a critique of philosophy's "madness," and by extension also of the early Benjamin, that is broadly consonant with the critical project outlined by North.

18. See Kant, *Critique of the Power of Judgment*, 193 (*AA* 5:315).

19. The affinity is surprising in light of Benjamin's disparaging remarks on Hegel and probably cannot be chalked up to influence. See Jan Urbich, "Das Ausdruckslose: Zur Dialektik des Scheins bei Benjamin," in *Benjamins Wahlverwandtschaften: Zur Kritik einer programmatischen Interpretation*, ed. Helmut Hühn, Jan Urbich, and Uwe Steiner (Frankfurt: Suhrkamp, 2015), 95–97.

20. On aesthetic pleasure as involving a "feeling of life" attendant on the animation of mental faculties, see Kant, *Critique of the Power of Judgment*, 90, 104, 192 (*AA* 5:204, 219, 313). On the embodied character of all pain and pleasure, see 159 (*AA* 5:277–78).

21. "We linger over the consideration of the beautiful because this consideration strengthens and reproduces itself," writes Kant in *Critique of the Power of Judgment*, 107 (*AA* 5:222).

22. Kant, *Critique of the Power of Judgment*, 191–93 (*AA* 5:313–15).

23. North, "Apparent Critique," 81. Here, however, I must also note a point of divergence from North's argument. North draws on Benjamin's short 1919 text "Analogie und Verwandtschaft," published in English as "Analogy and Relationship" (*SW* 1:207–9), to argue that the kinship in terms of appearing that connects the artwork with the ideal of the problem must be distinguished from a formal analogy. In my view, however, the connection posited by Benjamin between art and philosophy only becomes fully intelligible in light of his theory of the beautiful, and therefore requires the Kantian, analogical interpretation that I just outlined.

24. Some of Benjamin's more obtuse contemporaries evidently did read him along Heideggerian lines. Uwe Steiner writes: "The intellectual proximity of Benjamin's work to positions espoused by conservative cultural criticism seemed

evident not during these years only. As late as 1938 he read with annoyance that, in regard to the *Elective Affinities* essay, he was 'presented as a follower of Heidegger' "; Uwe Steiner, *Walter Benjamin: An Introduction to His Work and Thought*, trans. Michael Winkler (Chicago: University of Chicago Press, 2010), 63.

25. On the relation between philosophy as an empirical, historical practice and the dream of systematic totality, see North, "Apparent Critique," 77.

26. On this point see Winfried Menninghaus, "Das Ausdruckslose: Walter Benjamins Kritik des Schönen durch das Erhabene," in *Walter Benjamin, 1892–1940*, ed. Uwe Steiner (Bern: Peter Lang, 1992), 52–53. For Adorno, as J. M. Bernstein explains, it is the abstraction of disenchanted Enlightenment morality that cuts off the path of "material inference" from a concrete state of affairs disclosed in experience to the course of action it calls for. See Bernstein, *Disenchantment and Ethics*, 163 and 179.

27. Walter Benjamin, "Moral Education," in *Early Writings, 1910–17*, ed. Howard Eiland et al. (Cambridge, Mass.: Belknap, 2011), 108, translation modified. For the original, see *GS* 2/1:48.

28. Among Goethe's contemporary readers, only K. W. F. Solger noted the way in which this backstory casts doubt on the marriage between Eduard and Charlotte: "The *prótarchos áté* [original transgression] lies here not just in the decision to invite the captain and Ottilie, but already in the wavering state [*schwankenden Zustande*] in which the relationship, wisely dissolved by God, between Eduard and his former lover, who on top of it intended Ottilie for him, was nevertheless actualized" (*GHA* 6:635).

29. Thomas Mann, *Death in Venice*, trans. Michael Henry Heim (New York: Ecco, 2004), 137.

30. Kant, *Critique of the Power of Judgment*, 112 (*AA* 5:217). This way of putting the matter simplifies things. In describing aesthetic pleasure as a free harmonious interplay between the imagination and the understanding, Kant tends to stress the productive (as opposed to the reproductive) function of the former, that is, the function involved in the free projection of what he calls "schemata." The fact that the free harmonious play of the faculties must also involve the reproductive imagination is evident, however, from Kant's cautious formulation: in the pure judgment of taste, he writes, the imagination is "*in the first instance* [*erstlich*] taken not as reproductive . . . but as productive" (124 [*AA* 5:240], my italics).

31. Kant, *Critique of the Power of Judgment*, 171 (*AA* 5:290–91). For a more detailed account of this possibility, see my *Receptive Spirit: German Idealism and the Dynamics of Cultural Transmission* (New York: Fordham University Press, 2016), 46–48.

32. See Uwe Steiner, *Die Geburt der Kritik aus dem Geiste der Kunst: Untersuchungen zum Begriff der Kritik in den frühen Schriften Walter Benjamins* (Würzburg: Königshausen & Neumann, 1989), 287.

33. The comment occurs in book 11 of *Poetry and Truth*.

34. Kant, *Critique of the Power of Judgment*, 116–20 (*AA* 5:231–36). I attempt to make sense of this rarely discussed doctrine in *Receptive Spirit*, 49–59.

35. See Novalis, "Miscellaneous Observations," in *Philosophical Writings*, trans. Margaret Mahony Stoljar (Minneapolis: University of Minnesota Press,

1997), 31; Friedrich Schlegel, "Ideas," in *Friedrich Schlegel's Lucinde and the Fragments*, trans. Peter Firchow (Minneapolis: University of Minnesota Press, 1971), 247; and Friedrich Schlegel, "Athenaeum Fragmens," no. 389, in *Philosophical Fragments*, trans. Peter Firchow (Minneapolis: University of Minnesota Press, 1991), 79. On the role of Rosenzweig's recently published book *The Star of Redemption*, which Benjamin began to read at the end of 1920 under Scholem's influence, see Steiner, *Die Geburt der Kritik aus dem Geiste der Kunst*, 291–94.

36. Eli Friedlander, *Walter Benjamin: A Philosophical Portrait* (Cambridge, Mass.: Harvard University Press, 2012), 57.

37. For Menninghaus's interpretation of the expressionless in terms of the Kantian dichotomy of the beautiful and the sublime, see "Das Ausdruckslose," 33–76, esp. 34–46. For another interpretation of this juncture along Kantian lines see Rainer Nägele, *Theater, Theory, Speculation: Walter Benjamin and the Scenes of Modernity* (Baltimore: Johns Hopkins University Press, 1991), 126.

38. Urbich, "Das Ausdruckslose," esp. 96–108 and 116–24.

39. Urbich, "Das Ausdruckslose," 100.

40. Urbich, "Das Ausdruckslose," 104.

41. Urbich, "Das Ausdruckslose," 104.

42. Urbich, "Das Ausdruckslose," 107.

43. Urbich, "Das Ausdruckslose," 106–7.

44. Urbich, "Das Ausdruckslose," 97–98.

45. Urbich, "Das Ausdruckslose," 119.

46. See Kant, *Critique of the Power of Judgment*, 192–93 (*AA* 5:314–15). Another indication of Kant's approximation of beauty to sublimity can be found in his claim that the aesthetic idea by virtue of which an artwork is beautiful promotes "spirit," defined as "the animating principle in the mind" (192–93 [*AA* 5:314–15]); in the "First Introduction" of the third *Critique*, Kant provisionally identifies "the feeling of spirit" as "the capacity for representing sublimity in objects" (50 [*AA* 20:251]).

47. Urbich, "Das Ausdruckslose," 118.

48. Friedrich Nietzsche, *The Birth of Tragedy and Other Writings*, ed. Raymond Geuss and Ronald Speirs, trans. Ronald Speirs (Cambridge: Cambridge University Press, 1999), 16, 50.

49. Nietzsche, *Birth of Tragedy*, 103–4.

50. Nietzsche, *Birth of Tragedy*, 104–5.

51. Nietzsche, *Birth of Tragedy*, 104.

52. See Winfried Menninghaus, "Die Polarität von Mythos und Freiheit in Gesellschaft und Kunst" (Tragödie, Märchen, Goethes Wahlverwandtschaften)," in *Schwellenkunde: Walter Benjamins Passage des Mythos* (Frankfurt: Suhrkamp, 1986), 73–93. See also Winfried Menninghaus, "Romeo und Julia auf dem Dorfe: Eine Interpretation im Anschluss an Walter Benjamin," in *Artistische Schrift: Zur Kompositionskunst Gottfried Kellers* (Frankfurt: Suhrkamp, 1982), 97.

53. Gershom Scholem, *The Story of a Friendship*, trans. Harry Zohn (New York: New York Review of Books Classics, 2003), 73.

54. In this paragraph I draw on T. V. F. Brogan, "Caesura," in *The New Princeton Encyclopedia of Poetry and Poetics*, ed. Alex Preminger and T. V. F. Brogan (Princeton, N.J.: Princeton University Press, 1993), 158–60; and Reuven Tsur,

Poetic Rhythm: Structure and Performance—An Empirical Study in Cognitive Poetics, rev. and exp. 2nd ed. (Sussex, Eng.: Sussex University Press, 2012), 109.

55. Samuel E. Bassett, "The Theory of the Homeric Caesura according to the Extant Remains of the Ancient Doctrine," *American Journal of Philology* 40, no. 4 (1919): 343.

56. Friedrich Hölderlin, "An Casimir Ulrich Boehlendorff: Abschrift Sinclairs Nürtingen bei Stutgard. d. 4 Dec. 1801" (*HBA* 9, Location 2942–2954). The centrality of this second aim to Benjamin's thinking is evident from his citation from the relevant part of the letter to Böhlendorff: "The 'occidental Junoian sobriety'—which Hölderlin, several years before he wrote this, conceived as the almost unattainable goal of all German artistic practice—is only another name for that caesura . . ." ("GEA" 341).

57. See Hölderlin's explanation to his publisher Friedrich Wilmans, to the effect that he aimed to render Greek art "more vividly than usual" (*lebendiger als gewöhnlich*) by highlighting "the Oriental" moment that Greek art had repudiated (*verläugnet*) (Friedrich Hölderlin, "28. September. An Friedrich Wilmans. Nürtingen bei Stutgard. d. 28 Sept. 1803" [*HBA* 11, Location 1549–1551]).

58. Friedrich Hölderlin, "Anmerkungen zum Ödipus" (*HBA* 10, Location 2760).

59. Hölderlin, "Anmerkungen zum Ödipus" (*HBA* 10, Location 2790).

60. Here I follow Urbich's explication of Hölderlin's concept of caesura in terms of the understanding of temporality developed in the fragment "Das untergehende Vaterland." See Urbich, "Das Ausdruckslose," 114–16.

61. Friedrich Hölderlin, "Anmerkungen zum Ödipus" (*HBA* 10, Location 2754–2789). The idea that the caesura confers the stability and simultaneity of aesthetic form on historical transience is the upshot of Joshua Billings's analysis of the Hölderlinian conception. See his *Genealogy of the Tragic: Greek Tragedy and German Philosophy* (Princeton, N.J.: Princeton University Press, 2014), 203–5. In my exposition of Hölderlin's notion of the caesura I cannot follow the lead of Philippe Lacoue-Labarthe's influential essay, in which an overly loose employment of such key terms as "mimesis" and "speculative" yields a reading of the key passages that is itself speculative in the nontechnical sense. See Philippe Lacoue-Labarthe, "The Caesura of the Speculative," in *The Solid Letter: Readings of Friedrich Hölderlin*, ed. Aris Fioretos (Stanford, Calif.: Stanford University Press, 1999), 234ff.

62. *GS* 6:126, quoted in Steiner, *Die Geburt der Kritik aus dem Geiste der Kunst*, 291.

63. Hölderlin, "Anmerkungen zum Ödipus" (*HBA* 10, Location 2775).

64. "GEA" 341. In his 1919 piece "Fate and Character," Benjamin claims that in tragedy "pagan man" falls silent when, confronted with a fateful nexus of necessity that condemns him to guilt, he "becomes aware that he is better than his gods," a moment whose sublimity is owing to the "birth of genius in moral speechlessness, moral infantility" (*SW* 1:204, translation modified).

65. David Constantine's translation effectively highlights the ambiguity of Goethe's formulation by intimating a conjunction of falling and rising. This counterpoint of falling and rising seems especially apt in view of the correspondence established by Benjamin between the falling star of the caesura and the rising stars mentioned in Sulpiz Boisserée's recollection of his conversation with Goethe ("GEA" 354).

66. Wittgenstein's dictum reads: "*The limits of my language* mean the limits of my world" (Ludwig Wittgenstein, *Tractatus Logico-Philosophicus* [5.6], trans. D. F. Pears and B. F. McGuinness [London: Routledge, 2001], 68).

67. As Gerhard Richter writes in connection with Ernst Bloch's reflection on the disappointability of hope, "the hope that is disappointable is the hope that cannot be fully annihilated"; Gerhard Richter, *Afterness: Figures of Following in Modern German Thought and Aesthetics* (New York: Columbia University Press, 2011), 167.

68. As Peter Fenves points out, the "nonsynthesis" of hope in Benjamin corresponds to Kant's claim that the question "What may I hope?" "combines" the questions "What can I know?" and "What should I do?" See Fenves, "Kant in Benjamins Wahlverwandtschaften-Essay," 234.

69. I cite the passage in the New King James Bible version. The image of the falling star recurs in Revelation 9:1–2, but that passage is less pertinent here.

70. On the significance for Hölderlin's hymn of the conflict between Pietist doctrine and biblical criticism, see Jochen Schmidt, *Hölderlins geschichtsphilosophische Hymnen 'Friedensfeier,'–'Der Einzige'–'Patmos'* (Darmstadt: Wissenschaftliche Buchgesellschaft, 1990), 189ff.

71. On the hermetic significance of water, see Schmidt, *Hölderlins geschichtsphilosophische Hymnen*, 203n.

72. To quote Heidegger's relevant comments: "taking the dying of others as a substitute theme for the ontological analysis of the finished character of Da-sein and its totality rests on an assumption that demonstrably fails altogether to recognize the kind of being of Da-sein. That is what one presupposes when one is of the opinion that any Da-sein could arbitrarily be replaced by another, so that what cannot be experienced in one's own Da-sein is accessible in another Da-sein. . . . In 'ending,' and in the totality thus constituted as Da-sein, there is essentially no representation. The way out suggested fails to recognize this existential fact when it proposes the dying of others as a substitute theme for the analysis of totality" (Heidegger, *Being and Time*, 222–23).

73. M. M. Bakhtin, "Author and Hero in Aesthetic Activity," in *Art and Answerability: Early Philosophical Essays by M. M. Bakhtin*, ed. Michael Holquist and Vadim Liapunov, trans. Vadim Liapunov (Austin: University of Texas Press, 1990), 4–256. Although the study remained unfinished, Bakhtin held on to the notebooks throughout his life, making possible a posthumous publication in 1979. On the composition history and the neo-Kantian background of the treatise, see Michael Holquist's "Introduction: The Architectonics of Answerability" in the volume, ix–xviii.

74. Bakhtin, "Author and Hero," 103.

75. Bakhtin, "Author and Hero," 106–7.

76. Bakhtin, "Author and Hero," 117.

77. Bakhtin, "Author and Hero," 127.

78. Bakhtin, "Author and Hero," 131.

79. See Pauline Kleingeld, "Kant on the Unity of Theoretical and Practical Reason," *Review of Metaphysics* 52 (December 1998): 311–39.

80. M. M. Bakhtin, "Art and Answerability," in *Art and Answerability: Early Philosophical Essays by M. M. Bakhtin*, ed. Michael Holquist and Vadim Liapunov, trans. Vadim Liapunov (Austin: University of Texas Press, 1990), 1.

81. Bakhtin, "Art and Answerability," 1.

82. Menninghaus, "Das Ausdruckslose," 54.

83. In his detailed analysis of Benjamin's essay from the standpoint of the pragmatics of interpretation, Thomas Zabka claims that Benjamin's construal of the narrator's remark "dispenses with the analytical demonstration of the putative caesura" and rests "solely" on Benjamin's invocation of the astral imagery in a parallel passage from the poem "Urworte, orphisch." Yet Zabka ignores the more prominently deployed evidence of Sulpiz Boisserée's recollection, presumably because he thinks that Benjamin's recourse to this bit of anecdotal evidence runs counter to his critique of reductive biographical criticism. Such a worry would be misplaced, since Benjamin's deliberate and non-reductive transgression of the boundary between life and work is central to his critical undertaking. See Zabka, *Pragmatik der Literaturinterpretation*, 149 and 165.

84. This is how Menninghaus describes Benjamin's marking of a caesura in "Das Ausdruckslose," 55. See also Urbich, "Das Ausdruckslose," 110–11. Ulrich Rüffer's conclusion is worth quoting: "The shattered narrator, the structure of his experience, and the singular quote from him to which the essayist has confined the narrator give the dialectical image of hope. If in the novel it is 'the most paradoxical, most fleeting' hope, its image is supposed to be definitively fixed through emphatic citation in the essayistic text. Through such citational practice, which introduces potentially violent forms of overinterpretation, the essay itself becomes vulnerable to criticism. However, through this vulnerability and the overtness of the essay's esotericism, the essayist maintains loyalty to the narrator"; Ulrich Rüffer, "Zur Physiognomie des Erzählers in Benjamins Wahlverwandtschaften-Essay," in *Goethes Wahlverwandtschaften: Kritische Modelle und Diskursanalysen zum Mythos Literatur*, ed. Norbert W. Bolz (Hildesheim: Gerstenberg Verlag, 1981), 49.

85. Rodolphe Gasché correctly points out that Benjamin does not simply posit a mutual exclusion between critique and biographical investigation, since he allows the work to shed light on the hidden truth of the author's biography. See Rodolphe Gasché, "Critique, Authentic Biographism, and Ethical Judgment," in *The Honor of Thinking: Critique, Theory, Philosophy* (Stanford, Calif.: Stanford University Press, 2007), 68–69. However, Gasché elides the point—equally important for Benjamin's project but, at least on the face of it, harder to square with his repudiation of biographical criticism—that the critical fracturing of the work requires recourse to biographical evidence. See Gasché's dismissive comment on Benjamin's quotation of the biographical episode recollected by Boisserée ("Critique," 101).

86. On this undertaking, see Peter Fenves, *The Messianic Reduction: Walter Benjamin and the Shape of Time* (Stanford, Calif.: Stanford University Press, 2011), 178–79.

87. See entry N9,4 in Walter Benjamin, *The Arcades Project*, trans. Howard Eiland and Kevin McLaughlin (Cambridge, Mass.: Belknap, 1999), 473.

88. See, for instance, Walter Benjamin, *The Origin of German Tragic Drama*, trans. John Osborne (London: Verso, 2003), 33. The first known use of the formula is in a text by Plutarch, who makes no reference to Plato; that dubious attribution originates with the later Neoplatonist philosopher Simplicius. See James Evans and J. Lennart Berggren, *Geminos's Introduction to the Phenomena: A Translation and Study of a Hellenistic Survey of Astronomy* (Princeton, N.J.: Princeton University Press, 2006), 49–51.

89. Pierre Duhem, *To Save the Phenomena: An Essay on the Idea of Physical Theory from Plato to Galileo* (Chicago: University of Chicago Press, 1969). Angus Nicholls suggests that Benjamin "likely picked up Duhem's discussion" from Emile Meyerson's 1921 study, cited in the *German Tragic Drama* book. See Angus Nicholls, "Against Darwin: Teleology in German Philosophical Anthropology," in *Historical Teleologies in the Modern World*, ed. Henning Trüper, Dipesh Chakrabarty, and Sanjay Subrahmanyam (London: Bloomsbury, 2015), 141n.

90. Current scholarship no longer accepts Duhem's thesis that the principle of saving phenomena was uniformly understood throughout the Hellenistic and medieval periods in an "instrumentalist" sense, that is, as sanctioning merely the formation of heuristic hypotheses that remain noncommittal about reality. See Evans and Berggren, *Geminos's Introduction to the Phenomena*, 51. However, this historical point does not detract from the relevance of Duhem's understanding of the formula to its invocations by Benjamin.

91. Reuss, "Wo aber Gefahr ist, wächst das Rettende auch [. . .]," 33–34.

92. Friedrich Nietzsche, "279. Star friendship," in *Gay Science, with a Prelude in German Rhymes and an Appendix of Songs*, ed. Bernard Williams, trans. Josefine Nauckhoff and Adrian del Caro (Cambridge: Cambridge University Pres, 2001), 159. The preceding two aphorisms suggest that this "sublime hypothesis" is another testimony to "our own theoretical and practical skill in interpreting," easily mistaken for providence—a skill that here permits the postulation of an analogy between a human relationship and a natural one imagined as legible from a suprahuman standpoint—and that this hypothesis only becomes available through an awareness, ordinarily suppressed, of "the brotherhood of death" that finally awaits the estranged friends ("279. Star friendship," 158).

93. Thomas Zabka construes the astral motif in the third part of the essay in terms of his overarching hypothesis that the three parts of Benjamin's essay correspond to the doctrine (descended from Philo of Alexandria) of the threefold meaning of Scripture, which aligns physical, psychological, and pneumatic allegoresis with, respectively, the body, the soul, and spirit. See Zabka, *Pragmatik der Literaturinterpretation*, 143 and 147.

94. Foremost among these apologists was the theologian Andreas Osiander, the anonymous author of the preface to Copernicus's posthumously published foundational work. See Hans Blumenberg, *The Genesis of the Copernican World*, trans. Robert M. Wallace (Cambridge, Mass.: MIT Press, 1987), 200ff. and 224.

95. Benjamin, *The Arcades Project* [K1,2], 388–89.

Chapter Two

1. On Benjamin's influence on Adorno's thinking about *Wozzeck*, see Bernadette Meyler, "Adorno's Shifting *Wozzeck*," in *Modernism and Opera*, ed. Richard Begam and Matthew Wilson Smith (Baltimore: Johns Hopkins University Press, 2016), 154–55. In the conclusion, I will have more to say about Benjamin's remarks on music.

2. "Many measures in Beethoven sound like the sentence in *Elective Affinities*: 'Like a star hope fell from the heavens below'; this is true of the Adagio of the Sonata in D Minor, op. 31, no. 2" (AT 188).

3. Analyzing the use of the concept of caesura in Adorno's writings on Beethoven, Michael Spitzer shows that Adorno often uses the term, in line with

Hölderlin's and Benjamin's use of it, to designate a singular point in the development section of sonata form—namely, the moment of "subjective positing" in the heroic style of Beethoven's middle period, or, by the inverse logic of the late style, the "exit hole of escape" through which subjectivity "expressionlessly" withdraws from the work; Spitzer, *Music and Philosophy: Adorno and Beethoven's Late Style* (Bloomington: Indiana University Press, 2006), 60. Often, however, Adorno posits multiple caesuras at levels ranging from the local to the architectonic. Echoing the normative concept of "*Einschnitt*" in late-eighteenth-century compositional theory, this second use of the term reflects the "recursive" or "fractal" character of the classical style's musical language. This latter use of the term has little affinity with Hölderlin's, unless one counts Hölderlin's transferral of the concept of caesura from the prosodic to the architectonic level of analysis (*Music and Philosophy*, 227ff.). On Adorno's use of the concept of caesura in his 1963 essay "Parataxis" and in his early piece "Late Style in Beethoven," see Robert Savage, "The Polemic of the Late Work: Adorno's Hölderlin," in *Language without Soil: Adorno and Late Philosophical Modernity*, ed. Gerhard Richter (New York: Fordham University Press, 2010), 186–94.

4. Indeed, Benjamin points out that the beautiful figure of Ottilie conjured up by Goethe is closer to the Helen of the second part of Goethe's own Faust than to the Helen of the Iliad ("GEA" 338–39).

5. See Katie Fleming, "Odysseus and Enlightenment: Horkheimer and Adorno's *Dialektik der Aufklärung*," *International Journal of the Classical Tradition* 19, no. 2 (2012): 111.

6. "GE" 37–38. See also the comments on Wilamowitz in footnote 10 of the published text (*DE* 261).

7. On this development, see Georg Bollenbeck, *Bildung und Kultur: Glanz und Elend eines deutschen Deutungsmusters* (Frankfurt: Insel, 1994), 172–73.

8. For an in-depth examination of Borchardt's relevant writings, see Vincenzo Martella, "Dialectics of Cultural Criticism: Adorno's Confrontation with Rudolf Borchardt and Ludwig Klages in the Odyssey Chapter of *Dialektik der Aufklärung*" (Ph.D. diss., Justus-Liebig-Universität Giessen, 2012), 77–128.

9. Nietzsche, *Birth of Tragedy*, 29.

10. Nietzsche, to be sure, follows Friedrich Schlegel in identifying Plato's dialogues as the earliest proto-novelistic works. See Nietzsche, *Birth of Tragedy*, 69. On the affinity between Nietzsche's and Borchardt's views on the novel, see Martella, "Dialectics of Cultural Criticism," 133n.

11. Thomas Mann, *The Magic Mountain*, trans. John E. Woods (New York: Vintage, 1996), 243.

12. James I. Porter, "Odysseus and the Wandering Jew: The Dialectic of Jewish Enlightenment in Adorno and Horkheimer," *Cultural Critique* 74 (Winter 2010): 207–11. See also Wellmer, *Persistence of Modernity*, 3. See also the illuminating connection drawn by Ulrich Plass between the fearful, mimetic garrulousness of Odysseus and Heine's poetic facility, as characterized by Adorno, in Plass, *Language and History in Adorno's Notes to Literature*, 136–41.

13. For the published version, see Theodor W. Adorno, "Über epische Naivität," in *Gesammelte Schriften*, vol. 11 (Frankfurt: Suhrkamp, 1997), 34–40.

14. Theodor W. Adorno, "Der Standort des Erzählers im zeitgenössischen Roman," in *Gesammelte Schriften*, vol. 11 (Frankfurt: Suhrkamp, 1997), 45.

15. On Adorno's disenchantment with German *Kultur* as a result of his experience of America, see Detlev Claussen, *Theodor W. Adorno: Ein letztes Genie* (Frankfurt: Fischer, 2003), 228–29, 247.

16. Novalis, "General Draft," in *Philosophical Writings*, ed. and trans. Margaret Mahony Stoljar (Albany: State University of New York Press, 1997), 135.

17. On this aspect of Borchardt's agenda, see Martella, "Dialectics of Cultural Criticism," 110–11.

18. Georg Lukács, *Die Theorie des Romans: Ein geschichtsphilosophischer Versuch über die Formen der grossen Epik* (Neuwied-Berlin: Luchterhand, 1991), 31–32.

19. Vivian Liska, "Messianic Language and the Idea of Prose: Benjamin and Agamben," in *Messianic Thought Outside Theology*, ed. Anna Glazova and Paul North (New York: Fordham University Press, 2014), 99.

20. Albrecht Wellmer, "The Death of the Sirens and the Origin of the Work of Art," *New German Critique* 81 (Autumn 2000): 11–12.

21. Wellmer, "Death of the Sirens," 13.

22. This question raised by Wellmer points to a lacuna, or worse a circularity, in Adorno's account. As Peter Dews notes, "the notion of sacrifice invoked here presupposes that the proto-human being already has a capacity to restrain its impulses for the sake of later benefit, in other words has at least a rudimentary ego." See Peter Dews, "Dialectics and the Transcendence of Dialectics: Adorno's Relation to Schelling," *British Journal for the History of Philosophy* 22, no. 6 (2014): 1188. See also James I. Porter's characterization of the Adornian Odysseus as "self-pre-possessing (literally so)": "The strangeness of this founding gesture [of self-sacrifice] lies in the fact that for all its rationality it is unwilled" (Porter, "Odysseus and the Wandering Jew," 204). The worry that Adorno does not have a coherent account of the *Urgeschichte* of subjectivity can only deepen in view of the sketchiness of Adorno's relevant statements. See, for example, Adorno, "On Subject and Object," 258.

23. Wellmer, "Death of the Sirens," 15–16.

24. Borchardt describes Doric chant as "feierlich im allverbindenden Festsinne" ("solemn in the universally binding sense of celebration"): Rudolf Borchardt, *Pindarische Gedichte* (Stuttgart: Klett-Cotta, 1931), 108, quoted in Martella, "Dialectics of Cultural Cricisism," 127.

25. On retention and protention in the perception of melody, see Edmund Husserl, *Husserliana X: Zur Phänomenologie des inneren Zeitbewusstseins (1893–1917)*, ed. Rudolf Boehm (The Hague: Martinus Nijhoff, 1969), 35.

26. Homer, *The Odyssey*, trans. Emily Wilson (New York: W. W. Norton, 2017), 492.

27. Benjamin, *The Origin of German Tragic Drama*, 166, translation corrected and quoted in Theodor W. Adorno, "The Idea of Natural History," trans. Robert Hullot-Kentor, *Praxis* 4, no. 2 (July 1984): 120.

28. Hegel, *Phenomenology of Spirit*, 226, paragraph 565.

29. In a letter to Horkheimer dated November 28, 1936, Adorno wrote apropos of the blindness of classical philology to social history: "A disenchantment of antiquity is an unconditional necessity: the whole craft has significance only as concealment" ("Eine Entzauberung der Antike ist unbedingt notwendig: das ganze Handwerk hat bloß verhüllende Bedeutung," quoted in Martella, "Dialectics of

Cultural Criticism," 93). Adorno probably learned of Murray's work from the classical scholar Maurice Bowra, whom he befriended during his time in Oxford, and who was expected at the time to succeed Murray in his recently vacated Regius Professorship. Since Bowra was a liberal with a taste for conservative German authors such as George, Borchardt, Hofmannsthal, and Kantorowicz, Adorno recruited him for a disenchantment of antiquity which was to take the form of an article for the periodical of the Institute for Social Research. The *Zeitschrift für Sozialforschung* published Bowra's article in 1937, but Adorno's disappointment with the piece meant that in the end it fell to him to carry out the disenchantment of antiquity. On Adorno's contacts with Bowra, see Martella, "Dialectics of Cultural Criticism," 91–94.

30. Gilbert Murray, *The Rise of the Greek Epic, Being a Course of Lectures Delivered at Harvard University* (Oxford: Clarendon, 1911), 141–46.

31. Theodor W. Adorno, "Words from Abroad," in *Notes to Literature, Volume One*, 188, translation modified.

32. "What is at stake is not to portray literary works in the context of their age, but to represent [*zur Darstellung zu bringen*] the age that perceives them—our age—in the age during which they arose" (*SW* 3:290).

33. Benjamin's biographers plausibly suggest that the institute's decision and Adorno's critique were "probably the most crushing rejection of [Benjamin's] career." See Howard Eiland and Michael W. Jennings, *Walter Benjamin: A Critical Life* (Cambridge, Mass.: Belknap, 2014), 622.

34. Walter Benjamin, letter to Theodor W. Adorno, December 9, 1938 (trans. by Harry Zohn modified), in *Aesthetics and Politics*, by Theodor W. Adorno, Walter Benjamin, Bertolt Brecht, and Georg Lukács (London: Verso, 2007), 136–37.

35. "Your study of Goethe's *Elective Affinities* and your Baroque book are better Marxism than the wine duty and the deduction of phantasmagoria from the behaviour of the feuilletonists" (Theodor W. Adorno, letter to Walter Benjamin, November 10, 1938, in Adorno et al., *Aesthetics and Politics*, 131).

36. Katie Fleming writes: "In 1931, in one of many inflammatory and violently anti-Semitic articles in *Der Angriff*, Goebbels adopted the persona of Cicero, and called for the expulsion of the Jews from Germany: 'Wie lange noch, Catilina, willst du unsere Geduld und Langmut mißbrauchen?' " (Fleming, "Odysseus and Enlightenment," 125).

37. The preface by Kraus, along with the other relevant texts, can be found in *Karl Kraus—Rosa Luxemburg: Büffelhaut und Kreatur: Die Zerstörung der Natur und das Mitleiden des Satirikers*, ed. Friedrich Pfäfflin (Berlin: Friedenauer Presse, 2009).

38. Rosa Luxemburg, "To Sophie Liebknecht, December 1917," in *The Letters of Rosa Luxemburg*, ed. Annelies Laschitza, Georg Adler, and Peter Hudis, trans. George Shriver (London: Verso, 2013), 457.

39. Luxemburg, "To Sophie Liebknecht, December 1917."

40. Pfäfflin, ed., *Karl Kraus—Rosa Luxemburg: Büffelhaut und Kreatur*, 15.

41. Between 1920 and 1928, Kraus read the letter by Luxemburg (in lightly abridged form) at no less than ten public readings held in Berlin, Dresden, Prague, Vienna, and Karlsbad (see Pfäfflin ed., *Karl Kraus—Rosa Luxemburg*, 24). The importance for Benjamin of Luxemburg's letter and Kraus's polemical response to

von Lill-Rastern von Lilienbach may be assessed from the fact that he first mentioned it in his letter of December 29, 1920, to Gershom Scholem and returned to it in a letter of May 6, 1934. See Benjamin, *The Correspondence of Walter Benjamin*, 171 and 439. During Adorno's time in Vienna in 1925–26, he and Alban Berg attended several readings by Kraus. Although Adorno's first reaction to Kraus was guarded, his appreciation grew as he read Kraus's works. See Stefan Müller-Doohm, *Adorno: A Biography*, trans. Rodney Livingstone (Cambridge: Polity, 2005), 92.

42. Pfäfflin, ed., *Karl Kraus—Rosa Luxemburg: Büffelhaut und Kreatur*, 3.

43. For a version of the hypothesis that the caesura is a kind of "Atempause," see Otto Schröder, *Griechische Singverse* (Leipzig: Dieterich'sche Verlagsbuchhandlung, 1924), 8. For a counterargument, see Samuel Bassett, "The Theory of Homeric Caesura," 344. The mainstream position in current prosodic scholarship treats caesuras as metrical features introduced by the poet that should not to be conflated with optional performative pauses, although they may be marked in oral performance. See also Brogan, "Caesura," 159.

44. Examples include Benjamin's claim in the *German Tragic Drama* book that the contemplative discourse of the treatise moves among levels of meaning in a discontinuous manner, with an "incessant pausing for breath [*Atemholen*]," and his comment on Proust: "This asthma became part of his art—if indeed his art did not create it. Proust's syntax rhythmically, step by step, enacts his fear of suffocating. And his ironic, philosophical, didactic reflections invariably are the deep breath [*Aufatmen*] with which he shakes off the crushing weight of memories." See Benjamin, *Origin of German Tragic Drama*, 28; and *SW* 2/1:246.

45. Andrew Hewitt has argued that women are "included" in Horkheimer and Adorno's account "only by their exclusion," and always in relation to the male subject. See Andrew Hewitt, "A Feminine Dialectic of Enlightenment? Horkheimer and Adorno Revisited," *New German Critique* 56 (Summer 1992). Inasmuch as women represent a particularity leveled by identitarian thought and can still experience the domination that is thoroughly internalized and hence no longer experienceable by men, they embody a tenuous possibility of utopian escape. However, since women are denied the "honor of individualization" that comes with subjecthood, Horkheimer and Adorno end up, or so Hewitt argues, perpetuating the exclusion that they condemn. Rochelle Duford convincingly counters that *Dialectic of Enlightenment* unmasks the mechanisms by which "the weight of the representation of all those things non-masculine is forced upon" women, rather than participating in such essentializing thought. See Rochelle Duford, "Daughters of the Enlightenment: Reconstructing Adorno on Gender and Feminist Praxis," *Hypatia* 32, no. 4 (Fall 2017): 789.

46. This expressionlessness anticipates the symptom-free life of the "regular guy, the popular girl" described in *Minima Moralia*, denizens of a world without "dark closets," whose psyches have been so thoroughly normalized through "prehistoric surgical interventions" that a neurotic conflict between instincts and ego cannot even arise in the first place. See Adorno, "36. The Health Unto Death," in *MM* 58–59.

47. Goethe's comment to General von Rühle was recorded by Varnhagen von Ense. See his diary entry of June 28, 1843, quoted in the "Appendix" of the Hamburg edition of *Die Wahlverwandtschaften* (*GHA* 6:623).

48. To quote the relevant passage from Flaubert's letter to Louise Colet: "The author's comments [*réflexions*] irritated me continually. Does one have to make observations [*réflexions*] about slavery? Depict it: that's enough. . . . Look at *The Merchant of Venice* and see whether anyone declaims against usury. But the dramatic form has that virtue—of eliminating the author. . . . An author in his book must be like God in the universe, present everywhere and visible nowhere. Art being a second Nature, the creator of that Nature must behave similarly. In all its atoms, in all its aspects, let there be sensed a hidden, infinite impassivity [*impassibilité*]. The effect for the spectator must be a kind of amazement. 'How is all that done?' one must ask; and one must feel overwhelmed without knowing why. Greek art followed that principle, and to achieve its effects more quickly it chose characters of exceptional social conditions—kings, gods, demigods. You were not encouraged to identify with the dramatis personae: the divine was the goal"; Gustave Flaubert, "To Louise Colet, 9 December 1852," in *The Letters of Gustave Flaubert, Volumes I–II, 1830–1880*, ed. and trans. Francis Steegmuller (London: Picador, 2001), 238–39.

49. Emily Wilson, translator's note, in Homer, *The Odyssey*, trans. Wilson, 88–89.

50. On the Flaubertian taboo and its modernist rejection, see Adorno, "Der Standort des Erzählers im zeitgenössischen Roman," 45.

51. So Benjamin concludes his review "Das Problem des Klassischen und die Antike: Acht Vorträge gehalten auf der Fachtagung der klassischen Altertumswissenschaft zu Naumburg 1930" (GS 3:294). This claim, along with Adorno's later meditation on the execution scene, may be taken to counter the grim assertion made by Nietzsche, that authoritative forerunner of conservative *Kulturphilosophie*, to the effect that "slavery belongs to the essence of a culture." See Friedrich Nietzsche, "The Greek State [1871/72]," in *On the Genealogy of Morality*, ed. Keith Ansell-Pearson, trans. Carol Diethe (Cambridge: Cambridge University Press, 2006), 166. Nietzsche's views on this matter also surfaced in connection with the novel indirectly referenced in Adorno's citation of the Flaubertian term *impassibilité*, for Nietzsche dismissed Beecher Stowe as a "misguided disciple of Rousseau" and lamented the abolition of slavery in the United States. See Martin Ruehl, "Politeia 1871: Nietzsche 'Contra' Wagner on the Greek State," in *Bulletin of the Institute of Classical Studies, Supplement, No. 79, Out of Arcadia: Classics and Politics in the Age of Burckhardt, Nietzsche and Wilamowitz*, ed. Ingo Gildenhard and Martin Ruehl (London: Institute of Classical Studies, 2003), 84.

52. I modified Jephcott's translation of *Märchen* as "fable" because it is clear, for reasons that will become apparent shortly, that what Adorno has in mind is not a didactic story. Here is the place to note my disagreement with Britta Scholze's reading of Adorno's comments on the novel in his excursus. According to Scholze, Adorno means to counter Lukács's alignment of epic with totalization by showing that the content of the *Odyssey*, far from being a product of aesthetic totalization, actually shapes aesthetic form and includes moments of self-reflexive resistance to fiction that make the epic less ideologically deluded than the novel: "Gerade aufgrund seiner Formbestimmtheit kann das Epos nicht gänzlich dem Bereich des Fiktiven zugeordnet werden, sondern seine Aktualität als Geschichstdokument bewahren." See Britta Scholze, *Kunst als Kritik: Adornos Weg aus*

der Dialektik (Würzburg: Königshausen & Neumann, 2000), 83. Accordingly, Scholze claims that the final sentence of the excursus offers a critical paraphrase of the Lukácsian reading of the *Odyssey* as a consoling novelistic totality which, by relegating horror to a distant past, turns a blind eye to the ongoing horror of a world that remains captive to myth. This interpretation rests on the following implausible premises: that the final sentences of the excursus convey a thought that Adorno rejects; that the epic is more reflective and less fictional than the novel; that Adorno assumed that Lukács would read the *Odyssey* as a novel; and that such a Lukácsian reading of the *Odyssey* would produce a consoling impression of pastness, fictitiousness, or fatefulness (Scholze wavers between these suggestions).

53. Johann Wolfgang Goethe, "Über epische und dramatische Dichtung: Von Goethe und Schiller," *GHA* 12:249.

54. M. M. Bakhtin, "Epic and Novel," in *The Dialogic Imagination: Four Essays*, ed. Michael Holquist, trans. Caryl Emerson and Michael Holquist (Austin: University of Texas Press, 1996), 13–14.

55. Siegfried Kracauer, "The Mass Ornament," in *The Mass Ornament: Weimar Essays*, ed. and trans. Thomas Y. Levin (Cambridge, Mass.: Harvard University Press, 1995), 81.

56. Seyla Benhabib, *Critique, Norm, and Utopia: A Study of the Foundations of Critical Theory* (New York: Columbia University Press, 1986), 188.

57. This understanding of the caesura as the liberating remembrance of a traumatic past may be contrasted with the understanding of caesura as a mark of forgetting that was developed by Max Kommerell, an authoritative critic of the George circle. As Paul Fleming has shown, Adorno's implicit polemic with Kommerell in his 1959 essay "On the Final Scene of *Faust*" turns on this very issue. Kommerell argued that Faust's enigmatic salvation at the end of Goethe's play was made possible by the unreflectiveness of his striving: his lapses into oblivion, producing a rhythmic recurrence of caesuras in the play, allow him to be transformed and to forget his misdeeds. Adorno follows Kommerell in suggesting that the caesura of mercy at the end of the drama answers to Faust's nonidentity with himself owing to these caesuras of oblivion: the old Faust is "no longer the one who signed the pact." Yet Adorno corrects Kommerell by construing Faust's forgetfulness as the precondition for a subsequent involuntary remembrance of what has been destroyed, nourishing a hope for reconciliation. As Fleming notes, Adorno's essay itself becomes a site of such remembrance, since it ends with a meditation on hope that echoes the conclusion of Benjamin's essay on *Elective Affinities*. See Paul Fleming, "Forgetting–*Faust*: Adorno and Kommerell," in *Adorno and Literature*, ed. David Cunningham and Nigel Mapp (London: Continuum, 2006), 133–44. By way of extending Fleming's argument, I would argue that Adorno's uses of the concept of caesura in the excursus on Odysseus and in the later essay on *Faust* represent complementary sides of the dialectic of continuity and discontinuity that governs his thinking about utopia. Whereas the caesura marked in the excursus on Odysseus is a moment of remembrance that enables the present to free itself from compulsive recurrences, in the *Faust* essay the caesura marks a forgetting that allows for a subsequent remembrance charged with utopian hope.

58. Hegel, *Phenomenology of Spirit*, 38, paragraph 79.

59. On this parallel, see Rüdiger Bittner, "Does *Dialectic of Enlightenment* Rest on Religious Foundations?" in *The Early Frankfurt School and Religion*, ed. Margarete Kohlenbach and Raymond Geuss (New York: Palgrave Macmillan, 2005), 163–70.

60. This is my translation of the sentence, which is rendered unintelligible in Jephcott's translation (*DE* 31). The original reads: "Indem aber die Aufklärung gegen jede Hypostasierung der Utopie recht behält und die Herrschaft als Entzweiung ungerührt verkündet, wird der Bruch von Subjekt und Objekt, den sie zu überdecken verwehrt, zum Index seiner Unwahrheit und der Wahrheit"; Max Horkheimer and Theodor W. Adorno, *Dialektik der Aufklärung: Philosophische Fragmente* (Frankfurt: Fischer, 1993), 46.

61. On the inversion of the Spinozistic doctrine, originating in Scholastic thought, see Bittner, "Does *Dialectic of Enlightenment* Rest on Religious Foundations?" 165.

62. Hegel, *Phenomenology of Spirit*, 35–36, paragraphs 73–75.

63. Rüdiger Bittner arrives at a similar conclusion, though without having shown the unworkability of the Hegelian reconstruction that Horkheimer and Adorno's formulations gesture toward. See Bittner, "Does *Dialectic of Enlightenment* Rest on Religious Foundations?" 168–70.

64. See Rahel Jaeggi, "'No Individual Can Resist': *Minima Moralia* as Critique of Forms of Life," *Constellations* 12, no. 1 (2005): 73.

65. See James Gordon Finlayson, "Hegel, Adorno and the Origins of Immanent Criticism," *British Journal for the History of Philosophy* 22, no. 6 (2014): 1161. Adopting Uwe Justus Wenzel's framework, Rahel Jaeggi proposes that Adorno's critique of our form of life can be immanent by virtue of an "asymmetrical reciprocity" between negative diagnosis and positive utopia: although the diagnosis depends on an initially indeterminate utopian counterimage, the latter gains definite contours through the former. See Jaeggi, "'No Individual Can Resist,'" 75. However, while the "highly specific constellations" of *Minima Moralia* can indeed produce "situationally defined counterimages" (76), it is hard to see how this strategy could work in the more abstract context of *Dialectic of Enlightenment*.

66. Plato, *The Republic*, 414b-c; and Immanuel Kant, "Kritik der praktischen Vernunft," *AA* 5:30. Martella rightly notes that "in the *Odyssey* chapter, Adorno at times unintentionally exposes the idealistic premises and entailments of his philosophy, as for instance when he overvalues the role and power of individual consciousness in 'making' history" (Martella, "Dialectics of Cultural Criticism," 344n).

Chapter Three

1. Kant, *Critique of the Power of Judgment*, 192 (*AA* 5:313).

2. On reconciliation as "communication of what is differentiated," or "agreement between human beings and things," see Adorno, "On Subject and Object," 247.

3. Theodor W. Adorno, "Late Style in Beethoven," in *Essays on Music*, ed. Richard Leppert, trans. Susan H. Gillespie (Berkeley: University of California Press, 2002), 564.

4. Adorno, "Late Style in Beethoven," 565–66, translation modified.

5. Elsewhere Adorno explicitly notes the parallelism between the constitution of the subject and that of the artwork: "Expression is the gaze of artworks. Compared to significative language, the language of expression is older though unfulfilled: as if artworks, by molding themselves to the subject through their organization, recapitulated the way the subject originated, how it wrested itself free. Artworks bear expression not where they communicate [*mitteilen*] the subject, but rather where they are set atremble [*erzittern*] by the protohistory of subjectivity, of ensoulment, for which tremolo of any sort is a miserable surrogate. This is the affinity of the artwork to the subject and it endures because this protohistory survives in the subject and recommences in every moment of history" (*AT* 112–13, translation modified).

6. See Kant, *Critique of Pure Reason*, 235–36 (A113–14). This parallel lends support to Peter Uwe Hohendahl's provocative suggestion that "for Adorno's own aesthetic theory, the insights of Kant's First Critique turn out to be more valuable and demanding than Kant's discussion of the artwork." See Hohendahl, "Human Freedom and the Autonomy of Art: The Legacy of Kant," in *The Fleeting Promise of Art: Adorno's Aesthetic Theory Revisited* (Ithaca, N.Y.: Cornell University Press, 2013), 35.

7. I modified Hullot-Kentor's translation of the sentence "Die Homerische Erzählung von der Penelope, die nächtens auftrennt, was sie des Tages gewirkt hat, ist eine ihrer selbst unbewußte Allegorie von Kunst: was die Listige an ihren Artefakten verübt, das verübt sie eigentlich an sich selbst"; Theodor W. Adorno, *Ästhetische Theorie*, ed. Gretel Adorno and Rolf Tiedemann (Frankfurt: Suhrkamp, 1973), 278. Hullot-Kentor translates the last clause, erroneously in my view, as "she actually inflicts on herself." Since the idea of Penelope undoing herself makes as little sense in the Homeric context as in the context of Adorno's argument, the pronoun "sie" must refer to "art" ("die Kunst"), not Penelope. The adverb "actually" (*eigentlich*) highlights the difference between the literal meaning (Penelope undoing her artifact) and the allegorical one (art undoing itself).

8. Rebecca Comay, "Adorno's Siren Song," *New German Critique* 81 (Autumn 2000): 46–47.

9. Comay, "Adorno's Siren Song," 280. See also Theodor W. Adorno, "Schöne Stellen," in *Gesammelte Schriften*, vol. 18: *Musikalische Schriften*, ed. Rolf Tiedemann and Klaus Schultz (Frankfurt: Suhrkamp, 1984), 695–718.

10. For adumbrations of the utopia of reconciliation, see *ND* 6; Adorno, "On Subject and Object," 247; and Theodor W. Adorno, "Lecture 8, 19 June 1958," in *An Introduction to Dialectics*, ed. Christoph Ziermann, trans. Nicholas Walker (Cambridge: Polity, 2017), 71.

11. See Bernard Williams, "The Makropoulos Case: Reflections on the Tedium of Immortality," in *Problems of the Self: Philosophical Papers 1956–1972* (Cambridge: Cambridge University Press, 1973), 82–100.

12. Theodor W. Adorno, "49. Morality and Temporal Sequence," *MM* 78–80.

13. Ovid, *Metamorphoses*, trans. Charles Martin (New York: W. W. Norton, 2004), 721.

14. The relevant passage reads: "What serves as a sign of the reconciliation of genius, which is no longer hardened and enclosed within itself, however, is that mortality—as opposed to mythic infinitude in the bad sense—is attributed to it . . . Genius itself is also nature. Its death 'im Ernste des Lebens,' in the

seriousness of life—that would be the extinction of reflection, and of art with it, in the moment when reconciliation passes out of the medium of the merely spiritual and into reality." Theodor W. Adorno, "Parataxis: On Hölderlin's Late Poetry," in *Notes to Literature, Volume Two*, trans. Shierry Weber Nicholsen (New York: Columbia University Press, 1992), 149.

15. See *ND* 395–97. On aesthetic experience as a training ground for fostering such experiential openness through a strengthening of the subject, see Wellmer, *The Persistence of Modernity*, 19.

16. Adorno, "On Subject and Object," 254. Conversely, Adorno claims that "what transcendental philosophy praised in creative subjectivity is the subject's own self-concealed imprisonment within itself. The subject remains harnessed within everything objective it thinks, like an armored animal in its layers of carapace it vainly tries to shake loose; yet it never occurred to those animals to vaunt their captivity as freedom" (252).

17. The idea that the gods envy humans' death-bound solidarity represents a reversal of Nietzsche's claim that the Olympian gods of the Homeric poems justified human life by living it in a transfigured form: "The same drive which calls art into being to complete and perfect existence and thus to seduce us into continuing to live, also gave rise to the world of the Olympians in which the Hellenic 'Will' held up a transfiguring mirror to itself. Thus gods justify the life of men by living it themselves—the only satisfactory theodicy! Under the bright sunshine of such gods existence is felt to be worth attaining, and the real pain of Homeric man refers to his departure from this existence, particularly to imminent departure, so that one might say of them, reversing the wisdom of Silenus, that 'the very worst thing for them was to die soon, the second worst ever to die at all' " (Nietzsche, *The Birth of Tragedy*, 24).

18. Emily Wilson, "A Translator's Reckoning with the Women of the Odyssey," *New Yorker*, December 8, 2017, https://www.newyorker.com/books/page-turner/a-translators-reckoning-with-the-women-of-the-odyssey.

19. Homer, *The Odyssey*, trans. Wilson, 441.

20. Seyla Benhabib, *Critique, Norm, and Utopia: A Study of the Foundations of Critical Theory* (New York: Columbia University Press, 1986), 40 and 61.

21. Benjamin, *GS* 5/2:1057. On the problem of the continuity versus discontinuity of awakening, see Winfried Menninghaus, "Walter Benjamin's Theory of Myth," in *On Walter Benjamin: Critical Essays and Recollections*, ed. Gary Smith (Cambridge: Cambridge University Press, 1988), 310. See also John McCole, *Walter Benjamin and the Antinomies of Tradition* (Ithaca, N.Y.: Cornell University Press, 1993), 250–52 and 298.

22. Theodor W. Adorno, *Hegel: Three Studies*, trans. Shierry Weber Nicholsen (Cambridge, Mass.: MIT Press, 1993), 6–7, 92–94. See also "Dedication," *MM* 16; and *ND* 7, 27.

23. See Theodor W. Adorno, "The Actuality of Philosophy," trans. Benjamin Snow, *Telos* 31 (1977): 129. For an illuminating interpretation of the program outlined in this key early text, see Henry W. Pickford, "Riddlework I," in *Der aufrechte Gang im windschiefen Kapitalismus: Modelle Kritischen Denkens*, ed. Rüdiger Dannemann, Henry Pickford, and Hans-Ernst Schiller (Wiesbaden: Springer, 2018), 667–91. Adorno's thinking about this problematic may be contrasted with the Hegelian claim that philosophical thought shows contradictions

to be self-dissolving and reconciled. For a programmatic statement of this view, see G. W. F. Hegel, *Aesthetics: Lectures on Fine Art*, vol. 1, trans. T. M. Knox (Oxford: Clarendon, 1988), 54–55.

24. Theodor W. Adorno, "Cultural Criticism and Society," in *Prisms*, trans. Samuel Weber and Shierry Weber (Cambridge, Mass.: MIT Press, 1983), 27–28.

25. See Adorno, "Cultural Criticism and Society," 29–33.

26. Finlayson, "Hegel, Adorno and the Origins of Immanent Criticism," 1157.

27. I address the way in which the Kantian problematic surfaces in this passage in *Receptive Spirit*, 209–11.

28. Kant, *Critique of the Power of Judgment*, 225–28 (*AA* 5:351–54).

29. Kant, *Critique of the Power of Judgment*, 156 (*AA* 5:274).

30. Although the noncoincidence between positive and negative presentation is a central tenet of Adorno's thinking about art, it is not an exceptionless one. In the final section of his essay on Proust, Adorno identifies a unique crack (Spalt) in Proust's work that affords a glimpse of the "last things" reserved for metaphysics. Commenting on a single sentence in which Proust tentatively entertains the possibility of Bergotte's immortality, Adorno tacitly fuses the positive with the negative variant of the caesura model. See Theodor W. Adorno, "Short Commentaries on Proust," in *Notes to Literature, Volume One*, ed. Rolf Tiedemann, trans. Shierry Weber Nicholsen (New York: Columbia University Press, 1991), 183–84.

Chapter Four

1. For discussions of Benjamin's essay that take him to posit two caesuras, see Ulrich Rüffer, "Zur Physiognomie des Erzählers in Benjamins Wahlverwandtschaften-Essay," 45; and N. K. Leacock, Character, Silence, and the Novel: Walter Benjamin on Goethe's Elective Affinities," *Narrative* 10, no. 3 (2002): 296.

2. Meyler, "Adorno's Shifting *Wozzeck*," 175.

3. Billings, *Genealogy of the Tragic*, 203ff.

4. Paul Fleming, "The Crisis of Art: Max Kommerell and Jean Paul's Gestures," *Modern Language Notes* 115, no. 3 (April 2000): 541–42.

5. Writing to Bettina Brentano in November 1809, Achim von Arnim takes the first half of *Elective Affinities* to portray "the boredom of unoccupied, inactive happiness" characteristic of educated noblemen who lack any direction (*GHA* 6:281).

6. A somewhat similar model is proposed in a musicological dissertation by Brent Andrew Wetters apropos of *Oedipus the King*. In addition to the caesura identified by Hölderlin, Wetters posits a "secondary articulation that occurs toward the end, where prophecy is proved true and the horrible truth of Oedipus's actions is revealed to him . . . The tension and resolution of what amounts to two complementary caesuras—the prophecy and its fulfillment—are what allow *Oedipus* to stand as a discrete work. The joining of these two moments has the effect of stopping the incessant flow of time. Instead of a mere succession of scenes, the play becomes a graspable object—something as clear as a single poetic line. It is as if, at the moment of *caesura*, the entire work pivots on the axis of time and can be understood (viewed) in its entirety." See Brent Andrew Wetters, "Darmstadt and the Philosophical Turn" (Ph.D. diss., Brown University, 2012), 6, https://repository.library.brown.edu/storage/bdr:297687/PDF/. Wetters's version

of the double caesura model differs from mine inasmuch as it construes the relation between the two caesuras as one of prophecy and fulfillment. Moreover, Wetters doesn't consider the applicability of his modification of the Benjaminian model to *Elective Affinities*; nor does he elaborate his thesis regarding Adorno's formative influence on the Darmstadt school in terms of Adorno's use of the concept of caesura.

7. The key formulation in the novella is "he seized her [*er faßte sie*], raised, and bore her," and in the scene interrupted by the hard caesura: "'I shall do as you ask,' Eduard cried . . . clasping her tightly in his arms. She enfolded him in hers and pressed him lovingly against her heart" (*EA* 191, 206). See Zabka, *Pragmatik der Literaturinterpretation*, 150–51.

8. EA 182. Exploiting the interchangeability of *englisch* and *engelisch* in archaic German usage, Jochen Hörisch has linked the camera obscura used by the English Lord to capture picturesque views of the estate to the "'*Lord* of Hosts (of angels)' beyond the human eye." This hint of transcendence is, as I shall suggest, not fortuitous. Quoted in Stanley Corngold, "Genuine Obscurity Shadows the Semblance Whose Obliteration Promises Redemption," in *Benjamin's Ghosts: Interventions in Contemporary Literary and Cultural Theory*, ed. Gerhard Richter (Stanford, Calif.: Stanford University Press, 2002), 163 and 330n.

9. J. W. von Goethe, Hermann und Dorothea, canto IX, l. 262–289 (*GHA* 2:512–13).

10. This nuance is lost in David Constantine's translation of "da alle Welt staunend verstummte" as "when for astonishment nobody spoke" (*EA* 211).

11. By intimating the necessity of an interminable retrogression into the past that undermines the possibility of a proper narrative beginning, Goethe's novel verges on a philosophical problematic. In the same year in which Goethe's novel appeared, Schelling—whose philosophy of nature had a considerable influence on the novel—published his *Philosophical Investigations into the Essence of Freedom*. Inaugurating Schelling's "Ages of the World" project, this work is literally groundbreaking: it culminates in a paradoxical theogony that narrates the formation of God's personality out of the divine "ground" and, in a further regressive step, the differentiation of both out of the "non-ground" (*Ungrund*). A similar retrogressive logic drove Richard Wagner to gradually expand his projected work about Siegfried's death into a mythological cycle encompassing the very origins of cosmic order.

12. Wolf Kittler, "Goethe Wahlverwandtschaften: Sociale Verhältnisse symbolisch dargestellt," in *Goethes Wahlverwandtschaften: Kritische Modelle und Diskursanalysen zum Mythos Literatur*, ed. Norbert W. Bolz (Hildesheim: Gerstenberg, 1981), 233; and Friedrich Kittler, "Ottilie Hauptmann," in *Goethes Wahlverwandtschaften*, ed. Bolz, 267–68. See also Alexander Honold, *Der Leser Walter Benjamin: Bruchstücke einer deutschen Literaturgeschichte* (Berlin: Vorwerk 8, 2000), 143.

13. Thomas Zabka finds this hypothesis plausible in view of the fact, recalled by Charlotte in chapter 1 of part 1, that Eduard's father had forbidden Eduard to marry Charlotte. Yet this inference, similarly to the entirety of Zabka's otherwise meticulous analysis, neglects to take into account the fact that the novella is based on an incident from the captain's, rather than Eduard's, life. See Zabka, *Pragmatik der Literaturinterpretation*, 167.

14. "Ist in der Novelle wirklich der Rettende, nicht der Abgewiesene der Hauptmann?" (*GS* 1/3:839). For the hypothesis that is being questioned here, see André François-Poncet, *Les Affinités Électives de Goethe: Essai de commentaire critique* (Paris: Félix Alcan, 1910), 187.

15. My argument in this section concurs with Helmut Hühn's critique that Benjamin's antithetical construction fails to acknowledge a "traumatic kernel" in the novella. However, whereas Hühn seems to think that this traumatic kernel is simply due to the unhappy outcome of the real-life incident, I am arguing for the opposite claim. Since the real-life incident is already known to Charlotte, what she evidently finds unbearable is its fictional transfiguration in the companion's narrative, and in particular the severe reproach implied by the ethical ideal that emerges from that narrative. See Helmut Hühn, "Einsicht in einen Lichtkern des erlösenden Gehalts: Benjamins *Wahlverwandtschaften*-Essay im Spiegel der Forschung," in *Benjamins Wahlverwandtschaften: Zur Kritik einer programmatischen Interpretation*, ed. Helmut Hühn, Jan Urbich, and Uwe Steiner (Frankfurt: Suhrkamp, 2015), 330.

16. The only discussion known to me that connects Benjamin's essay on *Elective Affinities* to his later essay on Leskov is Ulrich Rüffer's highly compressed essay from 1981, which also stands out for its attention to the relationship between the two caesuras. Rüffer argues that at both junctures the mystified novelistic narrator gives way to a genuine narrator. To be sure, the latter figure appears in a characteristically modern guise, inasmuch as he owes the precarious authority of his "stance" (*Haltung*) to his "being shattered" (*Erschütterung*) and disempowered. This genuine narrator becomes a stage for perilous and imperiled forces, whose critical situation is defined by the tension between two possibilities, corresponding to the two caesuras: on the one hand redemption, and on the other, doom that permits only hope for the sake of the hopeless. Focused on the sentence in chapter 13 of part 2, Rüffer's analysis does not work out the implications of this approach for the novella and its framing. See Rüffer, "Zur Physiognomie des Erzählers in Benjamins Wahlverwandtschaften-Essay," in *Goethes Wahlverwandtschaften*, ed. Bolz, 45–51.

17. Goethe himself learned of the incident that inspired the novella from an English newspaper, mentioned in *Italienische Reise*. See Hühn, "Einsicht in den Lichtkern des erlösenden Gehalts," 328. This detail appears significant in light of Benjamin's claim that the regime of information inaugurated by newspapers was one of the forces that brought about the supersession of integral experience by lived experience. When the novelistic narrator claims that the novella emerged through the kind of transmission that elevates an incident to the plane of integral experience, this may be viewed as an instance of Goethe's own attempt at a fictional transfiguration of *Erlebnis* into *Erfahrung*.

18. According to Gadamer's survey of the history of the word *Erlebnis*, the earliest documented use of the noun—still as an idiosyncratic coinage, as indicated by its being preceded by a feminine article rather than the now-customary neutral one—occurs in a letter by Hegel. See Hans-Georg Gadamer, *Truth and Method*, 2nd rev. ed., trans. and rev. Joel Weinsheimer and Donald G. Marshall (London: Continuum, 2004), 53, 95.

19. Ernst Bloch, *Erbschaft dieser Zeit: Erweiterte Ausgabe* (Frankfurt: Suhrkamp, 1962), 104–26.

20. Walter Benjamin, "On Some Motifs in Baudelaire," *SW* 4:331.

21. My argument about the positivity of the image of fulfillment that Benjamin sees in the novella complements Michael W. Jennings's emphasis on the "absolutely negative truth" conveyed by the apocalyptic decisions of the characters. See Jennings, *Dialectical Images*, 137. It is indeed significant that the image of redemption presented in the novella is replete with negative moments. Nevertheless, a basic moment of positivity attaches to the novella *as* a story that presents a definite scenario of decisive action and triumphant fidelity.

Chapter Five

1. On this topic Blanchot writes: "André Breton repudiates music because he wants to preserve in himself the right to hear the discordant essence of language, his unmusical music. And Kafka, who never ceases to acknowledge that he is deafer to music than anyone else in the world, does not fail to discover in this weak point one of his strengths. 'I am strong, really. I have a certain strength, and, to characterize it briefly and not very clearly, it is my unmusicalnes' "; Maurice Blanchot, *The Space of Literature*, trans. Ann Smock (Lincoln: University of Nebraska Press, 1989), 192. Rilke's fictional alter ego confesses to having been "distrustful" of music "even as a child . . . not because it lifted me out of myself more powerfully than anything else, but because I had noticed that it never put me back where it had found me, but lower down, somewhere deep in the uncompleted"; Rainer Maria Rilke, *The Notebooks of Malte Laurids Brigge, with an Introduction by William Gass*, trans. Stephen Mitchell (New York: Vintage, 1990), 125.

2. On this long-neglected aspect of Benjamin's work, see the essay collection edited by Tobias Robert Klein and Asmus Trautsch, *Klang und Musik bei Walter Benjamin* (Munich: Fink, 2013). On the role of music in the essay on *Elective Affinities*, see, in the same volume, Elio Matassi, "Trauerspiel und Oper bei Walter Benjamin," 70ff.; and Sigrid Weigel, "Die Geburt der Musik aus der Klage: Zum Zusammenhang von Trauer und Musik in Benjamins musiktheoretischen Thesen," 89ff.

3. Plato, *Phaedrus*, 258e–259d. This passage is mentioned in the chapter of Bachofen's *Das Mutterrecht* that Benjamin references via Carl Albrecht Bernoulli's book on Bachofen. See J. J. Bachofen, *Das Mutterrecht: Eine Untersuchung über die Gynaikokratie der alten Welt nach ihrer religiösen und rechtlichen Natur* (Stuttgart: Krais & Hoffmann, 1861), 330. On this passage in the *Phaedrus*, see G. F. R. Ferrari, *Listening to the Cicadas: A Study of Plato's Phaedrus* (Cambridge: Cambridge University Press, 1987), 25–34; Silvia Montiglio, *From Villain to Hero: Odysseus in Ancient Thought* (Ann Arbor: University of Michigan Press, 2011), 133; and, in connection with Adorno on Odysseus, Comay, "Adorno's Siren Song," 35n. Although the famous meditation on the sirens episode is found in the programmatic opening chapter of *Dialectic of Enlightenment* that Horkheimer coauthored with Adorno, it seems reasonable to credit Adorno, the undisputed author of the excursus on Odysseus, as its author.

4. *SW* 2/1:54. Remarkably, Benjamin does not note another, arguably more important, thematic connection between Goethe's and Keller's works, namely, the problematic of marriage as the guise in which the more fundamental problem of "continuance in love" appears in the bourgeois era ("GEA" 301–2). The

omission seems anything but accidental in light of Benjamin's claim that "the subject of *Elective Affinities* is not marriage" ("GEA" 302)—a gesture of disavowal that allows Benjamin to downplay a subject matter of utmost personal urgency for him and maintain the impersonality of his discourse. Winfried Menninghaus has developed a detailed and illuminating reading of Keller's novella in light of Benjamin's essay on *Elective Affinities*. However, Menninghaus focuses on the Benjaminian concepts of myth and fate and does not consider the relevance of the concept of caesura. See Winfried Menninghaus, "Romeo und Julia auf dem Dorfe: Eine Interpretation im Anschluss an Walter Benjamin," in *Artistische Schrift: Zur Kompositionskunst Gottfried Kellers* (Frankfurt: Suhrkamp, 1982), 91–163. It is worth noting here, finally, that the connections drawn to both Homer and Goethe have a prima facie plausibility in light of the genesis of Keller's novella, which grew out of an unrealized project modeled after Goethe's neo-Homeric epic poem *Hermann und Dorothea*. See Klaus Jeziorkowski, ed., *Dichter über ihre Dichtungen: Gottfried Keller* (Munich: Heimeran, 1969), 40.

5. Justus Fetscher, "Neutralität: Eine sachliche Lektüre von Gottfried Kellers 'Romeo und Julia auf dem Dorfe,'" *Zeitschrift für Religions- und Geistesgeschichte* 62, no. 2 (2010): 129.

6. Benjamin, "Gottfried Keller," *SW* 2/1:55.

7. Gerhard Kaiser, "Sündenfall, Paradies, und himmlisches Jerusalem in Kellers *Romeo und Julia auf dem Dorfe*," *Euphorion* 65, no. 1 (1971): 21–48.

8. Kaiser, "Sündenfall, Paradies," 41, 46.

9. Kaiser, "Sündenfall, Paradies," 41; see also 20.

10. Kaiser, "Sündenfall, Paradies," 48. The reference is to Adorno's discussion of the poem "Moonnight" ("Mondnacht") in the essay "In Memory of Eichendorff," in *Notes to Literature, Volume One*, trans. Shierry Weber Nicholsen (New York: Columbia University Press, 1991), 59–60.

11. See "VRJ" 76–77; and Heinrich Heine, *Sämtliche Schriften*, vol. 6/1, ed. Klaus Brieglieb (Munich: Carl Hanser, 1985), 129, 138–39.

12. On Feuerbach's importance for Keller, see Nicholas Saul, "Poetic Legitimacy after 1848: Keller, Feuerbach, and the Mirror of Nature," *Oxford German Studies* 40, no. 3 (2011): 303–15.

13. "VRJ" 98. Given the quote from Heine earlier in the novella, this phrase may well be a reminiscence of Heine's famous characterization of the Torah as the "portable fatherland" (*portatives Vaterland*) of the Jews in "Geständnisse," *Sämtliche Schriften*, 6/1:483. The image of the moving temple echoes the earlier passage in which Vrenchen's father justifies the dispossession of the Black Fiddler by recalling the fact that, since his parents had joined a group of vagabonds, he was not baptized: "what are we supposed to do, make our baptismal font portable and carry it around in the woods with us? No, it's in the church permanently, and what's portable is the bier we have outside on the wall" ("VRJ" 55). Kaiser also links the bedstead likened to a "moving temple" to the boat that the lovers will turn into a "floating bedstead." See Kaiser, "Sündenfall, Paradies," 35.

14. Stanley Corngold, "Genuine Obscurity Shadows the Semblance Whose Obliteration Promises Redemption: Reflections on Benjamin's 'Goethe's Elective Affinities,'" in *Benjamin's Ghosts: Interventions in Contemporary Literary and Cultural Theory*, ed. Gerhard Richter (Stanford, Calif.: Stanford University Press, 2002), 166.

15. Kaiser, "Sündenfall, Paradies," 48.

16. Besides the problems of myth, right, and "continuance in love" on which Benjamin's essay on *Elective Affinities* focuses and which are also central to Keller's novella, there are strikingly precise correspondences between the two works on the level of motifs. A case in point is the correspondence (and contrast) between the protagonists' daring plunge into the river from the boat in Goethe's embedded novella and the pair's seemingly passive slipping into the river from the barge at the end of Keller's novella. Consider also the fact that both Goethe's novel and Keller's novella conclude by ironically adopting a conventional, and obviously unreliable, perspective.

17. Thus it does not seem impossible that even Benjamin's idiosyncratic emphasis on the narrator's comparison of hope to a star that falls or speeds away might have been encouraged by an association to a sentence from Keller's novella: "They heard the larks singing high above them and watched for them with their sharp eyes, and when they thought they caught a momentary glimpse of one, flashing up [*aufblitzen*] in the sun like a star that suddenly lights up in the blue sky or shoots out of sight [*gleich einem plötzlich aufleuchtenden oder hinschießenden Stern*], they kissed again" ("VRJ" 83–84, translation modified).

18. Walter Benjamin, "141. To Gerhard Scholem, Berlin 6 April 1926," in *The Correspondence of Walter Benjamin*, 265, translation modified

19. For the chronology of Mann's work on the novel, see Hans Rudolf Vaget, "The Making of *The Magic Mountain*," in *Thomas Mann's The Magic Mountain: A Casebook*, ed. Hans Rudolf Vaget (Oxford: Oxford University Press, 2008), 27.

20. See especially the conclusion of the chapter "Operationes Spirituales" in Thomas Mann, *The Magic Mountain*, trans. John E. Woods (New York: Vintage, 1996), 459. See also 450–51 and 499 for Naphta's dialectical arguments.

21. "It was Pribislav, it was him all over. I never would have thought that I'd see him so clearly again. And he looked so strangely like her—that woman up here. Is that why I am so interested in her? Or maybe that's also why I was so interested in him" (Mann, *The Magic Mountain*, 121, translation modified).

22. Mann, *The Magic Mountain*, 484, translation modified.

23. Mann, *The Magic Mountain*, 487.

24. As Hans Rudolf Vaget notes, the projected novella about Davos that would eventually grow into *The Magic Mountain* was conceived by Mann as "a satirical counterpart" to *Death in Venice*, completed a year earlier. See Vaget, "The Making of *The Magic Mountain*," 18. It is not hard to recognize in Aschenbach's Dionysian dream the precursor to Castorp's dream in "Snow."

25. For the source of Mann's title, see this passage from Nietzsche's first book: "How does the world of the Olympian gods relate to this piece of popular wisdom [*i.e., the pessimistic wisdom of Silenus*]? The relationship is that of the ecstatic vision of a tortured martyr to his torments. The Olympian magic mountain [*Der olympische Zauberberg*] now opens up, as it were, and shows us its roots. The Greeks knew and felt the terrors and horrors of existence; in order to live at all they had to place in front of these things the resplendent, dream-born figures of the Olympians" (Nietzsche, *The Birth of Tragedy*, 23).

26. Mann, *The Magic Mountain*, 641, translation modified. Woods's translation obscures the musical connotation of the phrase "höchste Behutsamkeit der Intonation," which is especially conspicuous in light of the narrator's preceding

comments on the artful delivery of the singer performing "Der Lindenbaum." See Thomas Mann, *Grosse kommentierte Frankfurter Ausgabe*, vol. 5.1: *Der Zauberberg*, ed. Michael Neumann (Frankfurt: S. Fischer, 2002), 987.

27. Mann, *The Magic Mountain*, 642, translation modified.

28. Mann, *The Magic Mountain*, 643, translation modified.

29. In Woods's translation, we find the phrase "the song's best son may yet have been the young man," even though Mann's term for the best son is not "der junge Mann" but simply the pronoun "einer" (one). This renderring flies in the face of Mann's self-interpretation. In a letter, Mann himself identified the "enchanter of souls" in this passage with Wagner, the founder of an empire with Bismarck, and the "song's best son" with Nietzsche, who was not a young man when he died. See Thomas Mann, *Grosse kommentierte Frankfurter Ausgabe*, vol. 5.2: *Der Zauberberg: Kommentar von Michael Neumann* (Frankfurt: S. Fischer, 2002), 386–87. Although Mann's identification of the third figure with Nietzsche cannot be dismissed as irrelevant, we should not accept this self-interpretation at face value. No reader unfamiliar with Mann's humanistic appropriation of Nietzsche could think of imputing the "self-overcoming" dictated by "conscience" of which the narrator speaks here to Nietzsche, of all people. Note, also, that the "best son" is said to die "for" Schubert's song, which cannot be said of Nietzsche, whereas Castorp will indeed be portrayed at the end of the novel as singing "Der Lindenbaum" on the brink of death. Hans Vaget correctly suggests that the pronoun "one" in the passage at issue may actually refer to two persons: "little Hans Castorp may be said to tread in the colossal footsteps of Nietzsche the Hero as he stumbles toward his death in Flanders"; Hans Vaget, "'Politically Suspect': Music on the Magic Mountain'," in *Thomas Mann's The Magic Mountain: A Casebook*, ed. Hans Rudolf Vaget (Oxford: Oxford University Press, 2008), 127. On the profound significance of Schubert's song for Mann see Mann, *Der Zauberberg: Kommentar von Michael Neumann*, 383–85.

30. Mann, *The Magic Mountain*, 706.

31. Mann, *The Magic Mountain*, xi–xii, translation modified.

32. In a letter to Gershom Scholem written on July 21, 1925, Benjamin claims to have read Kafka's parable "Before the Law" ("one of the best German short stories") ten years earlier, which is when it was first published, separately, in the Jewish journal *Selbstwehr*. See *The Correspondence of Walter Benjamin*, 279. Note that neither the text published in 1915 nor its republication in the 1921 collection *Ein Landarzt* included the cathedral scene that would eventually frame the parable in the novel. Benjamin read *The Trial* for the first time in November 1927. See Eiland and Jennings, *Walter Benjamin: A Critical Life*, 294.

33. Franz Kafka, *The Trial*, trans. Mike Mitchell (Oxford: Oxford University Press, 2009), 164–65.

34. For Benjamin's formulation, see his explanation to Scholem: "I wish tentatively to characterize the relationship of my essay [on Kafka] to your poem as follows: you take the 'nothingness of revelation' as your point of departure . . . the salvific-historical perspective of the established proceedings of the trial. I take as my starting point the small, nonsensical hope, as well as the creatures for whom this hope is intended and yet who on the other hand are also the creatures in which this absurdity is mirrored" (Walter Benjamin, "240. To Gerhard Scholem, 11 August 1934," in *The Correspondence of Walter Benjamin*, 453).

35. Walter Benjamin, letter to Theodor W. Adorno, December 9, 1938 (trans. by Harry Zohn), in *Aesthetics and Politics*, by Theodor W. Adorno, Walter Benjamin, Bertolt Brecht, and Georg Lukács (London: Verso, 2007), 137.

36. See Wellmer, "The Death of the Sirens," 19.

37. Raymond Geuss, "Adorno's Gaps," in *Outside Ethics* (Princeton, N.J.: Princeton University Press, 2005), 247.

38. The extraneous character of the passage about reconciliation with God, for example, is shown by the fact, noted by Gábor Gángó, that it is an almost verbatim citation from *Sätze aus der erotischen Philosophie* (1828) by the Catholic theologian Franz von Baader, whose influence on the early Benjamin was pervasive. See Gábor Gángó, "A felvilágosodott ész határhelyzetei: Goethe-inspirációk Lukács Györgynél és Walter Benjaminnál" ["Boundary Situations of Enlightened Reason: Goethean Inspirations in György Lukács and Walter Benjamin"], in *Németföldről Németországba: Magyar kutatók tanulmányai a német történelemről*, ed. Frank Tibor (Budapest: Gondolat Kiadó, 2012), 161. On the parallel between Benjamin's pronouncements on reconciliation and Hermann Cohen's meditations on the rite of penance on Yom Kippur, see Rochelle Tobias, "Irreconcilable: Ethics and Aesthetics for Hermann Cohen and Walter Benjamin," *Modern Language Notes* 127, no. 3 (2012): 668, 678.

39. The only discussion known to me that highlights some of these points of contact is Kenneth S. Calhoon, "Of Non-Vital Interest: Art, Mimicry, and the Phenomenon of Life," *Konturen* 6 (2014): 90–95, http://journals.oregondigital.org/index.php/konturen/article/view/3503/3278.

40. Hans Jonas, *The Phenomenon of Life: Toward a Philosophical Biology* (Evanston, Ill.: Northwestern University Press, 2001), 15.

41. Jonas, *The Phenomenon of Life*, 191.

42. Jonas, *The Phenomenon of Life*, 203.

43. Jonas, *The Phenomenon of Life*, 193. See also Hans Jonas, *The Imperative of Responsibility: In Search of an Ethics for the Technological Age*, trans. Hans Jonas and David Herr (Chicago: University of Chicago Press, 1984), 9.

44. Jonas, *The Phenomenon of Life*, 210.

45. Jonas, *The Phenomenon of Life*, 203.

46. Jonas, *The Phenomenon of Life*, 234. On idealism and materialism as fission products of Cartesian dualism, see *The Phenomenon of Life*, 21.

47. Jonas, *The Phenomenon of Life*, 26, 87–88, 196, 210.

48. Jonas, *The Phenomenon of Life*, 233.

49. Bernstein, *Adorno: Disenchantment and Ethics*, 110–112.

50. Hans Jonas, "Technology and Responsibility: Reflections on the New Tasks of Ethics," *Social Research* 40, no. 1 (Spring 1973): 52–53. See also *The Imperative of Responsibility*, 22–23.

51. Günther Anders, "Reflections on the H Bomb," *Dissent* 3, no. 2 (Spring 1956): 148.

52. Günther Anders, "Commandments in the Atomic Age," in *Burning Conscience: The Case of the Hiroshima Pilot Claude Eatherly, Told in his Letters to Gunther Anders* (New York: Monthly Review Press, 1961), 11.

53. Anders, "Commandments in the Atomic Age," 20.

54. Jonas, *The Phenomenon of Life*, 1 and 53–58.

55. Jonas, *The Phenomenon of Life*, 4–5.

56. Jonas, *The Phenomenon of Life*, 106, 184, and 210.

57. Jonas, *The Phenomenon of Life*, 185–87.

58. Hans Jonas, "Toward an Ontological Grounding of an Ethics for the Future," in *Mortality and Morality: A Search for the Good after Auschwitz*, ed. Lawrence Vogel (Evanston, Ill.: Northwestern University Press, 1996), 102.

59. Jonas, *The Imperative of Responsibility*, 8.

60. Jonas, "Toward an Ontological Grounding," 106–7, italics in the original.

61. Jonas, *The Phenomenon of Life*, 262–81.

62. Hans Jonas, "The Concept of God after Auschwitz: A Jewish Voice," in *Mortality and Morality: A Search for the Good after Auschwitz*, ed. Lawrence Vogel (Evanston, Ill.: Northwestern University Press, 1996), 134–36. For an equally substantial paraphrase of and apologia for the creation myth, originally presented in a lecture in 1988, see Hans Jonas, "Matter, Mind, and Creation: Cosmological Evidence and Cosmogonic Speculation," in *Mortality and Morality*, 189–91.

63. The quotes in this passage are from Jonas, *The Phenomenon of Life*, 275–77.

64. Jonas, *The Phenomenon of Life*, 4.

65. Jonas, *The Phenomenon of Life*, 23–24. Although in the singular case of the divine, anthropomorphism obviously cannot be subtractive, even here, Jonas asserts, "anthropomorphism in thinking about God is as legitimate as it is irremovable. Of course it must know about its inadequacy, as Thomas Aquinas urged with his concepts of the *analogie entis* and the *modo eminentiae*" (Jonas, "Matter, Mind, and Creation," 182).

66. Jonas, *The Phenomenon of Life*, 272.

67. Jonas, *The Phenomenon of Life*, 278.

68. Hans Jonas, "Is Faith Still Possible? Memories of Rudolf Bultmann and Reflections on the Philosophical Aspects of His Work," in *Mortality and Morality*, 149.

69. Jonas, "Matter, Mind, and Creation," 189.

70. Jonas, "The Concept of God after Auschwitz," 142.

71. F. W. J. Schelling, *System of Transcendental Idealism (1800)*, trans. Peter Heath (Charlottesville: University Press of Virginia, 2001), 232.

72. For Schelling's account of the divine ground, see F. W. J. Schelling, *Philosophical Investigations into the Essence of Human Freedom*, trans. Jeff Love and Johannes Schmidt (Albany: State University of New York Press, 2006), 27–33. On the primordial "rotation," see F. W. J. Schelling, *The Ages of the World (Fragment), from the Handwritten Remains, Third Version (c. 1815)*, trans. Jason M. Wirth (Albany: State University of New York Press, 2000), 20–21. On the influence on Schelling, via Jakob Böhme and Friedrich Christoph Oetinger, of the Lurianic doctrine of *tzimtzum*, see the editor's introduction to F. W. J. Schelling, *Stuttgarter Privatvorlesungen*, ed. Vicki Müller-Lüneschloss (Hamburg: Felix Meiner Verlag, 2016), xxi–xxx and her editorial notes, esp. 155–56.

73. Hans Jonas, *Erinnerungen: Nach Gesprächen mit Rachel Salamander*, ed. Christian Wiese (Frankfurt: Insel Verlag, 2003), 132 and 215–42.

74. Hans Jonas, *Organismus und Freiheit: Ansätze zu einer philosophischen Biologie*, trans. Hans Jonas and Klaus Dockhorn (Göttingen: Vandenhoeck & Ruprecht, 1973), subsequently republished as *Das Prinzip Leben: Ansätze zu einer philosophischen Biologie* (Frankfurt: Suhrkamp, 1994).

75. Jonas, *Das Prinzip Leben*, 11.
76. Jonas, *The Phenomenon of Life*, 279–81.
77. Jonas, *Das Prinzip Leben*, 395–96.
78. Jonas, *Das Prinzip Leben*, 394.
79. Jonas, "The Concept of God after Auschwitz," 134.

BIBLIOGRAPHY

Adorno, Theodor W. "The Actuality of Philosophy." Translated by Benjamin Snow. *Telos* 31 (1977): 113–33.

———. *Aesthetic Theory*. Edited by Gretel Adorno and Rolf Tiedemann, translated by Robert Hullot-Kentor. London: Continuum, 2002.

———. *Ästhetische Theorie*. Edited by Gretel Adorno and Rolf Tiedemann. Frankfurt: Suhrkamp, 1973.

———. *Critical Models: Interventions and Catchwords*. Translated by Henry W. Pickford. New York: Columbia University Press, 2005.

———. *Essays on Music*. Edited by Richard Leppert, translated by Susan H. Gillespie. Berkeley: University of California Press, 2002.

———. *Gesammelte Schriften*. Volumes 1–20. Edited by Rolf Tiedemann. Frankfurt: Suhrkamp, 1997.

———. "Geschichtsphilosophischer Exkurs zur *Odyssey* [Frühe Fassung von Odysseus oder Mythos und Aufklärung]." In *Frankfurter Adorno Blätter V*, edited by Rolf Tiedemann, 27–88. Frankfurt: edition text + kritik, 1998.

———. *Hegel: Three Studies*. Translated by Shierry Weber Nicholsen. Cambridge, Mass.: MIT Press, 1993.

———. "The Idea of Natural History." Translated by Robert Hullot-Kentor. *Praxis* 4, no. 2 (July 1984): 97–124.

———. *An Introduction to Dialectics*. Edited by Christoph Ziermann, translated by Nicholas Walker. Cambridge: Polity, 2017.

———. *Minima Moralia: Reflections on a Damaged Life*. Translated by E. F. N. Jephcott. London: Verso, 2005.

———. *Negative Dialectics*. Translated by E. B. Ashton. New York: Continuum, 2007.

———. *Notes to Literature, Volume One*. Translated by Shierry Weber Nicholsen. New York: Columbia University Press, 1991.

———. *Notes to Literature, Volume Two*. Translated by Shierry Weber Nicholsen. New York: Columbia University Press, 1992.

———. *Prisms*. Translated by Samuel Weber and Shierry Weber. Cambridge, Mass.: MIT Press, 1983.

Adorno, Theodor W., Walter Benjamin, Bertolt Brecht, and Georg Lukács. *Aesthetics and Politics*. London: Verso, 2007.

Anders, Günther. "Commandments in the Atomic Age." In *Burning Conscience: The Case of the Hiroshima Pilot Claude Eatherly, Told in His Letters to Gunther Anders*, 11–20. New York: Monthly Review, 1961.

———. "Reflections on the H Bomb." *Dissent* 3, no. 2 (Spring 1956): 146–55.

Bachofen, J. J. *Das Mutterrecht: Eine Untersuchung über die Gynaikokratie der alten Welt nach ihrer religiösen und rechtlichen Natur*. Stuttgart: Krais & Hoffmann, 1861.

Bakhtin, M. M. *Art and Answerability: Early Philosophical Essays by M. M. Bakhtin*. Edited by Michael Holquist and Vadim Liapunov, translated by Vadim Liapunov. Austin: University of Texas Press, 1990.

———. *The Dialogic Imagination: Four Essays*. Edited by Michael Holquist, translated by Caryl Emerson and Michael Holquist. Austin: University of Texas Press, 1996.

Bassett, Samuel E. "The Theory of the Homeric Caesura according to the Extant Remains of the Ancient Doctrine." *American Journal of Philology* 40, no. 4 (1919): 343–72.

Benhabib, Seyla. *Critique, Norm, and Utopia: A Study of the Foundations of Critical Theory*. New York: Columbia University Press, 1986.

Benjamin, Walter. *The Arcades Project*. Translated by Howard Eiland and Kevin McLaughlin. Cambridge, Mass.: Belknap, 1999.

———. *The Correspondence of Walter Benjamin, 1910–1940*. Edited by Gershom Scholem and Theodor W. Adorno, translated by Manfred R. Jacobson and Evelyn M. Jackson. Chicago: University of Chicago Press, 1995.

———. *Gesammelte Schriften*. Volumes I–VII. Edited by Rolf Tiedemann and Hermann Schweppenhäuser. Frankfurt: Suhrkamp, 1991.

———. *The Origin of German Tragic Drama*. Translated by John Osborne. London: NLR Books, 1977.

———. *Selected Writings*. Volumes 1–4. Edited by Howard Eiland, Michael W. Jennings, Marcus Bullock, and Gary Smith. Cambridge, Mass.: Belknap, 2004–06.

Bernstein, J. M. *Adorno: Disenchantment and Ethics*. Cambridge: Cambridge University Press, 2001.

Billings, Joshua. *Genealogy of the Tragic: Greek Tragedy and German Philosophy*. Princeton, N.J.: Princeton University Press, 2014.

Bittner, Rüdiger. "Does *Dialectic of Enlightenment* Rest on Religious Foundations?" In *The Early Frankfurt School and Religion*, edited by Margarete Kohlenbach and Raymond Geuss, 57–70. New York: Palgrave Macmillan, 2005.

Blanchot, Maurice. *The Space of Literature*. Translated by Ann Smock. Lincoln: University of Nebraska Press, 1989.

Bloch, Ernst. *Erbschaft dieser Zeit: Erweiterte Ausgabe*. Frankfurt: Suhrkamp, 1962.

Blumenberg, Hans. *The Genesis of the Copernican World*. Translated by Robert M. Wallace. Cambridge, Mass.: MIT Press, 1987.

Bollenbeck, Georg. *Bildung und Kultur: Glanz und Elend eines deutschen Deutungsmusters*. Frankfurt: Insel, 1994.

Bolz, Norbert W., ed. *Goethes Wahlverwandtschaften: Kritische Modelle und Diskursanalysen zum Mythos Literatur*. Hildesheim: Gerstenberg, 1981.

Calhoon, Kenneth S. "Of Non-Vital Interest: Art, Mimicry, and the Phenomenon of Life." *Konturen* vol. 6 (2014): 82–102. http://journals.oregondigital.org/index.php/konturen/article/view/3503/3278.

Claussen, Detlev. *Theodor W. Adorno: Ein letztes Genie*. Frankfurt: Fischer, 2003.

Comay, Rebecca. "Adorno's Siren Song." *New German Critique*, no. 81 (Autumn 2000): 21–48.

Corngold, Stanley. "Genuine Obscurity Shadows the Semblance Whose Obliteration Promises Redemption." In *Benjamin's Ghosts: Interventions in*

Contemporary Literary and Cultural Theory, edited by Gerhard Richter, 154–68. Stanford, Calif.: Stanford University Press, 2002.

Deuber-Mankowsky, Astrid. *Der frühe Walter Benjamin und Hermann Cohen: Jüdische Werte, kritische Philosophie, vergängliche Erfahrung*. Berlin: Verlag Vorwerk 8, 2000.

Dews, Peter. "Dialectics and the Transcendence of Dialectics: Adorno's Relation to Schelling." *British Journal for the History of Philosophy* 22, no. 6 (2014): 1180–1207.

Dickinson, Colby, and Stéphane Symons, eds. *Walter Benjamin and Theology*. New York: Fordham University Press, 2016.

Dornbach, Márton. *Receptive Spirit: German Idealism and the Dynamics of Cultural Transmission*. New York: Fordham University Press, 2016.

Duford, Rochelle. "Daughters of the Enlightenment: Reconstructing Adorno on Gender and Feminist Praxis." *Hypatia* 32, no. 4 (Fall 2017): 784–800.

Duhem, Pierre. *To Save the Phenomena: An Essay on the Idea of Physical Theory from Plato to Galileo*. Translated by Edmund Dolan and Chaninah Maschler. Chicago: University of Chicago Press, 1969.

Eiland, Howard, and Michael W. Jennings. *Walter Benjamin: A Critical Life*. Cambridge, Mass.: Belknap, 2014.

Evans, James, and J. Lennart Berggren. *Geminos's Introduction to the Phenomena: A Translation and Study of a Hellenistic Survey of Astronomy*. Princeton, N.J.: Princeton University Press, 2006.

Fenves, Peter. *The Messianic Reduction: Walter Benjamin and the Shape of Time*. Stanford, Calif.: Stanford University Press, 2011.

———. "Kant in Benjamins Wahlverwandtschaften-Essay." In *Benjamins Wahlverwandtschaften: Zur Kritik einer programmatischen Interpretation*, edited by Helmut Hühn, Jan Urbich, and Uwe Steiner, 221–37. Frankfurt: Suhrkamp, 2015.

Ferrari, G. F. R. *Listening to the Cicadas: A Study of Plato's Phaedrus*. Cambridge: Cambridge University Press, 1987.

Fetscher, Justus. "Neutralität: Eine sachliche Lektüre von Gottfried Kellers 'Romeo und Julia auf dem Dorfe.'" *Zeitschrift für Religions- und Geistesgeschichte* 62, no. 2 (2010): 125–41.

Finlayson, James Gordon. "Hegel, Adorno, and the Origins of Immanent Criticism." *British Journal for the History of Philosophy* 22, no. 6 (2013): 1142–66.

Flaubert, Gustave. *Correspondance II*. Edited by Jean Bruneau. Paris: Gallimard, 1980.

———. *The Letters of Gustave Flaubert, Volumes I–II, 1830–1880*. Edited and translated by Francis Steegmuller. London: Picador, 2001.

Fleming, Katie. "Odysseus and Enlightenment: Horkheimer and Adorno's *Dialektik der Aufklärung*." *International Journal of the Classical Tradition* 19, no. 2 (2012): 107–28.

Fleming, Paul. "The Crisis of Art: Max Kommerell and Jean Paul's Gestures." *Modern Language Notes* 115, no. 3 (2000): 519–43.

———. "Forgetting—*Faust*: Adorno and Kommerell." In *Adorno and Literature*, edited by David Cunningham and Nigel Mapp, 133–44. London: Continuum, 2006.

Förster, Eckart. "'Was darf ich hoffen?' Zum Problem der Vereinbarkeit von theoretischer und praktischer Vernunft bei Immanuel Kant." *Zeitschrift für philosophische Forschung* 46, no. 2 (1992): 168–82.

François-Poncet, André. *Les Affinités Électives de Goethe: Essai de commentaire critique*. Paris: Félix Alcan, 1910.

Friedlander, Eli. *Walter Benjamin: A Philosophical Portrait*. Cambridge, Mass.: Harvard University Press, 2012.

Gadamer, Hans-Georg. *Truth and Method*. 2nd revised edition. Translated and revised by Joel Weinsheimer and Donald G. Marshall. London: Continuum, 2004.

Gángó, Gábor. "A felvilágosodott ész határhelyzetei: Goethe-inspirációk Lukács Györgynél és Walter Benjaminnál." In *Németföldről Németországba: Magyar kutatók tanulmányai a német történelemről*, edited by Tibor Frank, 151–67. Budapest: Gondolat Kiadó, 2012.

Gasché, Rodolphe. *The Honor of Thinking: Critique, Theory, Philosophy*. Stanford, Calif.: Stanford University Press, 2007.

Geuss, Raymond. "Review of *Negative Dialectics*, by Theodor W. Adorno and E. B. Ashton." *Journal of Philosophy* 72, no. 6 (1975): 167–75.

———. *Outside Ethics*. Princeton, N.J.: Princeton University Press, 2005.

Glazova, Anna, and Paul North, eds. *Messianic Thought Outside Theology*. New York: Fordham University Press, 2014.

Goethe, Johann Wolfgang von. *Elective Affinities*. Translated by David Constantine. Oxford: Oxford University Press, 1999.

———. *Goethes Werke: Hamburger Ausgabe in 14 Bänden*. Volume 6. Edited by Erich Trunz. Munich: C. H. Beck, 1981.

Hegel, G. W. F. *Aesthetics: Lectures on Fine Art*. Volume 1. Translated by T. M. Knox. Oxford: Clarendon, 1988.

———. *The Phenomenology of Spirit*. Translated with an introduction and commentary by Michael Inwood. Oxford: Oxford University Press, 2018.

Heidegger, Martin. *Being and Time: A Translation of Sein und Zeit*. Translated by Joan Stambaugh. Albany: State University of New York Press, 1996.

———. *The Fundamental Concepts of Metaphysics: World, Finitude, Solitude*. Translated by William McNeill and Nicholas Walker. Bloomington: Indiana University Press, 1995.

Heine, Heinrich. *Sämtliche Schriften*. Volume 6/1. Edited by Klaus Briegleib. Munich: Carl Hanser, 1985.

Hewitt, Andrew. "A Feminine Dialectic of Enlightenment? Horkheimer and Adorno Revisited." *New German Critique* 56 (Summer 1992): 143–70.

Hohendahl, Peter Uwe. *The Fleeting Promise of Art: Adorno's Aesthetic Theory Revisited*. Ithaca, N.Y.: Cornell University Press, 2013.

Hölderlin, Friedrich. *Sämtliche Werke, Briefe und Dokumente in zeitlicher Folge*. Volumes 1–20. Edited by D. E. Sattler. Munich: Luchterhand, 2004. Kindle edition.

Homer. *The Odyssey*. Translated by Emily Wilson. New York: W. W. Norton, 2017.

Honold, Alexander. *Der Leser Walter Benjamin: Bruchstücke einer deutschen Literaturgeschichte*. Berlin: Vorwerk 8, 2000.

Horkheimer, Max, and Theodor W. Adorno. *Dialectic of Enlightenment: Philosophical Fragments*. Edited by Gunzelin Schmid Noerr, translated by Edmund Jephcott. Stanford, Calif.: Stanford University Press, 2001.

———. *Dialektik der Aufklärung: Philosophische Fragmente*. Frankfurt: Fischer, 1993.

Hühn, Helmut, Jan Urbich, and Uwe Steiner, eds. *Benjamins Wahlverwandtschaften: Zur Kritik einer programmatischen Interpretation*. Frankfurt: Suhrkamp, 2015.

Husserl, Edmund. *Husserliana X: Zur Phänomenologie des inneren Zeitbewusstseins (1893–1917)*. Edited by Rudolf Boehm. The Hague: Martinus Nijhoff, 1969.

Jaeggi, Rahel. "'No Individual Can Resist': *Minima Moralia* as Critique of Forms of Life." *Constellations* 12, no. 1 (2005): 65–82.

Jauss, Hans Robert. *Ästhetische Erfahrung und literarische Hermeneutik*. Frankfurt: Suhrkamp, 1991.

Jennings, Michael W. *Dialectical Images: Walter Benjamin's Theory of Literary Criticism*. Ithaca, N.Y.: Cornell University Press, 1987.

Jeziorkowski, Klaus, ed. *Dichter über ihre Dichtungen: Gottfried Keller*. Munich: Heimeran, 1969.

Jonas, Hans. *Das Prinzip Leben: Ansätze zu einer philosophischen Biologie*. Frankfurt: Suhrkamp, 1994.

———. *Erinnerungen. Nach Gesprächen mit Rachel Salamander*. Edited by Christian Wiese. Frankfurt: Insel Verlag, 2003.

———. *The Imperative of Responsibility: In Search of an Ethics for the Technological Age*. Translated by Hans Jonas and David Herr. Chicago: University of Chicago Press, 1984.

———. *Mortality and Morality: A Search for the Good after Auschwitz*. Edited by Lawrence Vogel. Evanston, Ill.: Northwestern University Press, 1996.

———. *The Phenomenon of Life: Toward a Philosophical Biology*. Evanston, Ill.: Northwestern University Press, 2001.

———. "Technology and Responsibility: Reflections on the New Tasks of Ethics." *Social Research* 40, no. 1 (Spring 1973): 31–54.

Kafka, Franz. *The Trial*. Translated by Mike Mitchell. Oxford: Oxford University Press, 2009.

Kaiser, Gerhard. "Sündenfall, Paradies und himmlisches Jerusalem in Kellers *Romeo und Julia auf dem Dorfe*." *Euphorion* 65, no. 1 (1971): 21–48.

Kant, Immanuel. *Critique of Pure Reason*. Edited and translated by Paul Guyer and Allen Wood. Cambridge: Cambridge University Press, 2000.

———. *Critique of the Power of Judgment*. Edited by Paul Guyer, translated by Paul Guyer and Eric Matthews. Cambridge: Cambridge University Press, 2000.

———. *Lectures on Logic*. Edited and translated by J. Michael Young. Cambridge: Cambridge University Press, 1992.

———. *Practical Philosophy*. Edited and translated by Mary J. Gregor. Cambridge: Cambridge University Press, 1999.

Keller, Gottfried. "A Village Romeo and Juliet." Translated by Paul Bernard Thomas. In *Stories*, edited by Frank G. Ryder, 52–118. London: Bloomsbury, 1982.

———. *Sämtliche Werke*. Volume 4, edited by Thomas Böning. Frankfurt: Deutscher Klassiker Verlag, 1989.

Klein, Tobias Robert, and Asmus Trautsch. *Klang und Musik bei Walter Benjamin*. Munich: Fink, 2013.

Kleingeld, Pauline. "Kant on the Unity of Theoretical and Practical Reason." *Review of Metaphysics* 52 (December 1998): 311–39.

Kracauer, Siegfried. *The Mass Ornament: Weimar Essays*. Edited and translated by Thomas Y. Levin. Cambridge, Mass.: Harvard University Press, 1995.

Lacoue-Labarthe, Philippe. "The Caesura of the Speculative." In *The Solid Letter: Readings of Friedrich Hölderlin*, edited by Aris Fioretos, 208–35. Stanford, Calif.: Stanford University Press, 1999.

Leacock, N. K. "Character, Silence, and the Novel: Walter Benjamin on Goethe's *Elective Affinities*." *Narrative* 10, no. 3 (2002): 277–306.

Lukács, Georg. *Die Theorie des Romans: Ein geschichtsphilosophischer Versuch über die Formen der grossen Epik*. Neuwied-Berlin: Luchterhand, 1991.

Luxemburg, Rosa. *The Letters of Rosa Luxemburg*. Edited by Annelies Laschitza, Georg Adler, and Peter Hudis, translated by George Shriver. London: Verso, 2013.

Mann, Thomas. *Death in Venice*. Translated by Michael Henry Heim. New York: Ecco, 2004.

———. *Grosse kommentierte Frankfurter Ausgabe. Volume 5.1. Der Zauberberg*. Edited by Michael Neumann. Frankfurt: S. Fischer, 2002.

———. *Grosse kommentierte Frankfurter Ausgabe. Volume 5.2. Der Zauberberg: Kommentar von Michael Neumann*. Frankfurt: S. Fischer, 2002.

———. *The Magic Mountain*. Translated by John E. Woods. New York: Vintage, 1996.

Marquard, Odo. *Abschied vom Prinzipiellen: Philosophische Studien*. Stuttgart: Reclam, 1981.

Martella, Vincenzo. "Dialectics of Cultural Criticism: Adorno's Confrontation with Rudolf Borchardt and Ludwig Klages in the Odyssey Chapter of *Dialektik der Aufklärung*." Ph.D. dissertation, Justus-Liebig-Universität Giessen, 2012.

McCole, John. *Walter Benjamin and the Antinomies of Tradition*. Ithaca, N.Y.: Cornell University Press, 1993.

McFarland, James. *Constellation: Friedrich Nietzsche and Walter Benjamin in the Now-Time of History*. New York: Fordham University Press, 2013.

Menninghaus, Winfried. *Artistische Schrift: Zur Kompositionskunst Gottfried Kellers*. Frankfurt: Suhrkamp, 1982.

———. "Das Ausdruckslose: Walter Benjamins Kritik des Schönen durch das Erhabene." In *Walter Benjamin, 1892–1940*, edited by Uwe Steiner. 33–76. Bern: Peter Lang, 1992.

———. *Schwellenkunde: Walter Benjamins Passage des Mythos*. Frankfurt: Suhrkamp, 1986.

———. "Walter Benjamin's Theory of Myth." In *On Walter Benjamin: Critical Essays and Recollections*, edited by Gary Smith, 292–328. Cambridge, Mass.: MIT Press, 1988.

Meyler, Bernadette. "Adorno's Shifting *Wozzeck*." In *Modernism and Opera*, edited by Richard Begam and Matthew Wilson Smith, 148–85. Baltimore: Johns Hopkins University Press, 2016.

Montiglio, Silvia. *From Villain to Hero: Odysseus in Ancient Thought*. Ann Arbor: University of Michigan Press, 2011.

Müller-Doohm, Stefan. *Adorno: A Biography*. Translated by Rodney Livingstone. Cambridge: Polity, 2005.

Murray, Gilbert. *The Rise of the Greek Epic, Being a Course of Lectures Delivered at Harvard University*. Oxford: Clarendon, 1911.

Nägele, Rainer. *Theater, Theory, Speculation: Walter Benjamin and the Scenes of Modernity*. Baltimore: Johns Hopkins University Press, 1991.

Nicholls, Angus. "Against Darwin: Teleology in German Philosophical Anthropology." In *Historical Teleologies in the Modern World*, edited by Henning Trüper, Dipesh Chakrabarty, and Sanjay Subrahmanyam, 89–113. London: Bloomsbury, 2015.

Nietzsche, Friedrich. *Beyond Good and Evil*. Edited by Rolf-Peter Horstmann and Judith Norman, translated by Judith Norman. Cambridge: Cambridge University Press, 2015.

———. *The Birth of Tragedy and Other Writings*. Edited by Raymond Geuss and Ronald Speirs, translated by Ronald Speirs. Cambridge: Cambridge University Press, 2006.

———. *The Gay Science, with a Prelude in German Rhymes and an Appendix of Songs*. Edited by Bernard Williams, translated by Josefine Nauckhoff and Adrian del Caro. Cambridge: Cambridge University Press, 2001.

———. *On the Genealogy of Morality*. Edited by Keith Ansell-Pearson, translated by Carol Diethe. Cambridge: Cambridge University Press, 2006.

North, Paul. "Apparent Critique: Inferences from a Benjaminian Sketch." *Diacritics* 40, no. 1 (2012): 70–97.

Novalis. *Philosophical Writings*. Edited and translated by Margaret Mahony Stoljar. Albany: State University of New York Press, 1997.

Ovid. *Metamorphoses*. Translated by Charles Martin. New York: Norton, 2004.

Pfäfflin, Friedrich, ed. *Karl Kraus—Rosa Luxemburg: Büffelhaut und Kreatur: Die Zerstörung der Natur und das Mitleiden des Satirikers*. Berlin: Friedenauer Presse, 2009.

Pickford, Henry W. "Riddlework I." In *Der aufrechte Gang im windschiefen Kapitalismus: Modelle kritischen Denkens*, edited by Rüdiger Dannemann, Henry Pickford, and Hans-Ernst Schiller, 667–91. Wiesbaden: Springer, 2018.

Plass, Ulrich. *Language and History in Adorno's Notes to Literature*. London: Routledge, 2007.

Plato. *Complete Works*. Edited by John M. Cooper. Indianapolis, Ind.: Hackett, 1997.

Porter, James I. "Odysseus and the Wandering Jew: The Dialectic of Jewish Enlightenment in Adorno and Horkheimer." *Cultural Critique* 74 (Winter 2010): 200–213.

Preminger, Alex, and T. V. F. Brogan, eds. *The New Princeton Encyclopedia of Poetry and Poetics*. Princeton, N.J.: Princeton University Press, 1993.

Reuss, Roland. *"Wo aber Gefahr ist, wächst das Rettende auch [. . .]": Philologie als Rettung*. Frankfurt: Stroemfeld, 2016.

Richter, Gerhard. *Afterness: Figures of Following in Modern German Thought and Aesthetics*. New York: Columbia University Press, 2011.

———, ed., *Language without Soil: Adorno and Late Philosophical Modernity*. New York: Fordham University Press, 2010.

Rilke, Rainer Maria. *The Notebooks of Malte Laurids Brigge, with an Introduction by William Gass.* Translated by Stephen Mitchell. New York: Vintage, 1990.

Ruehl, Martin. "Politeia 1871: Nietzsche 'Contra' Wagner on the Greek State." In *Bulletin of the Institute of Classical Studies, Supplement No. 79, Out of Arcadia: Classics and Politics in the Age of Burckhardt, Nietzsche and Wilamowitz,* edited by Ingo Gildenhard and Martin Ruehl. London: Institute of Classical Studies, 2003.

Saul, Nicholas. "Poetic Legitimacy after 1848: Keller, Feuerbach, and the Mirror of Nature." *Oxford German Studies* 40, no. 3 (2011): 303–15.

Schelling, F. W. J. *The Ages of the World (Fragment), from the Handwritten Remains, Third Version (c. 1815).* Translated by Jason M. Wirth. Albany: State University of New York Press, 2000.

———. *Philosophical Investigations into the Essence of Human Freedom.* Translated by Jeff Love and Johannes Schmidt. Albany: State University of New York Press, 2006.

———. *Philosophische Untersuchungen über das Wesen der menschlichen Freiheit und die damit zusammenhängenden Gegenstände.* Edited by Thomas Buchheim. Hamburg: Meiner, 2011.

———. *Stuttgarter Privatvorlesungen.* Edited by Vicki Müller-Lüneschloss. Hamburg: Felix Meiner Verlag, 2016.

———. *System of Transcendental Idealism (1800).* Translated by Peter Heath. Charlottesville: University Press of Virginia, 2001.

Schlegel, Friedrich. *Friedrich Schlegel's Lucinde and the Fragments.* Translated by Peter Firchow. Minneapolis: University of Minnesota Press, 1971.

———. *Kritische Schriften und Fragmente.* Volumes 1–6. Edited by Ernst Behler and Hans Eichner. Paderborn: Ferdinand Schöningh, 1988.

———. *Philosophical Fragments.* Translated by Peter Firchow. Minneapolis: University of Minnesota Press, 1991.

Schmidt, Jochen. *Hölderlins geschichtsphilosophische Hymnen 'Friedensfeier,'–'Der Einzige'–'Patmos.'* Darmstadt: Wissenschaftliche Buchgesellschaft, 1990.

Scholem, Gershom. *The Story of a Friendship.* Translated by Harry Zohn. New York: New York Review of Books Classics, 2003.

Scholze, Britta. Scholze, *Kunst als Kritik: Adornos Weg aus der Dialektik.* Würzburg: Königshausen & Neumann, 2000.

Schröder, Otto. *Griechische Singverse.* Leipzig: Dieterich'sche Verlagsbuchhandlung, 1924.

Spitzer, Michael. *Music and Philosophy: Adorno and Beethoven's Late Style.* Bloomington: Indiana University Press, 2006.

Steiner, Uwe. *Die Geburt der Kritik aus dem Geiste der Kunst: Untersuchungen zum Begriff der Kritik in den frühen Schriften Walter Benjamins.* Würzburg: Königshausen & Neumann, 1989.

———. *Walter Benjamin: An Introduction to His Work and Thought.* Translated by Michael Winkler. Chicago: University of Chicago Press, 2010.

Tobias, Rochelle. "Irreconcilable: Ethics and Aesthetics for Hermann Cohen and Walter Benjamin." *Modern Language Notes* 127, no. 3 (2012): 665–80.

Tsur, Reuven. *Poetic Rhythm: Structure and Performance—An Empirical Study in Cognitive Poetics*, revised and expanded 2nd edition. Sussex, Eng.: Sussex University Press, 2012.

Urbich, Jan. "Das Ausdruckslose: Zur Dialektik des Scheins bei Benjamin." In *Benjamins Wahlverwandtschaften: Zur Kritik einer programmatischen Interpretation*, edited by Helmut Hühn, Jan Urbich, and Uwe Steiner, 90–127. Frankfurt: Suhrkamp, 2015.

Vaget, Hans, ed. *The Magic Mountain: A Casebook*. Oxford: Oxford University Press,2008.

Warminski, Andrzej. *Readings in Interpretation: Hölderlin, Hegel, Heidegger*. Minneapolis: University of Minnesota Press, 1987.

Wellmer, Albrecht. "The Death of the Sirens and the Origin of the Work of Art," *New German Critique* 81 (Autumn 2000): 5–19.

———. *The Persistence of Modernity: Essays on Aesthetics, Ethics, and Postmodernity*. Translated by David Midgley. Cambridge: Polity, 2007.

Wetters, Brent Andrew. "Darmstadt and the Philosophical Turn." Ph.D. dissertation, Brown University, 2012. https://repository.library.brown.edu/storage/bdr:297687/PDF/.

Williams, Bernard. *Problems of the Self: Philosophical Papers 1956–1972*. Cambridge: Cambridge University Press, 1973.

Wilson, Emily. "A Translator's Reckoning with the Women of the *Odyssey*." *New Yorker*, December 8, 2017. https://www.newyorker.com/books/page-turner/a-translators-reckoning-with-the-women-of-the-odyssey.

Wittgenstein, Ludwig. *Philosophical Investigations*. Oxford: Blackwell, 1999.

———. *Tractatus Logico-Philosophicus*. Translated by D. F. Pears and B. F. McGuinness. London: Routledge, 2001.

Zabka, Thomas. *Pragmatik der Literaturinterpretation: Theoretische Grundlagen–kritische Analysen*. Tübingen: Max Niemeyer Verlag, 2005.

Zuckert, Rachel. "Is Kantian Hope a Feeling?" In *Kant and the Faculty of Feeling*, edited by Kelly Sorensen and Diane Williamson, 242–59. Cambridge: Cambridge University Press, 2018.

INDEX